MIDLAND
LOCOMOTIVES

This beautiful picture of a Johnson 'single' with its driver somehow typifies an age of railways which we, in this later part of the 20th century, find difficult to imagine. The locomotive is in magnificent condition with every detail of lining clearly visible. Built in 1892, this locomotive became No. 634 in 1907 and was withdrawn in 1922. *National Railway Museum*

AN ILLUSTRATED REVIEW OF

MIDLAND LOCOMOTIVES

FROM 1883

BY

R. J. ESSERY & D. JENKINSON

VOLUME ONE
A GENERAL SURVEY

WILD SWAN PUBLICATIONS LTD.

Designed by Paul Karau
Typesetting by Berkshire Publishing Services
Photo reproduction and offset plates by Oxford Litho Plates Ltd.
Printed by Blackwells, Oxford

Published by
WILD SWAN PUBLICATIONS LTD.,
Hopgoods Farm Cottage, Upper Bucklebury, Berks.

CONTENTS

Taken at Bradford, this picture of No. 1579 depicts a 6′ 8½″ wheel 4—4—0 (built at Derby in 1883) in full crimson livery. Whilst we cannot be certain, it would seem that c.1905 is a reasonable date for the picture since the locomotive carries the post 1903 lamp irons and received an 'H' boiler in 1906. It was renumbered 345 in 1907 and withdrawn in 1925.

J. H. Wright

INTRODUCTION

Well over twenty years ago (astonishing thought!), the two of us made our mutual acquaintanceship and discovered that we both shared common interests in matters concerning the LMS Railway and its constituents. Moreover, as model makers, we were equally frustrated at the lack of useful information available to us in those far off days — so we resolved to try and do something about it. Since then and fortified by the encouragement of our friends, we have tried to make our growing collection of information available to those of like mind. As a result, we have collaborated happily in a number of joint publishing projects and in this series of volumes we turn our attention to one of our most favourite topics — the Midland Railway and its locomotives.

One of us spent his early working years on the footplate of ex-Midland engines (amongst others) and the

other half of the partnership, by virtue of his job since the early 1970s, has been closely involved with the re-presentation to modern enthusiasts of, amongst others, some of the residual full size artefacts of the Midland Railway — not least its engines. Consequently, and with the active encouragement of our publisher, we resolved to 'have a go' at some aspects of the complex story of the Midland Railway locomotives, in particular those aspects which most appeal to us.

We should, however, state from the outset (as we have done in some of our previous works) that this is not meant to be the 'last word' on the subject, much less a 'total' history of Midland engines. Even though our publisher has generously allowed us a three-volume format, overall space constraints and our own acknowledged lack of detailed specialist knowledge in certain areas would

Photographed at Manningham, Bradford, this glorious picture of No. 1546 in full Crimson Lake livery, typifies, to the authors, the Edwardian era of the Midland Railway. No. 1546 was built at Derby in 1881 and is shown here in its c.1900 condition. Becoming No. 1280 in 1907, this locomotive was an early casualty, being withdrawn in 1924.   *J. H. Wright*

make this impossible. Instead, we have drawn up rather more limited terms of reference and these should be made clear from the outset.

The Midland Railway began its corporate existence in the 1840s and we came to the subject 'in reverse' as it were, from the LMS period, with a particular interest in the engines which survived to the grouping of 1923. Indeed, it was our original intention to include, in the title of this work, the words, '20th Century' and to begin the story in 1900; however, it soon became apparent that this was not a good idea.

An alternative starting point would have been to take up the story with the arrival of Samuel Waite Johnson at Derby as the new Locomotive Superintendent in 1873 following the death of Matthew Kirtley, but this too was rejected in favour of the year 1883, ten years into the Johnson era. At that time all Midland engines were green but in that year it was decided to paint Midland Railway locomotives red, a colour which was to become closely associated with the company, a colour described by other authors as warm and glowing, a colour which the LMS continued to use, even though changes in paint manufacture probably altered its final appearance on locomotives as they weathered in traffic, and overall a gorgeous shade to paint any engine.

We decided that the emphasis of our work would be on visual appearance, with livery and external detail as the underlying themes, therefore an obvious starting point was the Locomotive Committee minute which approved the proposal to paint all the locomotive stock in a new colour. Throughout this work the terms, MR Red, Oxide of Iron and Lake and Crimson Lake have been used — they all refer to the same basic colour.

The work has been broken down into three volumes and after this general survey, the detailed descriptions of the various classes, together with many drawings especially produced, will be found as below:

Volume 2 — Passenger Tender and Tank Locomotives plus absorbed LT & SR Locomotives.

Volume 3 — Goods Tender and Tank Locomotives plus absorbed S & DJR Locomotives.

In determining which locomotives to describe and the depth of treatment they are to be given, we have been guided by two factors. Firstly, note has been taken of a volume which is currently under preparation by members of the Midland Railway Society, and second has been the livery question, with the green period not being considered in any great detail.

Thus, the companion work will describe in detail the Midland Railway locomotives built up to the end of the Kirtley era, leaving the Johnson, Deeley and Fowler locomotives for our consideration. There are, however, some crossover points.

Our survey will not describe in detail any of the green liveries used prior to 1883, therefore those Johnson locomotives which were originally painted green (and in their green livery), will be found in the companion work, while many of the Kirtley locomotives which were in service *after* 1883 will be found within these volumes. At this point the 1907 renumbering enters the scene (see page 20). In that year the entire MR locomotive stock was renumbered and, by and large, Kirtley locomotives which did not survive until this date are more fully described in the companion volume, whilst those which acquired 1907 numbers have their final years described within our own compilation.

What this, therefore, amounts to is that we offer here a reasonably detailed study of the locomotive situation during the Midland's 'red engine' period — i.e. its last forty years or so. Inevitably we must refer to the pre-1883 state of affairs where it affects our survey and, indeed, we must also go beyond 1923 as well for similar reasons. In essence, however, we have left the detailed study of the pre-1883 period to other writers, whilst we ourselves have covered the LMS period in our own books on LMS locomotive matters.

In a work of this nature it is impossible to avoid errors. However, with the help of our many friends, without which life would have been very difficult, we hope they are at a minimum, and we invite corrections and comments via the publisher so as to be able to include them in one of the later volumes.

It is, perhaps, inappropriate to single out any particular names from a very long list but we cannot but express our thanks to the library staff of the National Railway Museum (and their predecessors in the Public Relations Offices of British Railways [LMR]) for their assistance and, in particular, to record our indebtedness to David Tee, whose formidable advice and assistance has been invaluable. Others who have assisted in a variety of ways to make these three volumes possible are:

Brian Badger, Roger Carpenter, the Late A. G. Ellis, Terry Essery, Geoff Goodfellow, David Hunt, Bernard Matthews, Mike Peascod, the Late W. O. Steel, Bill Stubbs, Peter Truman, Laurie Ward, David White and Ken Woodhead.

Finally, and as usual, we should record our indebtedness to the forbearance of our respective wives and families and in particular to Wynne and Steven Essery who typed the manuscript. We think they are used to us by now but it's always nice to have it confirmed on a regular basis.

RJE   *DJ*
Orpington   *Knaresborough*
1984   *1984*

EXPLANATORY NOTES

LOCOMOTIVE NUMBERS

Prior to the great 1907 renumbering, the Midland Railway practice for locomotive numbers was somewhat irregular, with some classes having consecutive numbers whilst others were scattered throughout the entire number series. With the allocation of new locomotives to capital or replacement stock being reflected in the numbers allocated, it was not even a 'lowest available number' system as on the LNWR. To help readers sort matters out, a full list of the 1907 renumbering will be found in Appendix 1 (see also page 74). It should also be realised that prior to 1907 some locomotives were renumbered more than once, with some of them being allocated to the duplicate list. Indeed, it was not unknown for locomotives to be built, renumbered, go onto the duplicate list, return to the capital list and go back again onto the duplicate list before being renumbered in 1907. Duplicate numbers carried an 'A' suffix.

The principle of this renumbering in 1907 was to divide the locomotive fleet into three categories namely Passenger Tender, Tank and Freight Tender by allocating the lowest number in each series to the oldest locomotives. This principle was followed through the various wheel arrangements as shown on page 20. The principle followed throughout these volumes is always to relate post 1907 numbers to the pre 1907 numbers and of these the one given is always that which was carried immediately prior to 1907.

ENGINE DIAGRAMS EXPLAINED

Many Midland Railway locomotives are difficult to identify and from time to time engine diagrams have been used and published. They lack, in many cases, the detail to be found in the carriage diagrams of the Midland Railway, nevertheless they are useful when related to the post 1910 period. Although diagrams of Midland Railway locomotives existed prior to 1910, in that year a new series of ED drawings was issued and these ED diagram numbers are listed in Volumes 2 and 3 and related to the 1907 renumbering scheme. In 1919 a further series of engine diagrams was issued but in many instances the original 1910 diagrams were taken and used to cover, with but one diagram, a number of locomotive classes previously covered by several of the 1910 diagrams! For this reason *all* diagrams should be treated with caution and, although they give certain basic information, their value for modelling purposes is restricted. Furthermore their detail accuracy is frequently open to question. Notwithstanding these limitations, the diagrams provide a useful 'shorthand' index for locomotives which received 1907 numbers, and we shall therefore use these diagram numbers for identification purposes throughout the detailed chapters in Volumes 2 and 3. Finally, in order to familiarise readers with the 1910 and 1919 series, we illustrate one of each series at *Fig. 1* (1910) and *Fig. 2* (1919).

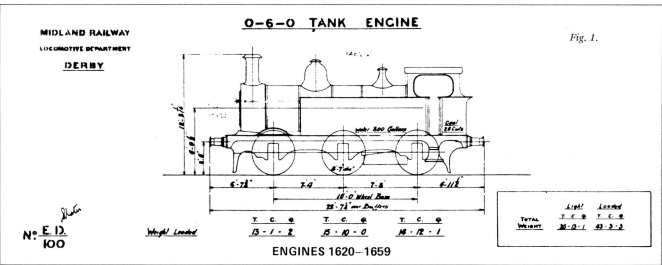

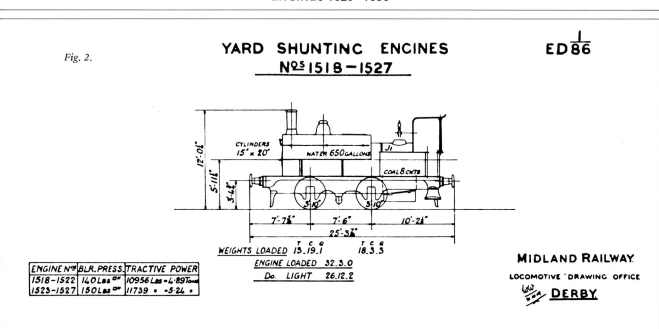

ix

Plate 1. The Johnson 'front end' is well displayed in this picture of an unidentified 'single' in Works Grey livery.

National Railway Museum

CHAPTER ONE

THE CHANGING FACE
OF MIDLAND LOCOMOTIVES

THE Midland Railway had both presence and style. It was large, profitable and generally well organised, whilst its lines stretched throughout the kingdom. It was held in high regard by contemporary travellers for both the quality of its carriages and the services it offered, and it pulled its passenger trains with beautiful red engines — most of the other trains, too, for much of the period with which we are concerned. It is the story of these engines which we are attempting to cover in these pages and it is no simple task.

For one thing, although the Midland embraced standardisation — any large organisation would inevitably have to do so — the story of its locomotives is most complex. Rebuilding, renumbering, changes in train weights and operating procedures, differences in emphasis by the various men in charge, the longevity of some designs and the sheer effect of the large numbers of locomotives involved, all combined, along with many other factors, to produce a very confusing picture — especially during the Edwardian era when the company was in process of change from 19th to 20th century conditions.

In this respect, the Midland was not unique — most of the British railway systems were faced with the same or similar problems — but the Midland probably showed more outward and visible evidence of the changes than most comparable sized companies. Take, for example, its closest rival, the LNWR. This system, too, had to modernise its locomotive activities in the light of Edwardian era changes, but it did so by producing new and larger machines which were self-evidently from the same 'stable' as their predecessors. This was not so on the Midland, where, quite regularly, changed circumstances often produced a changed approach to locomotive affairs and frequently imparted new visual lines to the fleet as well. In consequence, one can detect in the locomotive story periods of some degree of stability followed by 'spasms of some turmoil' before the next stable period began. Therefore to understand fully the detailed development of the Midland's engines, it is first necessary to have some sort of overall perspective — hence this preliminary chapter.

We have stated, in our introduction, why we have chosen to start the story in the 1880s and that our decision was made largely on visual grounds since this is where we are choosing to place the emphasis in this work. However, the early 1880s has some logic from a more purely technical standpoint. By this time, Johnson had been in charge for some ten years (with another twenty to go) and was well on the way to stamping his 'mark' on the scene just as his famous predecessor, Matthew Kirtley, had done before him. In other words, the early 1880s marks the end of one of the

'spasms of turmoil' mentioned above, which, from our point of view, was additionally and conveniently marked by the livery change of 1883.

The Johnson 'look' of the 19th century was marked in two main ways as far as the Midland's locomotives were concerned, namely the gradually increasing number of locomotives built to his own harmonious designs and the 'Johnsonising' of existing Kirtley designs — mostly but not exclusively, those which still had a reasonable life expectation in revenue-earning terms. It is a matter of history that this 'life-expectation' often turned out to be longer than most people could ever have imagined at the time.

We start our general survey, therefore, with the Kirtley engines and Johnson's work thereon. Essentially, when most people envisage a Kirtley Midland engine, they probably imagine something like *Plate 3* — double-frames, outside cranks and all. In fact what they are actually calling to mind is the 'Johnsonised' version of a Kirtley engine. The genuine Kirtley article was a somewhat more primitive looking machine (*Plate 2*) and it is a measure of Johnson's influence that even as early as 1883, not too many of them were left in this form. Many would hold that as rebuilt by Johnson, the Kirtleys also gained in visual quality as well.

The Johnson changes were usually as much cosmetic as anatomical and will, of course, be covered in somewhat more detail in the later chapters and volumes. Essentially, however, they almost always took the form of replacing the chimney/smokebox with one to the Johnson style, together with the fitting of a Johnson pattern cab. The engine part was generally left largely unmodified, although boilers were regularly changed, and the original Kirtley tenders were usually left alone. As time went by, many Kirtley engines eventually acquired replacement Johnson designed tenders but some original Kirtley tenders could be seen in use well into LMS and even, on one example, BR days.

The Johnson modifications were applied 'across the board' to most wheel arrangements introduced by Kirtley and at *Plates 4-6* we give a few typical examples of the sort of treatment carried out. When we turn to Johnson's own designs, we are dealing with one of the 'artist-engineers' of the late 19th century. It has been said that Johnson could not have designed an ugly engine if he had tried and certainly his Midland creations would endorse that view. What is sometimes overlooked in this popular view of his engines is that they were also extremely fine designs *as locomotives*, quite apart from their visual harmony — moreover, they were bigger than they looked. Johnson was fully aware of the needs of his company and, although he often disguised the fact by superlative visual lines, he gradually

Plate 2. 0—6—0 No. 648 was built by Dübs & Co. in 1868 and in 1907 went on to become, after successive rebuildings, MR No. 2566, surviving until 1932. In this view we see the genuine Kirtley locomotive of the pre Johnson era. *National Railway Museum*

enlarged the physical power and dimensions of his loco-motives as years went by. The preserved 'single' No. 673 at the National Railway Museum (incidentally one of the first British designs to employ piston valves) is a large engine when put alongside its contemporaries yet only its Deeley smokebox differs significantly from the Johnson original.

Thus, in the passenger field, Johnson moved from the modest sized 2—2—2s and 2—4—0s of the Kirtley era to larger 2—4—0s and 4—4—0s, plus, of course, the celebrated bogie 'singles' of 1887 and later. Some of the newer Kirtley 2—4—0 engines were also 'beefed up' and virtually rebuilt to what amounted to full Johnson appearance, but he did not develop the 2—2—2 arrangement at all and the smaller Kirtley 2—4—0s were also gradually phased out.

In the goods field, the neat Johnson 0—6—0 design (*Plate 7*) became highly familiar, but, dainty proportions

Plate 3. 2—4—0 No. 158A represents a good example of a Johnsonised Kirtley locomo-tive dating from 1866. Photo-graphed at Cheltenham c.1905 in full Crimson Lake livery, this locomotive was to become, in 1907 MR No. 2, and later it was to be preserved in the National Collection as the sole surviving British double-framed 2—4—0 passenger locomotive. Regrettably, in its preserved form it is coupled to the 'wrong type' of tender for its Deeley condition and it seems unlikely that this can now be rectified.

National Railway Museum

Plates 4-6. These three pictures illustrate Johnson features on original Kirtley designs. *Plate 4* illustrates 2—4—0 No. 14 photographed at some date between June 1877 and December 1884. Almost certainly the locomotive is in MR green livery but the lining is almost precisely the same as adopted later for the red livery. Note the Johnson cab and chimney. Becoming No. 14A in 1890, this locomotive was withdrawn in 1892.

The second picture shows 2—4—0 No. 151, built in 1874 after Kirtley had died, but to his basic design. When constructed it was fitted with the flush fitting smokebox door and dart, a feature of Johnson's design until his final years. Becoming MR 110 in 1907, this locomotive was to remain in service until the end of 1930.

The last view of this trio, shows 0—6—0 No. 711, a 'Johnsonised' version of an old Kirtley double frame 0—6—0 built in 1869 by Dübs & Co. Seen here in full Crimson Lake livery, this locomotive was to become No. 2603 in 1907 and was to remain in service until 1936.

Collection Bernard Mathews
National Railway Museum
Authors' collection

4

Plate 7. 0—6—0 No. 1357 is seen here in full Crimson Lake livery at Skipton in 1905. Built in 1878 by Dübs & Co., this locomotive was the first of the larger-wheeled Johnson 0—6—0s which were rapidly multiplied during the next twenty or so years. Becoming MR No. 3020, the engine lasted until 1927.

Collection David White

notwithstanding, it was more powerful than its Kirtley predecessor, as interpreted by the fact that when the MR classified its fleet for power (see page 22) the Johnson engines became class 2 whereas the Kirtleys by and large became class 1, unless carrying Johnson designed boilers/cylinders with a sufficiently high boiler pressure and cylinder size to qualify for the '2' power classification.

Until the end of the 19th century, Johnson's engines all shared many visual features — the famous chimney, the stylish, albeit somewhat spartan cab, the safety valves and dome and the tender design being typical cases in point,

and at *Plates 7-9* we give some characteristic examples of his work during this period.

By the turn of the century, even Johnson's modest enhancement of engine power was proving inadequate for some tasks. His last and physically largest series of bogie 'singles' (the 'Princess of Wales' type — see *Plate 11*) lasted for a considerably shorter period than their predecessors and were also considered by many to have gone 'over the top' in terms of visual harmony. More drastic changes were needed and thus the Midland embarked on its next period of 'turmoil', as it were. Like the Kirtley/Johnson transition

Plate 8. '115' class 4—2—2 No. 116, later to become MR 671, is depicted here in the Works Grey version of the full Johnson livery. The classic Johnson lines can be clearly seen in this locomotive which, to the authors, represents his most attractive variant in the 4—2—2 series.
National Railway Museum

Plate 9. A Johnson 4—4—0 No. 356, originally No. 1665, c.1906/7 with the locomotive in full livery. Note that all boiler lagging bands are lined but the engine is carrying the new heraldic emblem on the cab side. The tender has simplified lining and undoubtedly carries the locomotive number on its side panels. Note the power class numerals on the upper cab side.
National Railway Museum

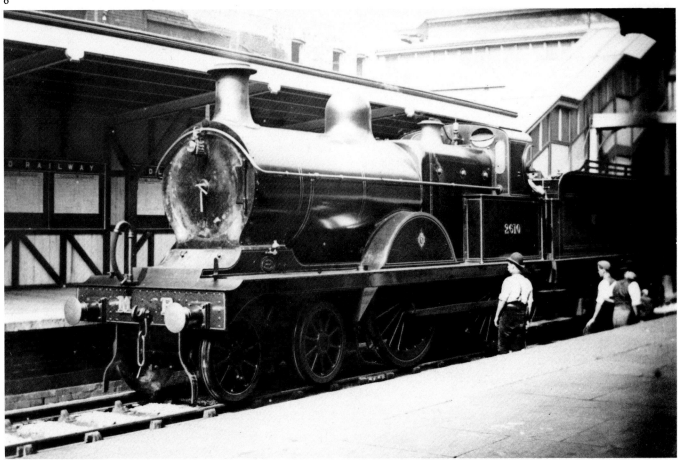

Plate 10. This picture shows Johnson 'Belpaire' No. 2610 at Kentish Town soon after building. The visual differences between the design 'as built' and as later modified by Deeley can readily be appreciated by comparing this view with, for example, *Plate 26.* No. 2610 became No. 704 in 1907 and was superheated in 1914. It was an early withdrawal (1927). Note the seriffed 'MR' on the front buffer plank — somewhat unusual (see page 100).   *Collection Bernard Mathews*

(1873-83), it was to last for about ten years or so and, again like the previous period of change, it gave new visual lines and a considerably altered livery to the locomotive fleet, although the 'red engine' theme remained — at least in part.

The beginning of the change was initiated by Johnson himself in the last few years of his period of office and, visually was heralded in 1900/02 by two, totally new, 4—4—0 designs, the 2 cylinder simple 'Belpaires' and the first 3-cylinder 'Compounds'. Gone were the slim boilers, elegant chimneys, Salter safety valves and all, to be replaced by an altogether more massive concept. They did not look like Johnson engines at all — but the Midland needed them for its heavier trains which now included corridor coaches and dining cars. A year later, Johnson put a much larger boiler onto a series of new 0—6—0s (later class 3) and, although the design retained a round-top firebox and a cab of traditional Johnson shape (*Plate 15*), things were obviously never going to be the same again. Even the full Johnson livery (see Chapter 5) never looked quite so splendid on these latest engines.

We do not and probably never will know just how much Johnson himself wanted to make these changes, but it is a fact that he left the Midland at the end of 1903 and was succeeded in 1904 by the real instigator of most of the Edwardian alterations — Richard Mountford Deeley.

Deeley only held the top locomotive post for some six years (1904-9) and it is generally reckoned that he eventually left the Midland as a result of internal disagreements, but by the time he went, he had set Midland locomotive development on a totally different course. His successor, Henry Fowler, was no great innovator (as the LMS also discovered in the 1920s!) and seems to have been content to condone further examples of the 'Deeley' approach. In consequence, it seems to us that we can bracket the 'Deeley/Fowler' régimes together as representing the final part of our story and this we have done in this survey.

What is undoubtedly true is that the new visual lines, which now came to prominence, owed little, if anything, to Fowler. They were, in fact, to hold sway well beyond the Midland period largely because of the locomotive policy adopted by the LMS in 1923 which perpetuated the Midland style for the new company. Quite apart from the continuation of the almost pure MR types ('Compounds', class '2' 4—4—0s, 0—6—0s, 0—6—0Ts), most of the new LMS 'standards' introduced before 1932 (2—6—2Ts, 2—6—4Ts, class '7F' 0—8—0s, 'Royal Scot' 4—6—0s, and even the 'Patriot' 4—6—0s) carried many 'Deeley' inspired visual lines. It was only with the advent of Stanier in 1932 that this final Midland 'face' became obsolescent and even Stanier built some class '4' 0—6—0s in 1941!

Plate 11. The last of the 'classic' Johnson slim boiler designs was his fifth and largest series of bogie 'singles', the so-called 'Princess of Wales' class, introduced in 1900. This view shows the second member of the series, No. 2602 (later No. 686), in totally unlined livery — probably plain crimson during its ex-works running-in period. The lack of lining serves to emphasise the somewhat ungainly look of these ultimate 4—2—2s, and this was only partially offset when they received lining (*see Plate 149*). The engine itself still showed some graceful lines but the large 'watercart' bogie tenders were somewhat ungainly and grotesque when attached to the typical original Johnson style locomotive. The end product displayed such a considerable loss of balance to the whole ensemble that, by previous Johnson standards, it almost constituted an aesthetic disaster area!

Collection Bernard Mathews

Plate 12. When the bogie tenders were coupled to the new, larger 4—4—0 types, the visual balance was vastly better than with the 4—2—2s, a fact readily apparent in this rear three-quarter view of 'Compound' No. 2633 (later No. 1002) in its original condition and taking water at Appleby c.1904/5. The engine is less than pristine in terms of cleanliness but seems to be carrying the full Johnson livery, modified only in respect of the tender side panels (see page 151). The new cab shape, Belpaire firebox and reduced height boiler mountings, were all clearly featured on these engines and, although not copied exactly by Deeley in later years, obviously formed the basis of Deeley's later changes. As built, however, these final Johnson 4—4—0s (including the visually somewhat similar 'Belpaires' [see *Plate 10*]) were, in their own way, as well proportioned and balanced in appearance as any of the previous Johnson designs, even if this was not fully appreciated at the time.

Collection Bernard Mathews

Plate 13. Deeley's large passenger locomotives are represented by Nos. 1011 and 990. 'Compound' 4—4—0 No. 1011 was built in 1905 as No. 1006 and became 1011 in 1907. Photographed c.1920, this locomotive was to remain in a saturated condition until the end of 1922 and lasted in service until 1951.

Authors' collection

Deeley seems to have been at times a difficult man, but he also appreciated some of the fundamental problems of the MR system. Firstly he realised that engines had to get bigger and more powerful and secondly he seems to have appreciated that locomotive costing needed attention. In consequence, and in pursuance of the first of these needs, the engines changed their physical appearance in terms of what might be called 'anatomy'. Secondly, in pursuance of more economical costing, they began to lose much of their previous decorative 'finery' as well. The LMS was to pursue this latter aspect throughout its life until virtually everything was unrelieved black (and pretty scruffy with it), but we feel the first steps on this road began with Deeley.

Turning first to the physical 'shape' of the engines, Deeley's new designs had a more severely functional character than their predecessors and are well exemplified by the first of his own version of the 'Compound' 4—4—0 and his own class '4' 2-cylinder simple 4—4—0 (*Plates 13 & 14*). The cab profile was clearly derived from Johnson's 'Belpaires' and 'Compounds' but the cab itself was made larger and more protective for the crew — early industrial relations, perhaps? At the smokebox end, the whole character changed with the introduction of the 'dog-ring' door fixing, strap hinges and new chimney design, and we go into this in more detail in Chapter 3. A new larger, flat-sided tender design also appeared on these 4—4—0s.

These structural changes were combined in 1905/6 with a new basic livery, incorporating smokebox numberplates,

large numerals on the tender side and a considerable simplification of lining treatment. The body colour may have remained the same at least on passenger and vacuum fitted goods engines, but the overall effect was distinctly new. When this was later, in and after 1907, combined with a completely re-cast locomotive numbering and power classification scheme (see page 22) based on the needs of the new train control system, the Midland really had changed its image.

The new livery style (with its large numbers) was adopted, amongst other reasons, in order to enable signalmen more readily to identify engines when reporting to 'control', and the changes were further emphasised with the introduction of a new MR heraldic emblem in 1906 and a decision to paint all goods engines black in 1910.

In fact, the decorative changes started somewhat before Deeley's time and took some time to become established in standard form. From c.1900-10 there were to be seen, therefore, many 'experimental' or non-standard practices which we have tried to analyse in Chapters 4 to 6. Contemporary observers were confused to say the least!

Had Deeley's changes been confined simply to the new visual lines for his own design of engines and a new style livery for the whole fleet, it would have been change enough, but overlaying all that has been said so far, was the start, c.1903/4, of a massive 'face lift' for very many of the older engines. Just as Johnson had, during the 1870s and 1880s, rebuilt and restyled Kirtley's engines, so did Deeley

Plate 14. This second picture shows one of 10 simple expansion 4−4−0s built to compare the merits of simple v. compound propulsion. These '990' class locomotives entered service between 1907-1909, all in saturated condition, but they were soon to be superheated as seen in this picture. No. 990 was the last to be built and the first to be withdrawn, in 1925. Whilst the majority of this class were renumbered in the 800-809 series, No. 990 never carried its allotted number 800.   *National Railway Museum*

Plate 15. Although not built until 1906, under the superintendency of R. M. Deeley, class 3 0−6−0 No. 281 is, to all intents and purposes, a Johnson locomotive and representative of his final years. Note the flowerpot chimney and longer cab which should be compared with those fitted to his smaller goods engines, which were to be classified as 2. Seen here as built and fitted with an 'H' boiler, No. 281 was to become No. 3811 in 1907 and received a Belpaire boiler in 1920. As such it remained in service until withdrawal in 1951 as British Railways No. 43811.

National Railway Museum

Plate 16. This and, indeed, most of the next few pictures illustrate various Kirtley and Johnson locomotives after receiving Deeley and/or Fowler modifications. This view shows 4–2–2 'single' No. 624 with a Deeley 'front end', smokebox and chimney. The flat smokebox door with horizontal handrail is a variation further discussed on page 59. *National Railway Museum*

Plate 17. In this picture we see a member of the old Kirtley '156' class 2–4–0s in its final Midland condition, now fitted with a Deeley chimney and smokebox. Photographed at Radlett, probably just after the end of the First World War, this locomotive did not survive to become an LMS locomotive, being withdrawn in 1921. *Collection the late A. G. Ellis*

get to work on his predecessor's machines. This time, however, it was products of *both* the Johnson and Kirtley régimes which received attention. We try to deal with these changes as they affect specific types in the class chapters in Volumes 2 and 3, but we feel it would be helpful to give a general summary here.

In essence and discounting livery/renumbering aspects, Deeley's innovations took three forms and we will deal with them in order.

Firstly was the question of replacement of worn-out components on engines which could otherwise expect to have further useful life. In these cases, the changes usually took the form of replacement 'front end' components (see also Chapter 3) on otherwise largely unaltered engines. Thus many Kirtley and Johnson engines found themselves with Deeley pattern smokeboxes and chimneys but otherwise little changed from the Johnson period (e.g. *Plate 16*).

Examples from most classes can be identified in this category but they included virtually all of the 4—2—2s (including the preserved No. 673) and many 2—4—0s, 0—6—0s, 0—6—0Ts and 0—4—4Ts. Many of these locomotives were actually given new boilers as well (to the old dimensions) and some of the early 4—4—0s were similarly dealt with, but most of the latter group of engines fell into the second category of Deeley's work. In this second category, a more comprehensive and at times utterly confusing rebuilding took place and we must give this aspect a reasonable amount of space.

The Midland was always a great 'rebuilder' of its engines and it is frequently difficult to determine how much of the original was left. In some cases, the only thing remaining unchanged was the locomotive number (!) — and then not always — and we have found it expedient to refer to the process as 'renewal' in many instances in this survey.

The single most noticeable example of this sort of practice was the 'renewal' of most of the 'slim-boilered' Johnson 4—4—0s dating from the 1880s and 1890s. The aim was to get more power output without building new engines (after all, most of them were well under twenty years old). In essence, and bearing in mind the dangers of over-simplified generalisation, this took the form of fitting the new larger 'H' round-topped boiler (first introduced by Johnson on his 0—6—0s of 1903) and a new rounded eaves cab on the old engines, frequently accompanied by enhanced boiler pressure and cylinder dimensions. These 'H' boiler rebuilds displayed much simpler visual lines (see *Plate 19*) and totally destroyed the elegant Johnson lines of the original engines.

Slightly later in the story (c.1908-9) a Belpaire firebox development of this larger boiler made its appearance and was applied to other 4—4—0s (*Plate 25*). Some engines received both types, in turn! Examples of all of these variants reached the LMS.

A somewhat similar process was also applied to *some* of the Johnson 0—6—0s. Many became class '3' when given round-top 'H' boilers and/or Belpaire equivalents like the 4—4—0s, but others, confusingly, were rebuilt with smaller Belpaire boilers from 1917 (a new innovation) and remained class '2' — these also included some Kirtley engines as well!

Plate 18. This and the next two pictures have been selected to illustrate very clearly the confusing story of certain Midland Railway 4—4—0s which changed in a few years from slim-boilered locomotives of the Victorian period to the Belpaire locomotives which survived into the British Railways era. No. 403, photographed in 1907 after renumbering using brass cabside numbers, was built in 1892 as No. 2183, the first of the series of Sharp Stewart 4—4—0s. This locomotive was rebuilt with an 'H' boiler in 1907 but regrettably the authors have not been able to trace a picture of No. 403 in this condition.   *National Railway Museum*

Plate 19. This picture of No. 410 in simplified Crimson Lake livery has been included to illustrate a '2183' class in 'H' boiler condition. Originally No. 2190, this locomotive received an 'H' boiler in 1906 and was renewed as a '483' class locomotive in 1920. Withdrawal was in 1953 as No. 40410.   *National Railway Museum*

Plate 20. No. 403 in its final form as a '483' class rebuild. This rebuild took place in 1920 and the locomotive is shown here as an oil burner. No. 403 lasted until 1950 when it was withdrawn still carrying its LMS number.   *Collection Bernard Mathews*

Plate 21. The 'Deeley' visual lines began to appear in the mid-Edwardian period and, apart from *new* locomotives, were probably best exemplified by the rebuilt examples of the slim-boilered Johnson 4—4—0s such as No. 1579 (later No. 345) seen here at Leeds c.1906/7. The engine has the new round-topped 'H' boiler, new Deeley style smokebox and fittings and the new cab design. The livery is also to the new simplified Deeley style with large tender numerals, new cabside emblem and front numberplate, all of which came into use more or less simultaneously in 1905-7. No. 1579 was rebuilt in 1906 so was probably an early example to receive the new paint treatment and, of course, was renumbered in 1907. It was never subsequently modified and was withdrawn by the LMS in this form in 1925.

Collection Bernard Mathews

Many of these 0—6—0s, rebuilt with either class '2' or class '3' boilers, *also* got new rounded eaves cabs (including a few Kirtley engines) and confusion became more widespread (*Plate 30*). This newer class '2' Belpaire boiler was later applied (by both the MR and later the LMS) to some formerly class '3' 'H' boilered round-tops, making things even worse!

As if this was not enough, superheating had also made its appearance. By now, Fowler was in charge and, although the visual characteristics of the engines remained 'Deeley',

the 'superheating factor', if we may thus describe it, caused further changes.

Dealing first with the 4—4—0s, the class 3 and 4 engines ('Belpaires', 'Compounds' and '990' class 'simples') gradually received superheaters with *relatively* little change in general appearance characteristics, save for the original 'Johnson' engines, especially the 'Compounds', which now assumed purely 'Deeley' looks, e.g. the preserved ex-Johnson No. 1000 at the National Railway Museum. This superheating in the case of the 'Belpaires' and 'Compounds', was not com-

Plate 22. This view of 4—4—0s Nos. 338/535 coaling at Derby in 1909, well exemplifies the first/second stage rebuilding of the original slim-boilered Johnson engines. The first stage rebuild, with round-top 'H' boiler is represented by No. 535 (formerly No. 6) in the background (with 3,500 gallon tender) whereas No. 338 (No. 1572 until 1907) has a saturated Belpaire boiler and is coupled to a 2,950 gallon tender. It carried a round-top 'H' boiler from 1907-9 only, before assuming the condition shown. Note the lack of bottom beading on the side and rear of tender of No. 338. The lining is applied as if beading had been present.

National Railway Museum

Plate 23. Many of the slim-boilered Johnson 4—4—0s, having been rebuilt with 'H' boilers and/or saturated Belpaire boilers, were 'renewed' at a later stage as members of the superheated '483' class, and this picture of No. 505 illustrates such a renewal. Built in 1899 as No. 2423, it received an 'H' boiler in 1908 and was renewed to '483' class in 1912. This picture shows the engine in LMS pre 1928 livery, precisely the same as the final MR style, save for ownership markings.   *National Railway Museum*

Plate 24. Deeley's rebuilding of the original Johnson 'Compounds' is seen in this view of No. 1003. Built in 1903 as No. 2634 (see Volume 2), it became No. 1003 in 1907 and was rebuilt, with superheater as illustrated, in 1915. Withdrawal as British Railways No. 41003 was in 1951.
Collection Bernard Mathews

Plate 25. The old '1562' class of 4—4—0s dated from 1882 and commencing in 1904 began to be renewed with 'H' boilers. No. 1573 became No. 339 in 1907, the same year that it received its 'H' boiler. Only two years later it was again rebuilt, as illustrated, with a saturated Belpaire boiler and in this condition it survived until 1928 when it was withdrawn by the LMS. *Collection Bernard Mathews*

Plate 26. The Johnson 'Belpaires' were all built between 1900 and 1905 and in due course began to receive Deeley smokeboxes and chimneys while still in a saturated condition, as seen in this view of No. 756. This picture is additionally interesting in that it shows a locomotive equipped for oil burning. From a livery standpoint the picture clearly shows how, at a time when the outsides of locomotive main frames were generally painted black, the inside cylinder 4—4—0s had the forward front of the frame painted Crimson Lake and lined out (see also page 151). No. 756 was superheated in 1923 and ran until 1949 when it was withdrawn without being renumbered by British Railways. *National Railway Museum*

pleted at the time of the railway grouping (1923) but *was* continued by the LMS. In the case of the 'Compounds', it was taken to completion but some of the 'Belpaires' were withdrawn in saturated state.

The other 4—4—0s, all of them 2-cylinder 'simples', and most already at the first or second stage of 'renewal' from their original Johnson 'slim boiler' state, were also affected by superheating. This took the form of further renewal or rebuild, depending on one's choice of words, to the '483' class — a high footplate, superheated version (*Plate 23*) which also became the basis of the LMS standard class 2 superheated 4—4—0 with 6 ft 9 in wheels, built new from

mostly but slowly assumed 'Belpaire' form and those which did not, were either scrapped as 'H' boiler round-top or received class 2 Belpaire boilers.

The tank engine story followed somewhat similar lines. The Deeley 'front end' became commonplace on all types and some of the smaller engines (class 1 0—6—0Ts and 0—4—4Ts) also received replacement Belpaire boilers. The class 3 0—6—0Ts all became Belpaired and the 0—6—4Ts were superheated (with Belpaire boilers) across the time of grouping.

The residual 2—4—0s, of both Kirtley and Johnson designs, mostly (probably wholly) received 'Deeley' style

Plate 27. The various reboilering and rebuilding of the old Kirtley 0—6—0s finally produced the visual style shows in this picture, which should be compared with *Plates 2 and 6* which show the earlier stages in their development. In this condition No. 2421 was to last until 1931.
Authors' collection

1928. In some cases this '483' class 4—4—0 renewal even involved a change of wheelbase and/or driving wheel size, 7' 0½" wheels and 9' 6" wheelbase, being the 'norm' for the '483' class.

Thus, in 1923, the LMS received in the 'below class 3' category not a simple series of 4—4—0 engines, but a highly 'mixed bag' of types. There were some 4—4—0 engines still class 1 and basically slim-boilered Johnson (save for Deeley smokebox/chimneys), others were 'H' boiler or saturated Belpaire (class 2) rebuilds dating from c.1905-9, and a further series were superheated '483' class renewals. All their numbers in the 'new' 1907 series were mixed together. The LMS continued the '483' class renewal programme to some extent, but the residual round-top 'H' boilered engines soon went to the scrapheap, followed more slowly by any surviving *saturated* Belpaire boilered types if not renewed as '483' class.

A somewhat similar story applied to the 0—6—0s, with the LMS continuing the former Midland rebuilding policy — to some extent — and scrapping the older, non-rebuilt engines. This was additionally influenced by the introduction of the class 4 superheated 0—6—0. What happened was, basically, that the superheated class 4 was built new during both late MR times and by the LMS until 1941. The class 2 engines continued, to some extent, to receive new class '2' Belpaire boilers — not all, however — and the class 3 engines

'front-ends' and many of the Johnson breed also received Belpaire boilers in due course but with no enhancement in power class.

All told, therefore, virtually the whole of the MR fleet, if not actually scrapped, displayed at least some Deeley visual influences in its final days and certainly in the LMS period. We believe that the final Johnson pattern 'front-end' had, with few exceptions, disappeared by c.1917 although the overall Johnson (and indeed Kirtley) proportions remained to the end if the locomotive in question had not been rebuilt with larger capacity boiler or other enhanced proportions — and there we must leave this aspect until Volumes 2 and 3.

The third category of Deeley influence — carried out by Fowler — was, of course, that displayed on *new* engines. We have already mentioned the new 'Compounds' and '990' class 4—4—0s which 'set the style' as it were in 1905-7 and this was augmented by new Deeley built 'Belpaire' class 3 4—4—0s and, in 1908, by the advent of a series of *new* 0—6—0s which carried the 'Johnson' round-top 'H' boiler of 1903 but also displayed the new 'Deeley cab' style (*Plate 29*).

These developments clearly established the 'house style' for the various rebuildings and renewals already covered and were obviously instrumental in the development of Fowler's new superheated class '4' 0—6—0 of 1911

Plate 28. A few Kirtley double-frame 0–6–0s were further altered by Deeley and we have selected this picture of 0–6–0 No. 2818 to show a locomotive now equipped with a rounded-eaves cab and modified (upgraded) to Class 2 – a process further discussed in this volume.

Authors' collection

Plate 29. Deeley's development of the final Johnson 0–6–0 goods engines (*Plate 15*) incorporated a new rounded-eaves cab style whose cab sides included the rear driving wheel splasher. We think that a better visual balance resulted from Deeley's changes. Somehow, the traditional Johnson style did not suit the bigger engines. Built in 1908, No. 3834 was the last of the class 3s to be constructed and the locomotive remained in 'H' boiler, round-top condition until 1918, when it was rebuilt with a 'G7' Belpaire boiler to assume the visual characteristics shown in *Plate 31*. This is a particularly interesting picture and shows a locomotive which, although vacuum fitted, could possibly be in Locomotive Brown livery (see page 97).

Collection Bernard Mathews

Plate 30. Starting in 1917 Fowler began to reboiler some of the class '2' goods engines using a Belpaire boiler which was classified as 'G6' and this picture of No. 2998 has been selected as typical of the end product. Built in 1876 as MR No. 1230, it was rebuilt in 1920 and lasted until 1959 when it was withdrawn as British Railways No. 58171. *Authors' collectioon*

Plate 31. The familiar class '3F' 0−6−0 Belpaire boiler rebuild is shown in this picture of No. 3371, whose origins date from 1892 when it was built to the standard Johnson style (by Sharp Stewart), as MR No. 1892. Becoming MR 3371 in 1907, it was reboilered in 1921 and lasted until 1961 when it was withdrawn by British Railways as No. 43371. *Authors' collection*

Plate 32. The flat Deeley smokebox door is seen in this view of 0–4–4T No. 1263 in conjunction with a Johnson chimney and continuous handrail. Photographed in the post 1907 Deeley version of the Crimson Lake livery, this locomotive was to survive until 1936.

Collection the late A. G. Ellis

Plate 33. The final design of Johnson's 0–6–0Ts is seen in this view of condenser fitted No. 1909 as running with a Deeley chimney and smokebox door, but still retaining the old type of continuous handrail. This series of 0–6–0Ts were all to be equipped eventually with Belpaire boilers and in the case of 1909 this happened in 1941 by which date it had been renumbered (by the LMS c.1934) 7209. Withdrawal by British Railways as 47209 was in 1961.

Authors' collection

Plate 34. Many Johnson locomotives received Belpaire boilers during the LMS era and the next three plates illustrate three classes in this guise. 0—4—4T No. 1422 is seen at Kingscliffe in 1937 carrying the LMS 'intermediate' livery (see page 104). Built as MR No. 2622 in 1900, it received a Belpaire boiler in 1927. Withdrawal as British Railways No. 58085 was in 1955. Note the blended red shading to the insignia (see page 156).

H. C. Casserley

Plate 35. 'Open cab' 0—6—0T No. 1664 at Kentish Town in June 1935, displaying a Belpaire boiler. Built in 1878 as MR No. 1381, it was to run until 1953 when it was withdrawn by British Railways as 41664.

Authors' collection

Plate 36. During the 1920s quite a considerable number of the surviving Johnson 2—4—0s were reboilered by the LMS with Belpaire boilers, and this picture of No. 238 shows a locomotive so equipped and displaying LMS pre 1928 livery. Even the Deeley/Fowler front end and the Belpaire boiler cannot totally destroy the elegance! Built in 1880 as MR No. 1488, it was reboilered in 1927. Becoming LMS 20238 in 1934 it was to run until 1938.
                                                                                                                                    W. L. Good

(*Plate 37*) and, in visual terms, his '483' class rebuilds of the class '2' 4—4—0s in 1912, and even the new Somerset and Dorset 2—8—0s of 1914 (see *Plate 38* and Volume 3).

Consequently, by the outbreak of World War I, the Midland Railway had incurred a total change of visual face since 1900 — much of which stemmed from the Deeley period (1904-9). Not all of its engines had, at that time, acquired the new Deeley details but, just as Johnson had altered the Kirtley 'look' in the 1870s and 1880s, so too did Deeley initiate a further round of changes and by the grouping the Midland's engines bore the unmistakable stamp of the 'new' order.

Of course, when dealt with in detail, there were numerous exceptions to the generalised pattern we have tried to trace in the preceding few pages and one of the principal aspects of the remainder of this and the next two volumes will be to try and sort out the details as they affect both general matters (e.g. locomotive details and liveries) and specific classes. However, it is a measure of both Kirtley's and Johnson's stature that unless their engines had been totally rebuilt (renewed?) during the Deeley-Fowler era, they bore the unmistakable stamp of their original creator(s) right to the very end — no matter how much modification had taken place. Therein lies our fascination with the Midland and its locomotives. This railway did not pursue an uninterrupted line of evolution as did the GWR (post-William Dean) or the LNWR in the Webb-Whale-Bowen Cooke epoch. The Midland was different and, to purloin a well-worn cliché, 'Vive la difference!'

We conclude this preliminary chapter with a few general notes which readers may find helpful before studying the remaining chapters of this (and subsequent) volumes.

LOCOMOTIVE RENUMBERING (1907)

The great renumbering of 1907 was a first (and successful) attempt by a British company to organise engine numbers systematically. It brought the types together in general groups (by utilisation) and within each group, produced consecutive number series for each specific class. The LMS followed the same idea in 1923 and it stood the test of time.

The renumbering of the existing MR locomotive stock commenced in 1907 and was completed in December of that year. By the grouping in 1923 the scheme had encompassed the following MR locomotive numbers but within these series there were numerous gaps due to withdrawals. Also added onto this number series by 1923 were most of the LT & SR locomotives which had been absorbed by the Midland Railway in 1912. These locomotives are described in Volume 2.

Passenger tender locomotives	1-1044
Tank locomotives	1198-1430 — passenger types
	1500-1959 — freight types
	2000-2039 — passenger type
	(Deeley 0—6—4T)
	and added later
Freight tender locomotives	2200-4026

Within each overall number series, the numbers were arranged in either wheel arrangement or ascending power class — both, where applicable — with the oldest engines in any category getting the lowest numbers. Thus the smallest (least powerful) engines generally carried the lowest numbers in a series and the newest and generally more powerful designs took the highest numbers. All things being equal, this meant that new construction (being normally of the

Plate 37. The final design of goods engine built by the Midland Railway was known as the 'Big Goods' and in due course was classified as 4. Two were built in 1911 and then, in 1917, construction commenced in earnest until a further 190 had been built before the grouping. This picture of 0—6—0 No. 3892 illustrates a locomotive built in 1919 and which was withdrawn in 1958 as British Railways No. 43892. Other than tender changes and other minor visual alterations (see Volume 3) the class 4s remained visually far less variable than other MR 0—6—0 types.   *Authors' collection*

Plate 38. Although not built for the Midland itself, the S & DJR 2—8—0s, dating from 1914, entirely typified the final Deeley/Fowler lines adopted on most Derby built/rebuilt engines. Locomotive No. 81 (later LMS Nos. 9671 [1930], 13801 [1934]) is seen here in somewhat grimy condition — it was actually black at the time — and carrying a headlamp on the smokebox door denoting its version of the 'light engine code'. These were the only class of tender engines built at Derby in pre-LMS days with outside Walschaerts valve gear and it has always been a source of some surprise the Derby did not build any for purely Midland use. They were pretty good engines and would certainly have come in handy for the heavy main line coal trains of the period which regularly got two quite small 0—6—0s, not always of the latest or most powerful type either.   *Collection Bernard Mathews*

newest and most powerful types) would be added at the end of the series.

In specifically Midland terms, the 1907 system fell short of perfection in but two main areas. Firstly, the 4—4—0s, 4—2—2s and 0—6—0s were numbered in relation to their 1903/4 status (i.e. 4—4—0s ahead of the 4—2—2s, the latter although of the same power class, having arrived later on the scene; and 0—6—0s in order of first building — i.e. Kirtley ahead of Johnson). In 1903/4 terms this would indeed have put them all in ascending power class order as well (below), but subsequent rebuilding (some of which had in fact *preceded* the 1907 numbering) meant that all of the rebuilt/renewed 4—4—0s had a higher power class than the 4—2—2s (which carried *higher* numbers) and some of the rebuilt 0—6—0s carrying lower numbers, were, in their new form, of higher power class than unrebuilt engines of the same wheel arrangement which, in original form, had been built at a later date and therefore carried higher numbers! We try to sort this out in later parts of the work.

The second area of confusion affected the Deeley 0—6—4Ts. The Midland did not normally differentiate between passenger and freight tanks but, in 1907, it did put the various 0—4—4Ts (passenger) ahead of the 0—6—0Ts (freight). On this basis, the 0—6—4Ts (essentially passenger types) could have been given numbers in the vacant 1431-99 series but they were actually numbered after the whole of the tank engine series in the 2000 + zone. This in turn, gave rise to some confusion during the LMS period after 1922 with other pre-group types which were added to the system, but this is outside the scope of this survey. The assimilation to the MR 1907 system of the ex-LT & SR engines in 1912 is covered in Volume 2.

LOCOMOTIVE AND POWER CLASSIFICATION

Prior to the 1907 renumbering, Midland locomotives were referred to by a variety of terms. Those built by outside contractors were allocated an alphabetical letter, e.g. 'L' class, whilst those built at Derby were usually referred to by their order number. However, enthusiasts often used the number of the first locomotive of the class, e.g. '1698' class to identify a particular series. In 1910 the company introduced a new series of engine diagrams and this method of identity has much to commend it, particularly when coupled with the post 1907 locomotive number. The 1910 series of engine diagrams should not be confused with earlier 'locomotive diagrams' or the 1919 series which took some of the 1910 diagrams and used them to cover several series of similar but not identical locomotives.

Starting in 1905, power classification identity began to appear on Midland locomotives and this is more fully covered within the livery section (see page 163). The scheme after the grouping was as below, but for completeness it does include some locomotives classified from 1905 but scrapped by 1923.

Passenger tender locomotives

Power class 1	1-281, 300-327, 600-684	2—4—0, 4—4—0, 4—2—2
Power class 2	328-562, 685-694	4—4—0, 4—2—2
Power class 3	700-779	4—4—0
Power class 4	990-1044	4—4—0

Tank locomotives

Not classified	1198-1199	4—4—0T
Power class 1	1200-1430	0—4—4T
Power class 3	2000-2039	0—6—4T
Power class 0	1500-1537	0—4—0T
Power class 1	1600-1899	0—6—0T
Power class 3	1900-1959	0—6—0T

Freight tender locomotives
(all 0—6—0 except where stated)

Power class 2	2200-2239 (American 'Mogul', all 2—6—0, extinct by 1915)
Power class 1	2300-2867 (Some class 2 within this series)
Power class 2	2900-3764 (Three locomotives were class 1 and many were class 3 within this series)
Power class 3	3137-3764 (Many were class 2 within this series)
Power class 3	3765-3834
Power class 4	3835-4026
Not classified	2290 (0—10—0 banking engine)

To recapitulate, the problem of locomotive identity is very complex as we have indicated. For example the various 4—4—0 reboilerings and rebuilding from the early 1900s did not, in some cases, alter the power classification, but the 0—6—0 rebuilding did. During a few years many of the 4—4—0s changed from slim-boilered 'Johnson' locomotives to high pitched 'H' boiler types and then to Belpaire boilers, and some locomotives retained the same number in two out of the three guises.

Many of the 4—4—0s finally emerged, from 1912, as members of the '483' class which further and totally altered their appearance. Various authorities speak of reboilering and rebuilding but, as we have stated, 'renewal using the old number' would not be an inaccurate term to use when describing some members of this group of engines.

Of the Kirtley 0—6—0s numbered in 1907 between 2300-2867, some were reboilered and reclassified as '2'. These locomotives (36 in all) are easily identified on the engine diagrams. However, the Johnson inside frame 0—6—0s are a problem. Once again to recapitulate, some went from small roundtop to large roundtop boilers (and in so doing went from power class 2 to power class 3) whilst others also went from power class 2 to power class 3 but exchanged their small roundtop boilers for large Belpaires. A third change was from small roundtop to small Belpaire and in so doing the power classification remained unchanged. A fourth change was from large roundtop class 3 to small Belpaire class 2, whilst the final change to be described was the large roundtop class 3 to large Belpaire class 3. It is in this form as the class '3' (or '3F' as they became in 1928) that they are probably best known.

It is small wonder that locomotive historians find MR locomotive history confusing in the post-Johnson period, and that modellers have some difficulty in assigning a correct running number to an otherwise visually accurate model. It is our hope that in the subsequent chapters of this and the next two volumes, we can shed some light on the subject — and we start by analysing the basic composition of the locomotive fleet.

CHAPTER TWO

A BASIC REVIEW
OF LOCOMOTIVE TYPES

PASSENGER TENDER LOCOMOTIVES

COMMENCING with the passenger tender types, we now begin to consider the various classes of Midland Railway locomotives which existed from 1883 onwards. At that time there were a number of 2—2—2s still in service and, whilst their importance as a class type declined, there were, nonetheless, a sufficient number in traffic at the beginning of 1884 for them still to provide an important element in the tender locomotive story. They were, however, all of Kirtley origin and, in accordance with our declared criteria in Chapter 1, we have left their story for others to describe in detail. They are represented in this volume in *Plates 41-43*. By 1900 these 'singles' were a dying breed and really have no part in our particular story. The handful still in service as 2—2—2s were withdrawn shortly after the turn of the century.

A similar 'minimal' approach has been taken with those 2—4—0s which existed in 1883 but which did not survive to receive 1907 numbers. However, some pictures have been included within these volumes to 'bridge the gap' and to provide continuity between the Kirtley and Johnson periods.

In 1883 the bulk of the express passenger work was performed by 2—4—0s and by this time all the Midland Railway locomotives of this wheel arrangement had been built. Of the 4—4—0s, the first 60 Johnson locomotives were in

traffic (with more to come) but the Johnson 'singles' were a few years away and did not appear until 1887. The years between 1883 and 1901 saw the construction of all of the slim-boilered Johnson 4—4—0s and 'singles', and the new century dawned with the Midland Railway facing a considerable increase in train weights as corridor coaches began to appear in ever increasing numbers.

The most powerful express passenger tender locomotives employed by the Midland Railway in 1900 were the various classes of Johnson 4—4—0s built from 1882 onwards and, although they displayed driving wheels of varying diameters from 6' 6" to 7' 0½", they were all very similar in appearance (see *Plate 46* which illustrates a locomotive built in 1899). These locomotives were subjected to rebuilding and reboilering during the next few years to produce very different looking machines and these changes are given in outline in this volume and in considerably more detail in Volume 2.

In 1900 the last of the final ten 'singles' were constructed to bring the total of these locomotives up to 95 and they were very much in the front line of express passenger service during the early 1900s.

Given this background, it will readily be appreciated that the scene in 1900 was of underpowered locomotives trying to cope with trains of increasing weight. The obvious and

Plate 39. 2—4—0 No. 150A. Built at Derby in 1859 as the first member of the '150' class, the locomotive was later rebuilt into the Johnson condition and is pictured here in full Crimson Lake livery at St. Albans on 19th July 1902. It was broken up at the end of 1903.

Collection Ken Nunn

Plate 40. No. 68A was built at Derby in 1873 and was a member of the '890' class. All but five of this class were renumbered in 1907, three being withdrawn prior to 1907 and two retained their old numbers. No. 68A, withdrawn in 1905, was one of the three early withdrawals.
Collection Bernard Mathews

urgent need was for more powerful types, and these were soon forthcoming.

Although 20 additional slim-boilered 4—4—0s entered traffic as late as 1901, a year earlier the first of the more powerful Johnson 'Belpaires' had entered service (see *Plate 48*). Most of these were eventually rebuilt and all were altered during their lifetime, but as early as 1905 the class had been expanded to eighty locomotives which were working the bulk of the Midland Railway's principal express

services until the grouping, well outnumbering their more powerful descendants, the forty-five 'Compound' and the ten simple '990' class 4—4—0s, which were collectively the most powerful express locomotives the company owned.

As early as 1902 the first two 'Compounds' had entered traffic, to be followed by three more in 1903. They were subsequently rebuilt as detailed later. Further 'Compounds', to a Deeley modification of the original design, entered

Plate 41. Photographed at Derby at some date after September 1892 (when it was placed upon the duplicate list for the second time) and before 1904 when it was broken up, this Kirtley 2—2—2 is shown here in its rebuilt Johnson condition. Dating from 1863, when it emerged from Derby as No. 30 (the first of the class), it went onto the duplicate list as No. 30A, then was restored to the capital list as No. 16. Three years later it was back on the duplicate list again in the condition illustrated.
Collection David White

Plate 42. As seen in this photograph, carrying Works Grey livery, Kirtley 2–2–2 No. 29A was placed upon the duplicate list in June 1887, prior to rebuilding with a Johnson boiler. Built at Derby in 1865 as a member of the '30' class, these locomotives were originally employed upon the Midland expresses from Bedford to Kings Cross via Hitchin. In 1889 the locomotive was reinstated in the capital list as No. 4, but in 1892 it became 4A on the duplicate list again. It ran with this number until being withdrawn in 1904. This photograph is worth careful study in so far as it shows an early example of the most probable lining used at this period in conjunction with Crimson Lake (see Chapter 5).

Collection Bernard Mathews

Plate 43. No. 133A, built at Derby in 1864 as No. 31, was a member of the '30' class and by 1888 it had been reboilered. In that year it also went onto the duplicate list. Two years later it went back onto the capital list as No. 133 and at the end of 1892 it was on the duplicate list again in the condition as illustrated. Withdrawal was in 1902. Although not a very clear photograph, the lining on the tender shows a single panel with a top line of yellow under the coping similar to that in *Plate 146* (see Chapter 4).

National Railway Museum

Plate 44. A number of 2–4–0Ts were built by Beyer Peacock in 1868. They were side tank condensing locomotives built for working the Metropolitan 'Inner Circle' line to the city. However, they were reported to be unsatisfactory and in 1870 they were rebuilt as 2–4–0 tender locomotives numbered 230-239. In 1895 they all went onto the duplicate list and were withdrawn between 1896 and 1906. No. 238A illustrated was the final survivor and is seen here in full Crimson Lake livery.

Collection Roger Carpenter

Plate 45. A series of ten 7 ft driving wheel 4—4—0s emerged from Derby in 1884, but they were not very successful and were all renewed between 1896 and 1901. This picture of No. 1676 shows one of the two (1675/6) which were fitted with Westinghouse brakes as well as vacuum brakes, the others having vacuum brakes only. No. 1676 was 'renewed' in 1901 and in due course received an 'H' boiler. In 1907 it became No. 492 and in 1912 was renewed yet again as a member of the '483' class. In this guise it survived until 1948 when it was finally withdrawn from service.   *Authors' collection*

Plate 46. 4—4—0 No. 2434 was built in 1899 and is shown here before being renumbered 516 which was done prior to the locomotive receiving an 'H' boiler. Renewal to '483' class was in 1912 and withdrawal was in 1950 as 40516.   *Collection Roger Carpenter*

Plate 47. A typical late Johnson condition is represented by this illustration of No. 44 which later became No. 119 in 1907. The locomotive was withdrawn in 1929. In this picture the locomotive carries a 'Rebuilt 1901' plate and is seen in full Crimson Lake livery.

Collection Roger Carpenter

traffic between 1905 and 1909 and all were later super-heated, although many were not so treated until after the grouping.

The last new design was the '990' class 4—4—0 simple expansion class 4 type. The pioneer locomotive was built in 1907 with nine others being completed in 1909.

While these more powerful class '3' and '4' locomotives were being built, an extensive programme of rebuilding and renewal was proceeding with all but the first thirty of the slim-boilered Johnson 4—4—0s. This involved boiler changes, new cabs, splashers and the like, and frequently happened more than once in the lifetime of any particular locomotive. Thus, although the initial rebuilds were with round-top 'H' boilers, the majority were again renewed as members of the superheated '483' class, bearing the same 1907 numbers as the locomotives they replaced. How much of the original was left is open to some conjecture.

Adding complication to the "slim boiler — 'H' boiler — '483' class" progression, was the insertion of an intermediate stage on some other examples of Johnson 4—4—0s. These received *saturated* Belpaire boilers with extended smoke-boxes, and chronologically stand between the 'H' boiler phase and the final superheated '483' state.

By the grouping, the forty-five 'Compounds', ten '990s' and eighty ('700' class) class 3 'Belpaires' provided the power for the principal express trains, whilst the class '483' renewals provided the second line in conjunction with the other unrebuilt Johnson 4—4—0s still in service. The ranks of the 'singles' were rapidly being depleted by 1923 and the 2—4—0s were also decreasing in numbers, the survivors being very much employed upon secondary or local work, including piloting.

During the early years of the grouping, the final saturated 'Compounds' were superheated together with some, but not all, of the remaining saturated examples of the ('700' class) class 3 'Belpaires' and the final examples of class 2 loco-motives to be renewed as members of the '483' class.

Construction of LMS standard locomotives to what were in effect Midland designs comprised 195 'Compounds' and 138 class '2P' 4—4—0s. These locomotives were in service by 1932 and they enlarged the Midland family of tender passenger locomotives, the last of which survived into the 1960s. During LMS days the 'Compounds' continued to be employed upon top link work until the arrival of the 4—6—0s of class '5' and class '5XP', but from the mid to late 1930s the 'Compounds' went into a decline, often ending their days working parcels and local passenger trains. A similar story applied to the 'Belpaires', whilst the class '2P' 4—4—0s worked all manner of trains from local passen-ger to trip goods and ballast trains until they were finally all withdrawn.

The 2—4—0 types had, by the grouping, largely been relegated to local work, so the story of Midland Railway tender passenger locomotives during the LMS era was one of declining importance, especially from c.1934 onwards.

A number of pictures of Midland Railway passenger tender locomotives have been selected to illustrate the examples of some of the various classes which were running from 1883 onwards and, whilst they do not include all the varieties which were in service, they should provide the reader with a suitable cross-section until we describe them all in considerably greater detail in Volume 2.

Plate 48. No. 2788 was one of the second series of 'Belpaires' and became No. 717 in 1907. The later history of this locomotive included rebuilding with a G8AS boiler in 1919 and withdrawal by the LMS in 1935. It is seen here in its original condition in full Crimson Lake livery and the reader's attention is drawn to the apparent difference in hue of the firebox compared with the boiler, probably no more than a partial repaint or revarnish. Although not entirely apparent from the photograph, the locomotive is coupled to a bogie tender.

Collection Roger Carpenter

Plate 49. The first 'Compound' is illustrated in this picture which shows No. 2631 shortly after it was built. No. 2631 was to become No. 1000 and eventually it was preserved in its final superheated form as part of the National Collection. In this picture it has a bogie tender and is running with indicator shelters. Note that they have been lined out and liveried to harmonise with the locomotive.

Collection Roger Carpenter

Plate 50. The intermediate stage between the original slim-boilered Johnson 4—4—0 design and the final superheated Belpaire '483' class was the period when the engines carried the 'H' boiler, and this picture of No. 2587 clearly illustrates a locomotive in this condition c.1906. Built in 1900 as No. 2587, this locomotive became No. 479 in 1907, having been reboilered in the condition as shown in 1905. Renewed as a '483' class in 1917, the locomotive was withdrawn at the end of 1949.

Collection Roger Carpenter

Plate 51. The '483' class renewals formed, in effect, the basis of the LMS standard class '2' 4–4–0s, albeit with detail alterations in the LMS type when compared with the Midland Railway locomotives. Note the bogie brakes, typical for this period. No. 551 was rebuilt to '483' class in 1913 and withdrawn as No. 40551 in 1953. This locomotive was originally No. 2639 and was reboilered with an 'H' boiler in 1907 at about the time of renumbering.

Collection Roger Carpenter

Plate 52. The ten members of the '990' class were built as saturated locomotives, but within a few years they had all been superheated, and this picture of No. 995 shows a locomotive in this condition. Photographed at Derby in August 1920, the locomotive was to become No. 805 shortly before withdrawal in 1928.

H. C. Casserley

Plate 53. Built at Derby in 1886 as No. 1752, this locomotive received an 'H' boiler in 1906 and was renumbered in 1907, becoming 372. In 1911 it received a Belpaire boiler and ran in this condition until withdrawal in 1940.

Collection Bernard Mathews

Plate 54. No. 1008, which was to become No. 1013 in 1907, is seen here at Leeds Holbeck in 1906, a few months after it was built. As No. 1013 this locomotive was superheated in 1925 and was withdrawn by British Railways in 1949 without being renumbered.

J. H. Wright

Plate 55. The beautiful 'singles' of the 'old 115' class are represented by this picture of No. 130 which later was to become No. 683. Built in 1899, this locomotive was withdrawn in 1926. *Collection Roger Carpenter*

Plate 56. No. 615 in its final condition with a Deeley front end, dished smokebox door with a small vertical handle on the right-hand side of the locomotive. The engine is in fairly dirty condition and no doubt was approaching the end of its service which commenced in 1889 as No. 1858. Becoming No. 615 in 1907, the locomotive was withdrawn in 1922. *H. C. Casserley*

PASSENGER TANK LOCOMOTIVES

In 1883 there were relatively few passenger tank locomotives in Midland Railway stock. Those in service comprised the 0—4—4 well tanks built in 1869/70, the first of the long-lived Johnson 0—4—4Ts and some 4—4—0Ts built by Beyer Peacock, known as the Metropolitan Tanks. The latter were to a standard Beyer Peacock design supplied to a number of companies, the Midland examples surviving until 1912.

By 1900 the passenger tank locomotive stock had expanded considerably and consisted largely of Johnson design 0—4—4Ts of which a final 20 had entered traffic that year. The 0—4—4T group of locomotives were renumbered 1200 to 1430 in 1907, none having been withdrawn by that date. They included, of course, the original twenty-six well tanks of Kirtley design, whilst the remainder were to the Johnson design, exhibiting two different driving wheel diameters and variations of tank sizes, etc., as described in Volume 2.

The only other passenger tank locomotives still in service in 1900 were a handful of residual 'Metropolitan' 4—4—0Ts which did not survive over long, although two did manage to receive 1907 numbers.

A class of forty 0—6—4Ts was added to the Midland's stock in 1907 and these locomotives, known as 'flatirons' or 'hole in the wall tanks', were principally employed in the Birmingham and Manchester areas. A few were superheated prior to the grouping, with the remainder being superheated by 1927.

The Johnson 0—4—4Ts were long-lived with many surviving into the British Railways period. They were all of the round-top variety in Midland days, and superheating with Belpaire boilers, if done at all, was entirely in the LMS and subsequent period. During the LMS and BR period a number of 0—4—4Ts were motor-fitted and they survived on this type of duty until the end of their days.

The 0—6—4Ts were mostly used on the heavier local passenger trains but, coming under a cloud in the mid 1930s due to members of the class being involved in derailments, they were largely taken off passenger work and as a class were extinct by 1938. Only the Johnson 0—4—4Ts ran on into the British Railways period, the 0—4—4 well tanks having become extinct as early as 1935.

Plate 57. The oldest passenger locomotives in service during our period of survey were the Kirtley designs represented by this picture of No. 692 in early crimson livery. No. 692 was to become No. 1202 in 1907 and was withdrawn in 1928. As one of the Beyer Peacock locomotives it can be distinguished from the more numerous Dübs built machines by the bunker sides, the Dübs examples having an outward flare at the top.

Collection D. White

Plate 58. The Johnson 0—4—4Ts came with two principal driving wheel sizes, the larger wheel locomotives being less numerous. This picture, taken c.1900, illustrates larger-wheeled No. 1280 which was to become No. 1254 in 1907. Withdrawal was in 1937. Note the jack at the front of the running plate on the right-hand side. The engine is in full Crimson Lake livery. *Authors' collection*

Plate 59. Small wheeled 0—4—4T No. 1824, illustrated in this picture in full crimson livery, was built at Derby in 1889 and became No. 1332 in 1907. Withdrawal was in 1931 only three years after a Belpaire boiler had been fitted. *Collection Roger Carpenter*

Plate 60. No. 2222, seen here fitted with condensing apparatus and in full red livery, was built in 1893 by Dübs. The locomotive became No. 1375 in 1907, was fitted with a Belpaire boiler in 1925 and withdrawn by British Railways in 1953 as No. 58070. Note the 'X' plate at the front of the tank. We are not sure what this signified (possibly something to do with working over the Metropolitan lines?) and would welcome more details.
Authors' collection

Plate 61. The final passenger tank locomotives were the 'Flatirons' and No. 2032 represents this class in original condition. The locomotive was superheated in 1924 and was the last survivor, being withdrawn in 1938. The engine was photographed at Birmingham New Street (20th August 1921) in the simplified Deeley version of the Crimson Lake livery.
W. L. Good

Plate 62. This picture of 4–4–0T No. 206A was taken at Lancaster on 12th September 1902 some two years before it was withdrawn. Under close scrutiny there appears to be no evidence of any lining, so it possible that it is in plain Crimson Lake livery. The locomotive was a standard Beyer Peacock design used by the Metropolitan Railway and other companies. No. 206A was the only member of the class to retain the condensing apparatus until withdrawal, which occurred in 1904. Two achieved 1907 numbers but the class was extinct by 1912.
Collection Ken Nunn

Plate 63. This view of No. 1601 dates from late Midland Railway days and in due course the locomotive was renumbered 1605 by the LMS in 1923 and withdrawn in 1924. The official history of the locomotive begins in 1848 when as No. 80 it was built by E. B. Wilson as a 2—2—2 of the Jenny Lind type. In 1862 it was renumbered No. 102 and in 1867 it went onto the duplicate list as No. 722. The following year it was renumbered No. 1000 and was out of use from 1868-71. In 1872 it was renewed as an 0—6—0ST and renumbered 2000. The next change came in 1875 when it was rebuilt as an 0—6—0WT and renumbered No. 213. Matters remained thus until 1890 when it became No. 205A and then in 1907 it was renumbered 1601. As such it is depicted here in plain black livery. *Authors' collection*

GOODS TANK LOCOMOTIVES

By the end of 1883, the numerous Johnson 0—6—0Ts dating from 1874 and of which 110 were in service, were the largest single group of tank locomotives working on the Midland. Further construction continued until 1900. The only other class of any other significance in service in 1883 was the '880' class, a series of ten locomotives built in 1871, which survived until the late 1920s as Nos. 1610-19.

By the turn of the century, however, there had been a significant development in freight tank locomotive evolution. Although the final examples of the above-mentioned Johnson 0—6—0Ts (later to be known as class '1') entered traffic in 1900, the previous year had seen introduced the first of the much enlarged 0—6—0Ts (later to be known as class '3') which, in their rebuilt form, provided the basis for the standard LMS class '3F' shunting tank design which was to be built in considerable numbers. In 1907 the class '1' types became 1620-1899 and the class '3s' 1900-59.

These two classes provided the bulk of the freight tank locomotives owned by the Midland with all but one of the class '1s' becoming LMS property. Commonly, but incorrectly known as 'half-cabs', even though many had an enclosed cab, these class '1s' were in three distinct groups. The series, which in 1907 became 1620-1659, were all built with

enclosed cabs and had a flared rear bunker. The largest batch, Nos. 1660-1844 with flat-sided bunkers, were mostly built with open cabs (not all, however) and the entire series from 1620-1844 all employed a 7' 4"-7' 8" wheelbase. The final series, which were renumbered 1845-1899 in 1907, were all built with enclosed cabs, but with their wheelbase increased to 7' 4"-8' 2".

Many of these locomotives later received Belpaire boilers, and some fitted with vacuum train pipes were employed regularly upon passenger work. The class was long-lived and examples survived until 1965.

The larger Johnson 0—6—0Ts were built between 1899-1902 and many were condenser fitted, being allocated duties in the London area. Originally built with round-top boilers, they began to receive Belpaire boilers in 1919 but it was not until 1942 that the last of the class was rebuilt. In this form they resembled the standard LMS design, although, of course, none of the latter locomotives were fitted with condensers. These Midland locomotives were another long-lived class, lasting until 1966 in British Railways' ownership.

Additional to what might be called the 'standard' Johnson 0—6—0Ts, the Midland also had some absorbed 0—6—0T locomotives in service and they included some

Plate 64. Johnson 0—4—0ST No. 1142A was built in 1903 at Derby and four years later was renumbered 1527. The locomotive was not long-lived, being withdrawn by the Midland Railway in 1922. As seen here, in immaculate full Crimson Lake livery, these locomotives must have presented an attractive sight.

Authors' collection

well tank rebuilds of Bromsgrove bankers. Where possible this mixed assortment of engines has been illustrated with descriptive captions. Those still in service in 1907 occupied numbers within the 1600-09 series.

The other freight tanks in service and to feature in this section were 0—4—0Ts, the majority being of Johnson design, becoming Nos. 1500-1527 in 1907. However, although numbered in a consecutive series and visually very similar, this first group of engines were not all of the same design. The batch, renumbered 1500-1507, was the smallest of this series. Two had been withdrawn before the 1907 renumbering, the remainder, with one exception, were withdrawn during the 1920s but the final survivor lasted until 1949.

Plate 65. Deeley 0—4—0T No. 1531 at rest in an unidentified location. Built in 1907, it became No. 41531 following nationalization and withdrawal was in 1963. It is interesting to note that even though some locomotives were being painted black in 1906, this locomotive is in lined Crimson Lake livery. We assume that the cab roof would have been crimson up to the rain strip and black on top. However, there is no lining on the cylinder covers, footplate angle or footsteps.

National Railway Museum

Plate 66. No. 1122A was built in 1870 by the Avonside Engine Company for the Severn & Wye whose full title in 1894, the year it was vested jointly in the GWR and MR, was the Severn and Wye and Severn Bridge Railway. When constructed, the locomotive was built as a broad gauge 'convertible' and in 1872 it was converted to standard gauge. The Midland removed the name *Friar Tuck* by which it was known on the S & W and numbered it 1122A. It was rebuilt in 1895 and in 1907 it was renumbered 1605. The locomotive was broken up in 1911. No. 1122A did receive lined Crimson Lake livery at some time, albeit in a simplified form, as this picture confirms.

National Railway Museum

The second series, Nos 1508-1517, remained intact until 1921 and were extinct, with one exception, by 1936. Once again the final member of the class lasted for a considerable time on its own, not going until 1955.

The third series, Nos 1518-1527, were somewhat larger than the previous batches and only five were in service in 1900, the other five entering traffic in 1903. The first withdrawal was in 1922 and the final locomotive was withdrawn in 1958.

A final series of 0—4—0Ts was constructed by the Midland to Deeley's design, the first five entering service in 1907. Numbered 1528-32, they lasted, with one exception, until the 1960s. Five more almost identical locomotives with only minor detail alterations were built in 1921/2 and these were, with one exception, withdrawn in the 1960s (1533-37).

Plate 67. Although we cannot date this second photograph of No. 1122A, other than pre-1907, it is interesting to note that there is no sign of any lining on this locomotive whatsoever. Whether it is in black or any other colour we cannot be sure. *Authors' collection*

Plates 68 & 69. No. 1123A had an interesting history. Built in 1874 by Fletcher Jennings & Co., it had also been owned by the Severn and Wye Railway. Originally named *Little John,* it came into MR stock as No. 1123A and was later withdrawn in 1905. In the second view the locomotive is not particularly clean and there is no visible evidence of any lining, but there are some degraded letters 'MR' on the tank sides. Both sides of the engine are shown and we believe the left-hand side view to be the earlier.

Authors' collection

Plate 70. No. 1607 was built by the Vulcan Foundry in 1882 for the Severn & Wye. In due course this locomotive came into Midland Railway stock as No. 1125A. Renumbered 1607 in 1907, it survived until 1920.   *Authors' collection*

Plate 71. No. 1093A was built by Sharp Stewart in 1862 for the Swansea Vale Railway and named *Eagle*. In 1874 this line was leased to the Midland Railway and vested in that company from 1876. This locomotive first became No. 1093 and in 1876 No. 1093A, remaining in service until 1903. We are not able to date this picture or to confirm the livery but the picture probably dates from the late 1890s or even c.1900 so the engine is likely to be plain Crimson Lake. *Collection Bernard Mathews*

Plate 72. No. 2069A was built by Hunslet Engine Co. in 1880 for the Trowell Iron Company and was acquired by the Midland Railway in 1885. Originally numbered 1697 it was later placed upon the duplicate list as No. 2069A. Withdrawal was in 1903. It is seen here at Manningham in what appears to be plain Crimson Lake livery. *Collection Bernard Mathews*

Plate 73. 0—6—0T No. 882A, at Kentish Town in beautiful condition c.1900, was built by Beyer Peacock in 1871. The locomotive, originally No. 882, went onto the duplicate list in 1890, the 1907 number was 1612 and withdrawal was in 1920. Note the open rear cab of the other locomotive on the right. Almost certainly this is an 0—6—0T of the '2248' class.　　　　　*Authors' collection*

Plate 74. This picture was taken before 1891, the year the engine depicted was renumbered 2064A and placed upon the duplicate list. An 0—6—0WT built by Manning Wardle, it was taken over from the Sheepsbridge Iron Works in 1870 and carried the number 1064 until 1872 when it was numbered 2064. Withdrawal was in 1900. *Collection Bernard Mathews*

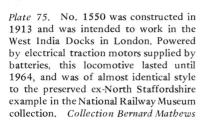

Plate 75. No. 1550 was constructed in 1913 and was intended to work in the West India Docks in London. Powered by electrical traction motors supplied by batteries, this locomotive lasted until 1964, and was of almost identical style to the preserved ex-North Staffordshire example in the National Railway Museum collection. *Collection Bernard Mathews*

Plate 76. Photographed at Manningham in full Crimson Lake livery, this engine represents the large series of 0—6—0Ts of Johnson design, many of which were built with 'open cabs' incorrectly called 'half cabs' by the majority of enthusiasts. No. 1115 was built in 1891 at Derby and in due course (1907) the locomotive became No. 1824. Three years later it received a 'closed cab' for service on the Worth Valley line and, as such, survived until 1951, being withdrawn as BR No. 41824.   *Authors' collection*

Plate 77. The largest shunting tank locomotives owned by the Midland Railway were the 0—6—0Ts built between 1899-1902 by the Vulcan Foundry. This picture of No. 2458 shows a locomotive built in 1900. No. 2458 was renumbered 1917 in 1907 and received a G5½ Belpaire boiler in 1924, being withdrawn in 1962 as No. 47217. Some references state that this locomotive was built with a condenser, but clearly at the time this picture was taken this was not so. Note the full Crimson Lake livery with considerable lining below the platform.

Collection Roger Carpenter

GOODS TENDER LOCOMOTIVES

Plate 78. Amongst the army of old double-frame goods engines withdrawn between 1900 and 1907 was this example built in 1856 by Robert Stephenson & Co., and this locomotive was originally numbered 381. It went onto the duplicate list as 381A and was then restored to the capital list as No. 338. Withdrawal was in 1903. The locomotive is shown here in full Crimson Lake livery and as rebuilt by Johnson.
Collection Bernard Mathews

In 1883 the freight tender locomotives of the Midland Railway were predominantly double-framed 0−6−0s of Kirtley design dating from the 1850s onwards, but by the commencement of our survey many of these had been rebuilt by Johnson during the ten years since he had taken office. Bearing in mind our stated criteria in the introduction, we find it difficult to decide how best to describe the early Kirtleys in simple fashion for this survey.

Locomotive historians generally consider that there were three Kirtley classes of 'Standard Goods' but successive rebuildings tended to merge them together. There was, however, one basic and obvious visual difference and this was in the shape of the frames. The earliest locomotives were of the straight-topped frame variety whereas the more numerous curved-topped frames belonged to the later locomotives. The 1907 straight frame number series was 2300-2397, 2459-2464. The curved frame series was 2398-2458, 2465-2867.

Unlike the Johnson class '2' 0−6−0s, regular reboilering and rebuilding was not quite so common with the Kirtley goods engines. Nevertheless, some were fitted with larger cylinders and upgraded to power class 2, while a few were fitted with 'H' boilers. A few others carried Belpaire boilers and, whereas the majority of Kirtleys retained their Johnson cabs, these rebuilds with larger boilers were fitted with Deeley style rounded eaves cabs.

The lowest number allocated in 1907, No. 2300, was given to a locomotive which originated as No. 240, built in

1850 by R. & W. Hawthorn. Just how much, if anything, of this locomotive remained by 1907 is open to conjecture, but as No. 240 it gave this number to the first of a class which, in a rebuilt form, can be considered the first of Kirtley's standard designs. Other elderly 0−6−0s from this period were also running in 1900 and so it is felt that the story of the early Kirtley 0−6−0s, as far as we are concerned, should be told by using as many illustrations as possible, including photographs of those locomotives withdrawn before 1907.

During these first ten years of Johnson's superintendency, inside-frame 0−6−0s had also been introduced, commencing with the '1142' class of 1875, followed by the '1357' class of 1878. By the end of 1883 some 213 locomotives of these two classes were in service. During the next nineteen years the inside-frame 0−6−0 fleet was enlarged until there were 864 in service by 1902.

In 1899, due to an extreme shortage of locomotives, the Midland Railway purchased forty 2−6−0s of American design. They were short-lived, the last locomotive being withdrawn in 1915, and had essentially been purchased as a stopgap resulting from the inability of any British locomotive builder to supply in a reasonable timespan. Two types were provided, by Baldwin and Schenectady, but they represented only a small part in the story of Midland freight locomotives.

The Midland itself in 1900 was building large numbers of 0−6−0s, which later were to be classified as power class 2.

Plate 79. No. 478 is seen here in Johnson condition in full Crimson Lake lined livery. Built in 1862 by W. Fairbairn & Son, this locomotive became No. 2385 in 1907 and was withdrawn from service in 1909. Whilst there is lining around the frame slots and edge of the framing, the tender has only twin panels with no lining upon the top coping.   *Authors' collection*

Plate 80. This early picture of No. 456 shows another W. Fairbairn & Son built locomotive, but here in earlier condition. Note the cabside panel. The locomotive is in Crimson Lake livery which dates it as post 1883 and it was again rebuilt by Johnson in 1888. As rebuilt, it almost certainly resembled No. 478 seen in the previous view.   *Authors' collection*

Plate 81. No. 555 was a Kitson & Co. built locomotive from 1866 and it is shown here in fully lined Crimson Lake livery as rebuilt by Johnson in its final condition prior to withdrawal in 1904. Note the smokebox lamp iron positions.   *Collection Bernard Mathews*

These were still to the basic Johnson design dating from 1875, with the final locomotive of this series entering traffic in 1902. In 1907 they became Nos. 2900-3764 and had two driving wheel sizes, those renumbered between 2900-3019 and 3130-3189 having driving wheels nominally 4′ 10½″ whilst all the others used a nominal 5′ 2½″ driving wheel.

In 1903 a new enlargement of the Johnson 0-6-0 type entered service. These locomotives with 'H' class boilers, became, in 1907, Nos. 3765-3814 with a final batch built in 1908 numbered 3815-3834. Rebuilding with Belpaire boilers was mostly between 1920-1924. This enlarged design, round-top or Belpaire, was placed in power class 3.

From about 1904 many of the small Johnson locomotives, built before 1902, began to be fitted with 'H' boilers and this programme was largely implemented during a four year period from that date, although there were examples fitted with 'H' boilers after 1908. These rebuilds were rated similarly to the new 1903 built engines as class '3' and the cab variations to be found on all of them are illustrated in the detailed analysis in Volume 3. Suffice to say in this preliminary review that with 'H' boilers there were:-

(a) Short cab, square rear splasher and cab lower half in one piece. These locomotives when built carried taper chimneys and centre handwheel on the smokebox door with a curved handrail over the smokebox. Their 1907 numbers were 3765-3794 and some earlier locomotives were converted into this style.

(b) As (a) but with a cab roof extension. These locomotives were numbered 3795-3814 in 1907.

(c) This batch had a rounded eaves cab with the rear splasher as part of the cab and to the full cab width, round spectacles in the cab front, and a Deeley Capuchon chimney. They were numbered 3815-3834.

Starting in 1916 these three variations began to be rebuilt with 'G7' Belpaire boilers with a Deeley cab (rounded eaves) and smokebox door held by dogs, together with a straight handrail on the smokebox door. The rear splashers were inset and not to full cab width. This style of locomotive ran in this form until the early 1960s, the principal modifications from the 1916 rebuilding being pop type safety valves for the original Ramsbottom variety and, very frequently replacement chimneys of Stanier or BR design. In this form they were, of course (to more modern day enthusiasts) the familiar class '3Fs'. In addition there were three class '2s' which ran on 6 ft driving wheels together with a brief experiment with superheated boilers (see Volume 3).

The rebuilding of locomotives to Belpaired class '3' had ceased by the mid 1920s but some locomotives equipped with large 'H' type boilers and classified as 3, were later altered to run with smaller 'G6' Belpaire boilers and reclassified 2. Examples of these rebuildings are to be found in Volume 3.

In 1917 a further reboilering programme of the Johnson class '2' locomotives began and many, but by no means all,

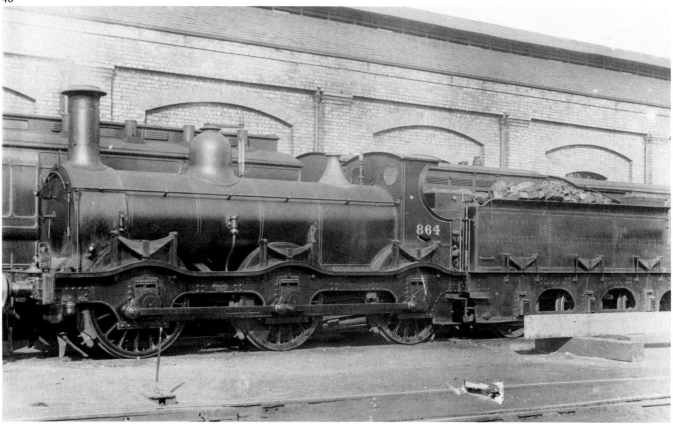

Plate 82. No. 864 was built in 1871 by Dübs & Co. and is seen here in its pre-1903 condition, after which date the lamp iron positions were altered. In 1905 the locomotive was renumbered to 555 and the following year it was sold to the Italian State Railways together with 49 other similar locomotives. At the time it was photographed the locomotive was in fully lined Crimson Lake livery.

Collection Bernard Mathews

Plate 83. Although No. 386 was from the same stable as No. 338 pictured in *Plate 78*, in its rebuilt form it displays considerable variations. Note the front sandbox positions and the shape of the slots at the front of the framing. Shown here in full Crimson Lake livery, this locomotive was withdrawn in 1904.

Collection Bernard Mathews

Plate 84. A post 1907 livery condition for the Kirtley goods engines is shown in this picture of No. 2758 seen here in black livery. Originally No. 974, built by Dübs & Co. in 1873, this locomotive became No. 2758 in 1907 and saw war service with the ROD. Withdrawal was in 1931.   *Collection Roger Carpenter*

of the small round-top boiler locomotives then received 'G6' Belpaire boilers. Consequently, whilst the class '3s', which survived beyond the late 1920s, only ran with Belpaire boilers (those with round-top class 'H' boilers having been either rebuilt or scrapped), many of the class '2' locomotives ran until scrapping with round-top boilers until well into the late 1950s in British Railways ownership, alongside their Belpaire boilered 'sisters'.

The bewildering story of the Midland 0–6–0s is only touched upon at this point in our survey — the more detailed

treatment being kept for Volume 3 — but an additional note on the numbering of 1907 may be helpful.

The 1907 numbers allocated to the Johnson engines reflected, essentially, the 1903 situation — i.e. after the *new* 'H' boilered engines had been introduced but before the 'H' boilered *rebuilds* had put in an appearance. It no doubt made some sort of logic to number all the original Johnson small-boilered engines *ahead* of the 1903 built types. However, by 1907, many of the original small-boilered engines had become class 3 rather than class 2. In consequence the

Plate 85. The American Moguls formed part of the Midland Railway scene from 1899 until the final locomotive was withdrawn some sixteen years later. No. 2215 was originally No. 2526. Built by Baldwin's Locomotive Works in 1899, this locomotive was withdrawn in 1909. There is no trace of lining on the locomotive which suggests a plain black livery.   *Authors' collection*

Plate 86. The standard Johnson goods engine in Johnson condition is depicted in this view of No. 2112 which was built by Sharp Stewart in 1892. Receiving an 'H' boiler in 1904, the locomotive was renumbered 3389 in 1907, and in 1924 the LMS rebuilt it with a 'G7' boiler and reclassified it '3'. Renumbered 43389 by British Railways, withdrawal was in 1962. *Authors' collection*

two power classes were hopelessly mixed together in the same series and remained thus throughout the MR and LMS period. It was only after nationalization that BR did what could have been done much earlier — number them in two separate series. The class 3s retained their LMS numbers (plus 40000) with one exception (below) and the class 2s were all given new numbers in the BR '58XXX' series.

The lowest number carried by a class 3 rebuild was No. 3137, which was renumbered 43750 by British Railways in 1951, when the number was required for an Ivatt design 2−6−0 which had just been built.

Within the number series 3137 (which became a class 3) and 3764 (which remained a class 2), locomotives to both these power classifications could be found. Those numbered above 3765 were all class 3 (until the class 4s commenced at 3835), whilst those numbered up to 3136 all remained in power class 2.

Prior to the commencement of Belpaire reboilering of the class 3s, the Midland Railway had produced two loco-

Plate 87. No. 2304 was built in 1896 and in 1904 was rebuilt into the condition as shown. This c.1905 photograph displays a locomotive in fully lined Crimson Lake livery. In 1907 this locomotive became No. 3490 and after nationalization No. 43490, with withdrawal in 1959. The locomotive was rebuilt as a class 3 'Belpaire' in 1924. *Authors' collection*

Plate 88. The later condition of the standard class '2' goods is seen in this view of No. 3149 in black livery heading a stopping goods train through Leicester. This view shows very clearly the narrow-bodied 'goods' engine tender. No. 3149 was originally No. 1717, built at Derby in 1885. The locomotive received a 'G6' Belpaire boiler in 1919, and was withdrawn as No. 43149 in 1954.
Collection Brian Badger

motives which were ultimately classified 4 (Nos. 3835-6). They were also the first new locomotives to be built with superheated boilers and entered service in 1911. No more examples were built until 1917, when No. 3837 was constructed and each year thereafter until 1922 saw further examples being completed so that by 1922 the class 4 number series was 3835-4026. The LMS expanded this class until as late as 1941, by which time the class 4 number series was 3835-4606, a total of 772 locomotives.

While all this new construction and rebuilding was proceeding in the inside framed class 2, 3 and 4 series,

the ranks of the old double-framed Kirtley 0–6–0s were only slowly being thinned. Consequently, even at the end of 1922 there were still in service 440 class 1 and 31 class 2 Kirtleys, the latter having been altered by reboilering. In total, these engines just exceeded the 453 class 2 Johnson types and almost equalled the 482 various class 3 locomotives of Johnson and Deeley origin. An additional 192 Fowler class 4 engines made up the grand total of 1598 freight tender locomotives handed over the the LMS.

Plate 89. The class 3's final form with a 'G7' Belpaire boiler is depicted in this illustration of No. 3297 photographed at Derby in July 1920. Built in 1891 as No. 1970 by Neilson & Co., it received an 'H' boiler in 1905 and a 'G7' boiler in 1920. Withdrawal as No. 43297 was in 1950.
W. L. Good

Plate 90. The 'Big Goods' which became known as the class '4s' or '4Fs' are represented by No. 3869 piloting a Kirtley 0—6—0 at Welsh Harp in July 1919. Note the single mechanical lubricator fitted to the earlier members of the class — later a second lubricator was fitted. No. 3869 was built in 1918, it was renumbered 43869 by British Railways and was withdrawn in 1962.   *Collection Roger Carpenter*

Plate 91. The largest Midland Railway locomotive was 0—10—0 No. 2290, the 'Lickey Banker' built in 1919 at Derby. Renumbered 22290 by the LMS in 1947 and No. 58100 by British Railways, withdrawal was in 1956. This picture was taken at Bromsgrove in February 1920 before the electric light was fitted to the smokebox door.   *W. L. Good*

MIDLAND LOCOMOTIVE STOCK AT THE GROUPING

The grouping of 1923 provides a convenient point to summarise the Midland Railway's stock and the existence of official documents provides the opportunity to illustrate to readers the 'official method' employed by the company.

It will be noted that the Midland Railway Company did not formally differentiate between goods and passenger tank locomotives; this distinction did not occur visually until 1928 when the LMS introduced the P & F suffix to power classifications.

The authors, whilst accepting this Midland classification, have placed the tank locomotives into Volume 2 and 3 and have divided them into two groups (of passenger and goods locomotives) using the post 1928 classifications.

Finally, the reader's attention is drawn to the fact that this return includes those locomotives which became Midland stock in 1912 following the absorption of the LT & SR in 1912. These locomotives will be more fully described in Volume 2.

MIDLAND RAILWAY ENGINE STOCK AT 31ST DEC. '22.

	TYPE	Nº OF ENGINES		ENGINE Nos	CLASS ENG	CLASS BOILER
PASSENGER TENDER ENGS	2-4-0	245		BETN 1 & 281	1	B & P
	4-4-0	16		BETN 300 & 327	1	B
		235	49	328–482	2	H
			44		2	G7
			142	328–562	2	G7S
	4-2-2	43	31	600–669	1	D
			12	670–683	1	E
	4-4-0	80	25	700–779	3	G8, G8A
			55		3	G8AS
		55	10	990–999	4	G9AS
			22	1000–1044	4	G9
			23		4	G9AS
	TOTAL	674				
TANK ENGINES	0-4-4	226		BETN 1200 & 1430		C
	0-4-0	33	16	BETN 1500 & 1517		J
			7	" 1518 & 1525		J1
			10	1528–1537		J2
	0-6-0	4		BETN 1601 & 1608		MISC.
		289		1610–1899		A
		60	56	1900–1959		C
			4			G5½
	0-6-4	40	37	2000–2039		H
			3			G7S
	4-6-4	8		2100–2107		5
	4-4-2	70	36	2110–2145		1
			12	2146–2157		3
			18	2158–2175		2
			4	2176–2179		3
	0-6-2	14		2180–2193		2
	TOTAL	744				
GOODS TENDER ENGS	0-10-0	1		2290		G10S
	D.F. 0-6-0	440		BETN 2300 & 2867	1	B
		31	15		2	B
			6		2	D
			1		2	E
			5		2	G6
			4		2	H
	0-6-0	2	1	2898	2	G5½ ALTD
			1	2899	2	4
	S.F. 0-6-0	453	378	2900–4026	2	B
			74		2	G6
			1		2	H
		482	238		3	H
			244		3	G7
		192			4	G7S
	TOTAL	1601				
	GRAND TOTAL	3019				

MIDLAND RAILWAY
LOCOMOTIVE DRAWING OFFICE
DERBY

M.R. PASSENGER ENGINES AT 31ST DEC. 1922

TYPE	ENGINE Nos	Nº OF ENGS		DRG WHEELS DIAMR	CYLRS DIA. STR.	CLASS OF BOILER	BLR PRESS LBS PER Dn	TRACTIVE POWER @85% LBS.	TONS	TENDER WATER CAPY	DIAGM Nº	REMARKS
2-4-0	1–22	21		6'-3"	18" × 24"	B or P.	140	12338	5.50	GALLONS	ED15 TYPICAL	
	24–67	24	14	6'-9"	18" × 24"		140	11424	5·10			
			4		18" × 24"		160	13056	5·82			
			5		18" × 26"		140	12376	5·52			
			1		18" × 26"		160	14144	6·31			
	68–126	50		6'-9"	18" × 24"		140	11424	5·10			
	127–156	27	26	6'-3"	18" × 24"		140	12338	5·50	2750		
			1				160	14100	6·29	2950		
	157–191	34		6'-6½"	18" × 26"		140	12770	5·70	3250		
	192–196	5		6'-9"	18" × 26"		140	12376	5·52			
	197–206	9		7'-0½"	18" × 26"		140	11863	5·29			
	207–216	10		6'-9"	18" × 26"		140	12376	5·52			
	217–221	5		6'-6½"	18" × 26"		140	12770	5·70			
	222–271	50		6'-9"	18" × 26"		140	12376	5·52			
	272–281	10		7'-0½"	18" × 26"		140	11863	5·29			
4-4-0	BETN 300 & 327	16	6	6'-6½"	18" × 26"	B	140	12770	5·70	2950	ED27 TYPICAL	
			7	7'-0½"			140	11863	5·29			
			3	7'-0½"			160	13558	6·05			
	BETN 328 & 482	49	14	6'-9"	18" × 26"	H	175	15470	6·90	3250	ED37 TYPICAL	
			9	7'-0½"	18" × 26"			14829	6·62			
			4	6'-6½"	18" × 26"			15962	7·12			
			22	6'-6½"	18½" × 26"			16862	7·52			
	BETN 328 & 482	44	16	6'-9"	18" × 26"	G7	175	15470	6·90	3250	ED64 TYPICAL	
			10	7'-0½"	18" × 26"			14829	6·62			
			16	6'-6½"	18" × 26"			15962	7·12			
			2	6'-6½"	18½" × 26"			16862	7·52			
	BETN 328 & 562	142		7'-0½"	20½" × 26"	G7S	160	17585	7·85	3250 & 3500	ED 69	Superheated
4-2-2	600–683	43	2	7'-4½"	18" × 26"	D	160	12945	5·78	3250	ED48 TYPICAL	
			19	7'-6½"	18½" × 26"			13372	5·96			
			10	7'-6½"	19" × 26"			14104	6·29			
			12	7'-9½"	19½" × 26"	E	170	15279	6·82	3500		
4-4-0	700–779	80	25	6'-9"	19½" × 26"	G8A	180	18674	8·33	3500	ED62 TYPL	
			55		20½" × 26"	G8AS	175	20065	8·96			Superheated
	990–999	10		6'-6½"	20½" × 26"	G9AS	180	21296	9·50	3500	ED 74	Superheated
	1005–1044	22		7'-0"	1 HP 19" × 26" 2 LP 21" × 26"	G9	220	24024 @ 80%	10·72 @ 80%	3500	ED 68	
	1000–1044	23		7'-0"	1 HP 19" × 26" 2 LP 21" × 26"	G9AS	200	21840 @ 80%	9·75 @ 80%	3500	ED 71	Superheated

M.R. TANK ENGINES AT 31st DEC. 1922

TYPE	ENGINE Nos	No OF ENGS.	DRG WHEELS DIAMr	CYLRS DIA. STR.	CLASS OF BOILER	BLR PRESS. LBS PER □″	TRACTIVE POWER @85% LBS	TONS	WATER CAPY GALLONS	DIAGM No	REMARKS
0-4-4	1200 – 1225	25	5'-3"			140	14688	6·55	1000		
	1226 – 1235	10	5'-4"			140	14458	6·45	950		
	1236 – 1265	29	5'-7"	18" x 24"	C	140	13811	6·16	1000	ED 82 TYPICAL	
	1266 – 1350	83	5'-4"			140	14458	6·45	1150		
	1351 – 1430	79	5'-4"			150	15491	6·91	1150 & 1270		
		226									
0-4-0	1500 – 1517	16	3'-10"	13" x 20"	J	140	8744	3·90	400	ED 88	
	1518 – 1522	4		15" x 20"	J1	140	11641	5·19	650	ED 86	
	1523 – 1525	3		15" x 20"	J1	150	12472	5·56	650		
	1528 – 1537	10		15" x 22"	J2	160	14635	6·53	650	ED 87	
		33									
0-6-0	1601	1	4'-3"	15" x 22"		140	11550	5·15	500		
	1604,1606,1608	3	4'-3"	17" x 24"		140	16184	7·22	500 to 896	ED104 TYPICAL	
	1610 – 1619	10	4'-3"	17" x 24"	A	140	16184	7·22	950		
	1620 – 1859	239	4'-7"	17" x 24"	A	140	15007	6·89	740 & 800		
	1860 – 1899	40	4'-7"	17" x 24"	A	150	16079	7·17	800		
	1900 – 1959	56	4'-7"	18" x 26"	C	160	20830	9·30	1000	ED 106	
		4	4'-7"	18" x 26"	G5½	160	20830	9·30	1000	ED106A	
		353									
0-6-4	2000 – 2039	37	5'-7"	18½" x 26"	H1	175	19756	8·82	2250	ED 114	
		3	5'-7"	18½" x 26"	G7s	175	19756	8·82	2250	ED114B	Superheated
		40									
4-6-4	2100 – 2107	8	6'-3"	20" x 26"	No 5	160	18858	8·42	2200	ED 200	Superheated
4-4-2	2110 – 2145	36	6'-1"	17" x 26"	No 1	160	13998	6·25	1240	ED 201	
	2146 – 2157	12	6'-6"	19" x 26"	No 3	170	17388	7·76	1620	ED 202	
	2158 – 2175	7	6'-6"	18" x 26"	No 2	170	15606	6·94	} 1565	ED 203	
		11	6'-6"	19" x 26"	No 2	170	17388	7·76			
	2176 – 2179	4	6'-6"	19" x 26"	No 3	170	17388	7·76	1873	ED 204	
		70									
0-6-2	2180 – 2193	14	5'-3"	18" x 26"	No 2	170	19322	8·62		ED 205	

M.R. GOODS ENGINES AT 31st DEC. 1922

TYPE	ENGINE Nos	No OF ENGs	DRG WHEELS DIAMr	CYLRS DIA. STR.	CLASS OF BOILER	BLR PRESS. LBS PER □″	TRACTIVE POWER @85% LBS	TONS	TENDER CAP GALLONS	DIAGRAM No	REMARKS
0-10-0	2290	1	4'-7½"	16½" x 28"	G10s	180	43315	19·33	2050	ED 123	4 CYL. SIMPLE (DEC.1919)
	BETWEEN 2300 & 2867	313	5'-3"	17" x 24"	B	140	13101	5·84	CHIEFLY 2000 A FEW 2200 to 2350	ED 124 TYPICAL	
		127		18" x 24"			14688	6·55			
		440									
	2898 & 2899	2	4'-7"	18" x 24"	G5½ ALT'D & 6	150	18026	8·05	2500	ED 206	
0-6-0	BETWEEN 2300 & 3764	15	5'-3"	17" x 24"	B, D, G6	160	14973	6·68		ED 124 & 161	
		97	5'-3"	18" x 26"	B, G6	140	15912	7·10		ED130A & 150	
		94	4'-11"	18" x 26"	B, G6	140	16990	7·58		ED 130	
		111	5'-3"	18" x 26"	B	150	17049	7·61	VARIOUS 2000 to 3250	ED 150	
		12	5'-3"	18" x 24"	B,D,E,G6	160	16786	7·49		ED 124 & 161	
		1	6'-0"	18" x 26"	H	175	17404	7·76			
		83	5'-3"	18" x 26"	B, G6	160	18185	8·11		ED130A & 150	
		4	5'-3"	18" x 24"	H	175	18360	8·19	*TYPICAL DIAGms		
		67	4'-11"	18" x 26"	B, G6	160	19417	8·66		ED130A & 150	
		484									
	BETWEEN 3130 & 3834	211	5'-3"	18" x 26"	H		19890	8·87		ED 146 TYPICAL	
		11	5'-3"	18½" x 26"	H		21010	9·37			
		16	4'-11"	18" x 26"	H	175	21238	9·48	VARIOUS 2750 to 3500		
		192	5'-3"	18" x 26"	G7		19890	8·87		ED 165	
		49	5'-3"	18½" x 26"	G7		21010	9·37			
		3	4'-11"	18" x 26"	G7		21238	9·48			
		482									
	3835 – 4026	192	5'-3"	20" x 26"	G7s	175	24555	10·96	3250 & 3500	ED 159	Superheated

EX-MR ENGINES AS AT 31st DECEMBER 1947

Wheel Arrangement	Engine Nos.	No. of Engines
2—4—0	20155, 20185, 20216	3
4—4—0	322-326 (ex S & DJR locomotives)	5
4—4—0	383-385-391 Saturated	3
4—4—0	Between 332-562 '483' class	157
4—4—0	Between 711-762 Class '3P' Belpaires	22
4—4—0	1000-1044 Compounds	45
0—4—4T	Between 1239-1261	9
0—4—4T	Between 1272-1430	56
0—4—0ST	1509, 1516, 1518, 1523	4
0—4—0T	1528-1537	10
0—6—0T	Between 1660-1895	95
0—6—0T	7200-7259	60
0—6—0	22630, 22846, 22853, 22863 Kirtley double frame	4
0—6—0	Between 22900-22984, 2987-2999, 23000-23018, 3130-3177 Small wheel class '2F'	96
0—6—0	Between 3021-3127, 3190-3764 Large wheel class '2F'	109
0—6—0	Between 3137-3189 Small wheel class '3F'	11
0—6—0	Between 3191-3773 Large wheel class '3F'. Includes 9 ex-S & DJR locomotives	332
0—6—0	Between 3775-3833	55
0—6—0	3835-4026 Class '4F' plus 5 ex-S & DJR locomotives numbers 4557-61	197
0—10—0	22290	1

TOTAL 1,274

EX-LT & SR LOCOMOTIVES AS AT 31st DECEMBER 1947

Wheel Arrangement	Engine Nos.	No. of Engines
4—4—2T	Between 2092-2109	17
4—4—2T	Between 2110-2160 Includes LMS. Built to LT & SR design	51
0—6—2T	1980-1993	14

TOTAL 82

54

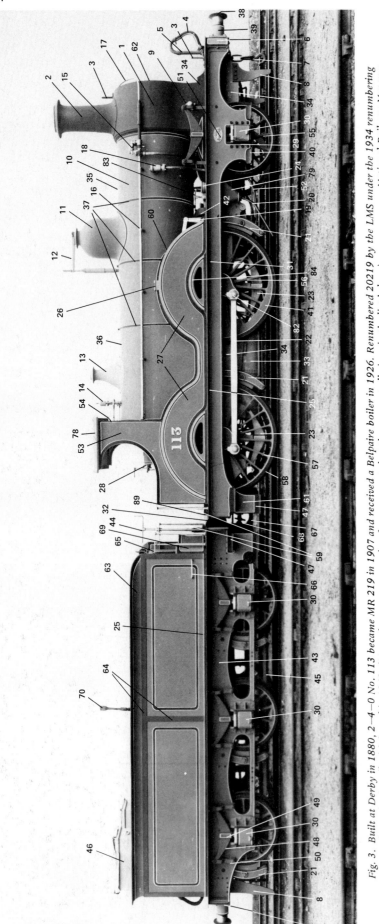

Fig. 3. Built at Derby in 1880, 2—4—0 No. 113 became MR 219 in 1907 and received a Belpaire boiler in 1926. Renumbered 20219 by the LMS under the 1934 renumbering scheme, it survived until withdrawal in 1943. (More than one name exists for some parts but they are not all given in the list below.)

National Railway Museum

1. Smokebox
2. Chimney
3. Lamp irons
4. Vacuum hose
5. Vacuum brake end train pipes
6. Buffer plank
7. Front coupling
8. Guard irons or wheel guards
9. Furness lubricator
10. Boiler
11. Steam dome
12. Salter safety valves
13. Direct loaded safety valve
14. Whistle
15. Large ejector
16. Combined ejector handrail
17. Handrail
18. Clack
19. Reversing lever
20. Sandpipe
21. Brake block hanger and brake block
22. Coupling rod
23. Driving wheel springs

25. Platform/running plate
26. Lubricator or oil trimming box
27. Driving wheel splashers
28. Screw reverser
29. Axlebox guide
30. Axlebox
31. Footplate angle/valance
32. Lap plate or fall plate
33. Ashpan
34. Main engine frames
35. Boiler clothing plates or lagging plates
36. Firebox clothing plates or   ,,
37. Boiler lagging bands
38. Buffer head
39. Buffer casing
40. Front steps
41. Wheel balance weights
42. Frame stay
43. Tender main frame
44. Tender hand brake
45. Tender brake pull rod
46. Rear mounted tool box
47. Engine/Tender footsteps
48. Tender spring

49. Spring buckle
50. Spring pillar
51. Works plate
52. Vacuum brake train pipe
53. Cab side sheets
54. Cab front or spectacle plate
55. Leading wheel
56. Leading driving wheels
57. Trailing driving wheels
    (On a six coupled locomotive the centre wheels are referred to as intermediate)
58. Tyre rim
59. Vertical handrails
    (sometimes referred to as 'uprights')
60. Splasher top
61. Footstep supports
62. Smokebox door
63. Tender flare
64. Vertical and horizontal beading
65. Tender front
66. Tender side handrail
67. Water pipe from tender to injector
68. Intermediate coupling (engine to tender)

69. Side pockets
70. 'Davits' (This was the LNWR name. MR name not known if different)
71. Ejector pipe
72. Leading bogie wheel
73. Trailing bogie wheel
74. Bogie brakes
75. Side tank
76. Bunker side
77. Bunker rear
78. Cab roof
79. Sandbox
80. Brake cylinder
81. Brake pull rod
82. Crankpins
83. Sandbox control lever
84. Coupling rod splasher
85. Coal plate
86. Cab rear (rear spectacle plate)
87. Bogie side frame
88. Engine hand brake
89. Footplate

CHAPTER THREE

DESIGN DETAILS ANALYSED

S O far, we have examined, in outline, the basic 'anatomical' development of Midland locomotives and given a four-fold breakdown of the fleet itself, divided into principal categories. This is to serve by way of background to our more detailed analysis later in both this and subsequent volumes and we start here with a more comprehensive look at the various visible detail features to be seen on Midland locomotives. For convenience, we have divided it into a series of main and sub-headings as follows:

A. **BOILER AREA**
   Boilers
   Smokeboxes ⎤
   Chimneys ⎦ Jointly referred to as 'the front end'
   Safety Valves
   Superheating
   Vacuum control gear for push and pull trains

B. **LOCOMOTIVE CABS AND FOOTPLATES**
   General layout
   Gauge glasses
   Lubricators
   Storm sheets
   Cab roof ventilators

C. **BRAKES**
   Steam brakes
   Westinghouse brakes

D. **COUPLINGS**

E. **SANDING**

F. **TENDERS**
   Coal rails
   Tool boxes
   Tender cabs
   Water pick-up
   Number plates
   Oil burning

A. THE BOILER AREA

BOILERS

Although the MR pursued standardisation, it employed a great number of boiler types and *Figs. 5 & 6* have been included to illustrate the principal variations of both the

Fig. 4. 0—4—4T No. 1540 was built at Derby in 1881, renumbered 1274 in 1907 and withdrawn in 1937.   *National Railway Museum*

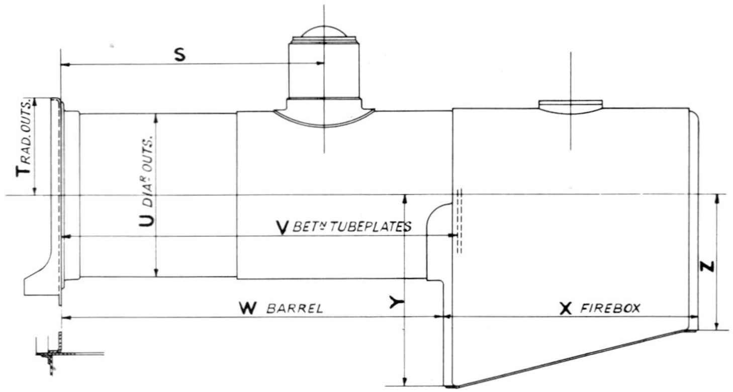

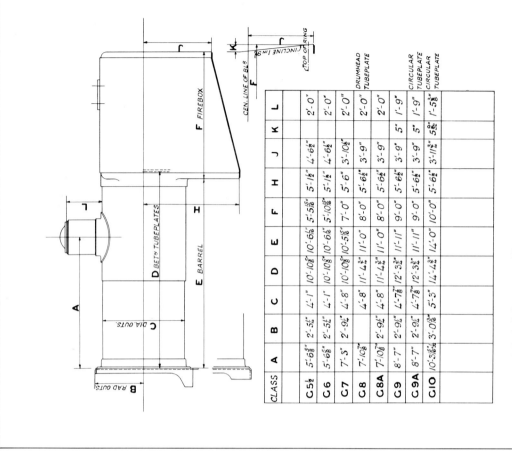

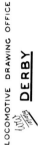

CLASS	S	T	U	V	W	X	Y	Z	REMARKS
A	5'-3 5/8"	2'-5 1/4"	4'-1"	10'-4 5/8"	10'-0"	5'-0"	4'-9 1/2"	4'-2 1/2"	THREE RINGS IN BARREL.
B	5'-6 5/8"	2'-5 1/4"	4'-1"	10'-10 5/8"	10'-6"	5'-11"	5'-1 1/2"	4'-6 1/2"	DITTO
C	5'-6 5/8"	2'-5 1/4"	4'-1"	10'-10 5/8"	10'-6"	5'-6"	5'-1 1/2"	4'-6 1/2"	DITTO
D	5'-4 5/8"		4'-1"	10'-8 5/8"	10'-4"	6'-6"	5'-2 1/2"	4'-7 1/2"	DRUMHEAD TUBEPLATE
E	5'-4 5/8"		4'-1"	10'-10 5/8"	10'-6"	7'-0"	5'-6 1/2"	4'-7 1/2"	DITTO
F	8'-7"		4'-1 7/8"	10'-10 11/16"	10'-6"	8'-0"	5'-9 1/2"	4'-10 1/2"	DITTO
H	7'-3"	2'-9 1/4"	4'-8"	10'-10 5/8"	10'-5 15/16"	7'-0"	5'-6"	3'-10 1/2"	
J	2'-4"	1'-10"	3'-0"	9'-4 7/16"	9'-0"	3'-0"	3'-8"	3'-8"	
J1	2'-9 11/16"	2'-2 11/16"	3'-8"	10'-8 5/8"	10'-4"	4'-0"	4'-1 1/2"	3'-8"	
J2	7'-4"	2'-2 11/16"	3'-8"	10'-8 5/8"	10'-4"	4'-0"	4'-1 1/2"	3'-8"	
P	5'-5 5/8"	2'-5 1/4"	4'-1"	10'-8 5/8"	10'-4"	5'-11"	5'-1 1/2"	4'-6 1/2"	THREE RINGS IN BARREL.

CLASSIFICATION OF BOILERS

WITH ROUND-TOPPED FIREBOX

MIDLAND RAILWAY

LOCOMOTIVE DRAWING OFFICE

WW 10/10/19 DERBY

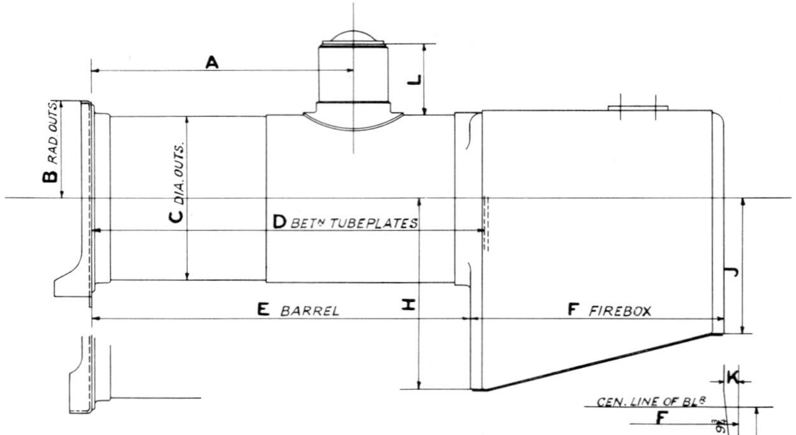

CLASS	A	B	C	D	E	F	H	J	K	L	
C5 1/2	5'-6 5/8"	2'-5 1/4"	4'-1"	10'-10 5/8"	10'-6 1/16"	5'-5 15/16"	5'-1 1/2"	4'-6 1/2"		2'-0"	
C6	5'-6 5/8"	2'-5 1/4"	4'-1"	10'-10 5/8"	10'-6 1/16"	5'-10 15/16"	5'-1 1/2"	4'-6 1/2"		2'-0"	
C7	7'-3"	2'-9 1/4"	4'-8"	10'-10 5/8"	10'-5 15/16"	7'-0"	5'-6"	3'-10 1/2"		2'-0"	
C8	7'-10 7/8"		4'-8"	11'-4 3/4"	11'-0"	8'-0"	5'-6 1/2"	3'-9"		2'-0"	DRUMHEAD TUBEPLATE
C8A	7'-10 7/8"	2'-9 1/4"	4'-8"	11'-4 3/4"	11'-0"	8'-0"	5'-6 1/2"	3'-9"		2'-0"	
C9	8'-7"	2'-9 1/4"	4'-7 7/8"	12'-3 3/4"	11'-11"	9'-0"	5'-6 1/2"	3'-9"	5"	1'-9"	
C9A	8'-7"	2'-9 1/4"	4'-7 7/8"	12'-3 3/4"	11'-11"	9'-0"	5'-6 1/2"	3'-9"	5"	1'-9"	CIRCULAR TUBEPLATE
C10	10'-3 15/16"+1/32	3'-0 13/16"	5'-3"	14'-4 3/4"	14'-0"	10'-0"	5'-6 1/2"	3'-11 3/4"	5 9/32"	1'-5 3/8"	CIRCULAR TUBEPLATE

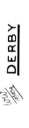

CLASSIFICATION OF BOILERS

WITH BELPAIRE FIREBOX

MIDLAND RAILWAY

LOCOMOTIVE DRAWING OFFICE

WW 10/10/19 DERBY

Figs. 5 & 6. The two drawings of round-top and Belpaire boilers, together with details of the standard heating surfaces, were taken from the 1919 Engine Diagram Book. Readers will note that by that date certain boilers, e.g. A1, C1, HX and H1, etc., are not listed and so presumably no longer formed part of the Midland Railway's boiler stock. It should be noted that these diagrams give the internal dimensions and not measurements over the cladding which are the areas required by modellers. The diagrams are mainly intended, therefore, to

STANDARD HEATING SURFACES

CLASS OF BOILER	FIREBOX SQ. FT.	TUBES Nº	TUBES EXTL. DIA.	TUBES SQ. FT.	FIREBOX AND TUBES SQ. FT.	SUPERHEATER ELEMENTS SQ. FT.	FIREBOX, TUBES AND ELEMENTS SQ. FT.	GRATE AREA SQ. FT.	NOTES
A	84·00	196	1¾"	932·50	1016·50			14·5	THESE SURFACES ARE CALCULATED AS AGREED ON BY ASSOCN OF RAILWAY LOCOMOTIVE ENGRS IN NOVR 1914, VIZ:- <u>FIREBOX</u> — WETTED SURFACES WITH DEDUCTIONS FOR AREAS OF TUBEHOLES & FIREHOLE RING. <u>TUBES</u> — LENGTH BETWEEN TUBEPLATES & ON UNIFORM OUTER DIAM. OF MIDDLE PORTION OF BOTH ORDINARY & SUPERHEATER FLUE TUBES. <u>ELEMENTS</u> — LENGTH TAKEN TO AND FROM SMOKEBOX END OF LARGE FLUE TUBES, ON INSIDE DIAM. OF ELEMENTS.
B	102·00	196	1¾"	977·50	1079·50			17·5	
C	96·00	196	1¾"	977·50	1073·50			16·0	
H	118·50	258	1¾"	1285·50	1404·00			21·1	
Hx & H1	118·75	242	1¾"	1205·75	1324·50			21·1	
G5									
G5½	97·00	196	1¾"	977·50	1074·50			16·0	
G6	103·00	196	1¾"	977·50	1080·50			17·5	
G7	122·75	254	1¾"	1265·50	1388·25			21·1	
G7s	123·50	148 21	1¾" 5¼"	1043·75	1167·25	252·75	1420·00	21·1	
G8A	136·75	249	1¾"	1298·75	1435·50			25·0	
G8AS	137·25	148 21	1¾" 5¼"	1092·75	1230·00	266·25	1496·25	25·0	
G9	146·75	216	1⅞"	1304·25	1451·00			28·4	
G9AS	147·25	148 21	1¾" 5¼"	1180·75	1328·00	290·75	1618·75	28·4	
G10	158·25	147 27	1⅞" 5¼"	1560·00	1718·25	445·00	2163·25	31·5	
J	44·00	106	1¾"	455·00	499·00			8·0	
J1 & J2	58·25	141	1¾"	692·50	750·75			10·5	MIDLAND RAILWAY
									LOCOMOTIVE DRAWING OFFICE
									WW 18·10·19 DERBY

round-top and Belpaire boilers used by the Midland Railway during the period covered by these volumes.

The figures have been reproduced from the Midland Railway's 1919 diagram book which does not include all the variations of boilers employed by the company. However, the locomotives upon which the listed varieties were all fitted are as below.

Class	
A	0–6–0T 1620-1844 as built. Rebuilds from 1600-8. 1610-19 as rebuilt.
A1	0–6–0T 1845-99 as built. Variant of A with 4" deeper firebox. Replaced by A or G5 boilers.
B	2–4–0 1-281 as rebuilt. 4–4–0 300-402, 473-92 as built. 0–6–0 2900-3764 as built. 2300-2867 as rebuilt. Kirtley 2–2–2 as rebuilt.
C	0–4–4T 1226-1380 as built. 1200-25 as rebuilt. Kirtley 2–2–2 and 2–4–0 and 0–4–4T as rebuilt.
C1	0–4–4T 1381-1430 as built. 0–6–0T 1900-59 as built. Variation of C boiler with 4" deeper firebox. Replaced by C or G5½ boilers.
D	4–4–0 403-72, 493-522 as built. 483-92 as rebuilt. 4–2–2 600-69 as built. 0–6–0 2846/47/49/52/53/58/61-3 as rebuilt.
E	4–4–0 523-62 as built. 4–2–2 670-84 as built. 0–6–0 2451/54/72/2567/79/89/2806/13/18/19/21/22/28 as rebuilt.
F	4–2–2 685-94 as built.
H	0–6–0 3765-3814 as built. Rebuilds from 3136-3764. 4–4–0 rebuilds from 328-562.
HX/H1	0–6–0 3815-34 as built. 2000-39 as built. Rebuilds from 328-562, 3136-3764. These HX and H1 boilers had the same external dimensions as the H boilers.
J	0–4–0T 1500-17 as built.
J1	0–4–0T 1518-27 as built.
J2	0–4–0T 1528-37 as built.
P	2–4–0 121-23, 125-26, 147-281 as built. 68-120, 124 as rebuilt.
G5	0–6–0T replacement for 'A' and 'A1' class boiler.
G5½	0–4–4T and 0–6–0T replacement for 'C1' and 'C' class boiler.
G6	2–4–0 rebuilds from 150-281. Sixteen rebuilds from '480' and '700' class Kirtley 0–6–0s. Rebuilds from 2900-3764.
G7	4–4–0 rebuilds from 328-393, 460-465 as rebuilt. 0–6–0 rebuilds from 3137-3764.
G7S	0–6–4T as rebuilt. 4–4–0 renewal from 332-562. 0–6–0 3835-4026.
G8	4–4–0 710-59 as built.
G8A	4–4–0 760-79 as built.
G8AS	4–4–0 '700' class rebuilds.
G8½	4–4–0 1000-4 as built.
G9	4–4–0 1005-44 as built.
G9A	4–4–0 990-9 as built.
G9AS	4–4–0 990-9 as rebuilt. 4–4–0 1000-4 as rebuilt.
G10S	0–10–0 as built.
GX	700-9 as built.

Plate 92. This picture of No. 71 was taken at Leeds Wellington and shows a number of interesting features, viz., the inside of the smokebox; arrangement of the Furness lubricator at the base of the smokebox; absence of any number on the locomotive headlamp and, from a livery standpoint, the lining and 'MR' on the buffer plank and lining on the cabfront. No. 71 was built in 1871 becoming No. 152 in 1907, and was withdrawn in 1925.

Collection David White

Plate 93. No. 854 illustrates a domed Johnson door but it is secured by dogs rather than a central wheel. This method was employed when a smokebox door number plate was fitted (in or after 1905) and of course the wheel was in the way. No. 854 was built at Derby in 1905 and was renumbered 764 in 1907. The year 1923 saw it fitted with a superheated boiler and withdrawal from service occurred at the end of 1934. *Collection Bernard Mathews*

THE 'FRONT END'

The expression 'front end' is a common way by which loco-motive historians refer to the combination of smokebox and chimney, although it is not an official description for this part of a locomotive. In more technical accounts, the phrase can also embrace a considerable discussion of the cylinder efficiency and draughting characteristics of a loco-motive but we shall confine our attention to visual changes.

Smokeboxes

The Johnson smokebox came in two principal styles with either the door held closed by a dart, together with plate hinges, or a dished door held shut by a wheel and using strap hinges. This later design arrived only in the final years of the Johnson era.

During the period c.1905-10 the Johnson front end was replaced and it is easy to appreciate that the locomotives reboilered by Deeley acquired quite different visual lines. First a flat smokebox door was utilised but this was later replaced with a dished door, both being held in the closed position by securing 'dogs' around the perimeter of the door. Flat doors usually had a small vertical handle whereas the dished doors usually featured a horizontal handrail. The flat door locomotives usually had a continuous handrail along the boiler side which curved upwards across the front of the smokebox, whereas locomotives with dished doors usually had straight handrails which did not extend around

Plate 94. The flat Deeley door is shown on this picture of 4–2–2 No. 647 which is noteworthy for the chimney which, while 'lipped', is not to the usual Deeley design. Indeed it appears to be a cut down Johnson design with a Deeley top. Another 'single', No. 613, ran with a 'flowerpot' chimney and these locomotives are at least two examples recorded by the authors showing unusual chimneys fitted to the 'singles'. *Collection Bernard Mathews*

Plate 95. The Johnson front end is seen in this picture of 0—4—4T No. 1266 which was to become No. 1240 under the 1907 renumbering scheme. The locomotive did not survive to become BR property. Withdrawal was in 1945. *Collection Roger Carpenter*

Plate 96. This close-up picture of the front end of 0—6—0 No. 1587, later to become No. 3085, has been selected to show the Johnson smokebox door which was closed with a dart, along with a typical front coupling used upon many Midland locomotives, three links and one hook. Note also the lamp irons, five in total. This picture also provides a good view of the sandbox pipes just in front of the brake blocks. *Authors' collection*

Plate 97. In comparison with *Plate 93* this picture shows the Johnson door closed by a wheel. It is not possible to identify the locomotive by number but it is a Belpaire 4—4—0. Here we have a different arrangement of the front three link coupling and just four lamp irons. Finally the reader's attention is drawn to the distinct taper on the 'Flowerpot' chimney. *Authors' collection*

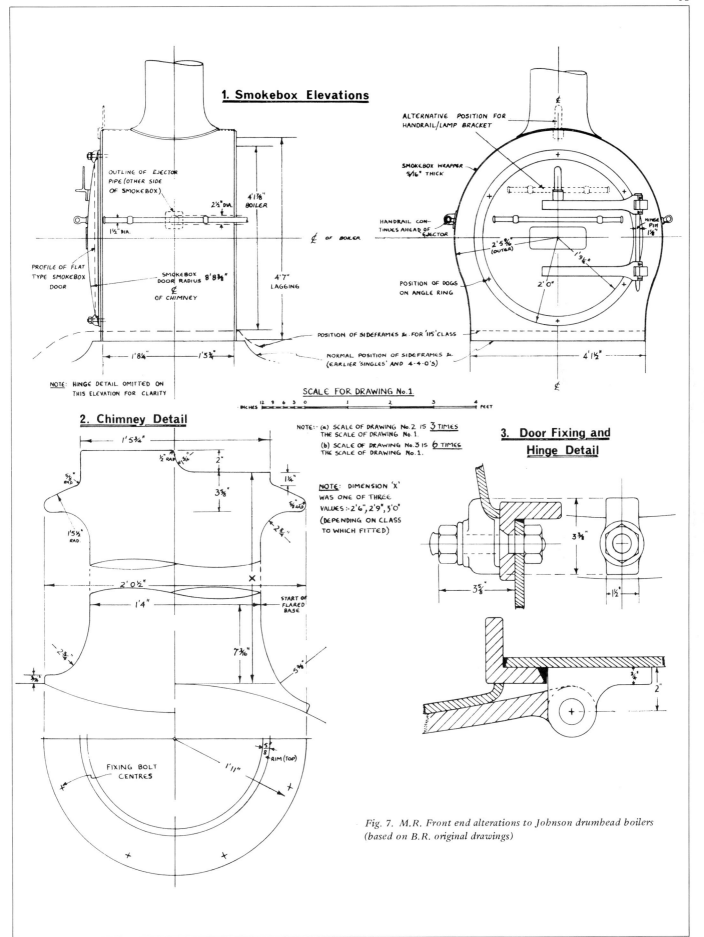

1. Smokebox Elevations

ALTERNATIVE POSITION FOR HANDRAIL/LAMP BRACKET

SMOKEBOX WRAPPER 5/16" THICK

OUTLINE OF EJECTOR PIPE (OTHER SIDE OF SMOKEBOX)

2½" DIA.

4'1⅞" BOILER

1½" DIA.

℄ OF BOILER

HANDRAIL CONTINUES AHEAD OF EJECTOR

HINGE PIN 1¾"

2'5⅞" (OUTER)

1'9⅞"

PROFILE OF FLAT TYPE SMOKEBOX DOOR

SMOKEBOX DOOR RADIUS 8'8½"

℄ OF CHIMNEY

4'7" LAGGING

POSITION OF DOGS ON ANGLE RING

2'0"

POSITION OF SIDEFRAMES &c. FOR '115' CLASS

NORMAL POSITION OF SIDEFRAMES &c. (EARLIER 'SINGLES' AND 4-4-0's)

1'8¼"

1'5¾"

4'1½"

℄

NOTE: HINGE DETAIL OMITTED ON THIS ELEVATION FOR CLARITY

SCALE FOR DRAWING No.1

INCHES 12 9 6 3 0   1   2   3   4 FEET

2. Chimney Detail

NOTE:- (a) SCALE OF DRAWING No.2 IS **3 TIMES** THE SCALE OF DRAWING No.1.

(b) SCALE OF DRAWING No.3 IS **6 TIMES** THE SCALE OF DRAWING No.1.

NOTE: DIMENSION 'X' WAS ONE OF THREE VALUES :- 2'6", 2'9", 3'0" (DEPENDING ON CLASS TO WHICH FITTED)

1'5¾"

½" RAD.

¾"

2"

1¼"

3⅜"

5/8" RAD.

⅝" RAD.

1'5½" RAD.

2¾"

2'0½"

1'4"

X

START OF FLARED BASE

7 3/16"

2⅜"

5¼"

FIXING BOLT CENTRES

1'11"

⅝" RIM (TOP)

3. Door Fixing and Hinge Detail

3⅜"

3⅝"

1½"

¾"

2"

Fig. 7. M.R. Front end alterations to Johnson drumhead boilers (based on B.R. original drawings)

Plate 98. This picture of 0—4—4T No. 1550 has been included to illustrate the Johnson three-piece built-up chimney in cast iron. In addition, the reader's attention is drawn to the lamp irons. The lower ones have extensions to carry the destination board. This locomotive was condenser fitted and worked in the London area. Later a cab was fitted and in due course No. 1550 became No. 1284 and was withdrawn in 1927.

Collection Roger Carpenter

the smokebox. There were exceptions to this principle and examples appear in various plates in Volumes 2 and 3. The dished door remained standard until the end of the Midland period and was used by the LMS for new construction of pre-Stanier types.

It is less easy to understand why the Johnson front end vanished so quickly from the non-reboilered locomotives, but the study of photographs clearly confirms that whilst the original Johnson front end did survive until the grouping on one or two locomotives, by and large its replacement by the Deeley pattern had taken place by 1917, thus giving a changed 'face' to the engine, even if its proportions remained 'Johnson'. Metal corrosion (by heat) may have been the reason. There were numerous exceptions to the general principles outlined above and these are mostly considered in detail in Volumes 2 and 3, but a few are given here.

Chimneys

Prior to 1889 the Johnson chimney was a three-piece built-up affair but from that date a single one-piece cast chimney was employed — but it took several years before the older style had been replaced. The 'Compounds' saw the arrival of the chimney with a lip, commonly referred to by enthusiasts as a 'capuchon', although 'windguard' was an official description for this chimney feature.

In 1903 a flowerpot chimney made an appearance. The 0–4–0Ts of the 1322 class, later 1500-1504, introduced a tall stovepipe chimney.

As far as we can establish, Johnson chimneys lasted until c.1917, after which date they were virtually extinct.

Plate 99. The later Deeley smokebox door on a Johnson locomotive is seen in this picture of 4–4–0 No. 320. This style is typical although there are examples of dished doors with a vertical handle on the right-hand side of the locomotive, similar to those which appeared on the flat doors. No. 320 was originally No. 1338, built in 1887, and was withdrawn in 1928, almost certainly in Crimson Lake livery. *Authors' collection*

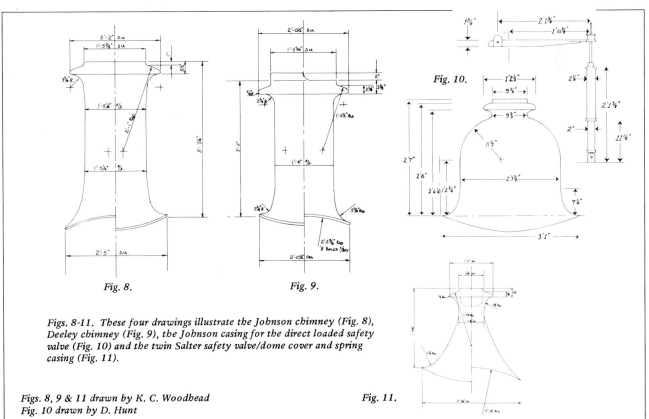

Fig. 8.   *Fig. 9.*   *Fig. 10.*   *Fig. 11.*

Figs. 8-11. These four drawings illustrate the Johnson chimney (Fig. 8), Deeley chimney (Fig. 9), the Johnson casing for the direct loaded safety valve (Fig. 10) and the twin Salter safety valve/dome cover and spring casing (Fig. 11).

Figs. 8, 9 & 11 drawn by K. C. Woodhead
Fig. 10 drawn by D. Hunt

Fig. 12.

— DETAILS OF SAFETY VALVES —

— MIDLAND RAILWAY. —

— FOR EXPRESS PASSENGER ENGINE. —

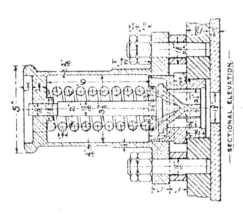

— SECTIONAL ELEVATION —

— PLAN —

FIG. 2.

The two larger valves, Fig. 1 (opposite page) are loaded by means of a crossbar or lever, and one central spring, in tension. This type of valve is generally known as the "Ramsbottom." The working pressure is 220 lbs. per square inch, and the total load on the valves is 3375 lbs.

The smaller independent valve, Fig. 2, is loaded directly by a spring in compression, and this valve is set to "blow-off" at a slightly higher pressure than the main valves. The load on this valve is 875 lbs.

The object of this additional valve is to act as a tell-tale and also to assist in preventing the accumulation of pressure which occurs when an engine, running at full power, is unexpectedly stopped by a signal.

Supplied by

Mr. R. M. DEELEY, M.I.M.E.

Late Chief Engineer, DERBY.

Reproduced from official records.

— DETAILS OF SAFETY VALVES —

MIDLAND RAILWAY.

— FOR EXPRESS PASSENGER ENGINE. —

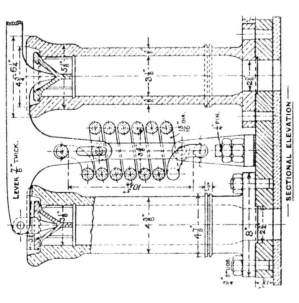

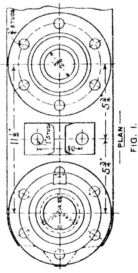

— SECTIONAL ELEVATION —

(SEE OPPOSITE PAGE.)

FIG. 1.

— PLAN —

Supplied by

Mr. R. M. DEELEY, M.I.M.E.,

Late Chief Engineer, DERBY.

SAFETY VALVES

The official drawing (Fig. 12) has been included to illustrate the workings of Ramsbottom and direct loaded safety valves.

Whilst the Ramsbottom safety valves of various styles fitted above the firebox of Belpaire boilered locomotives were replaced by 'pop' type safety valves during the 1930s, those locomotives with round-top boilers and fitted with Midland Salter safety valves on the dome retained them until the end of their existence. For further details see the plates which detail these safety valve variations.

The various styles of safety valves can be summarised as:

1. Twin Salter safety valves carried on the dome.

2. Direct loaded safety valve hidden within a brass casing on the firebox.

3. Ramsbottom safety valves on the firebox with lock-up valve (varies from class to class).

4. Direct loaded safety valve on the firebox behind or in front of the encased Ramsbottom safety valve.

5. Side by side as on the 0−4−0Ts.

6. 'Pop' valves.

SUPERHEATING

Superheating began in 1910 with the conversion of a class '990' 4−4−0 No. 998 and continued during the following year with two new 0−6−0s which later became class '4' locomotives, Nos. 3835 and 3836. The year 1912 saw the adoption of superheating on a wider scale with the commencement of the renewal of many 4−4−0 locomotives to the '483' class. Eventually a total of 157 locomotives were thus dealt with. Superheating of many other classes proceeded during the remainder of the Midland's separate existence.

The LMS policy for the first few years was to continue MR practice; then, starting c.1925, those locomotives with 'H' boilers, but not yet rebuilt with Belpaires, were gradually withdrawn. Additionally, the '700' class 4−4−0 superheated rebuilding programme ceased in 1925 and those locomotives which had not been rebuilt were quite speedily withdrawn. A less rapid withdrawal of saturated class '2' 4−4−0s numbered above 328, but not rebuilt to '483' class, took place. In general all those saturated 4−4−0 locomotives still running with 'H' boilers in the mid-1920s were soon taken out of service, but those which had been given saturated *Belpaire* boilers lasted quite a bit longer. Residual 'H' boilered 0−6−0s also went quite quickly to the scrap heap unless rebuilt.

What is probably not appreciated is that of the 45 'Compounds' to enter LMS service in 1923, 21 were still in saturated condition. It was not until 1928 that they were all superheated and this 'late' superheating also applied to the 0−6−4Ts, of which only three had been treated prior to 1923.

VACUUM CONTROL GEAR FOR PUSH & PULL TRAINS

Very few Midland Railway locomotives were equipped with a vacuum control regulator during the Midland Railway period but No. 1632 was one. Its purpose was to enable the locomotive to be braked by the driver when propelling motor-fitted coaches. 'Auto Trains', 'Reversible Trains', 'Motor Trains' and 'Push and Pull' trains were different terms used by various British railways for the system whereby a locomotive either pushed or pulled one or more coaches. The Midland appeared to favour the practice of placing the locomotive between the coaches with the driver controlling the brakes from the leading coach, leaving the fireman to open and close the regulator.

Plate 100. This picture illustrates a number of features − flat Deeley smokebox door with a horizontal handrail and vertical handle, vacuum control gear and, at the base of the smokebox, the Furness lubricator together with the knobs on the cylinder cover plates and the sandbox covers standing clear of the platform.

British Railways

Plate 101. This locomotive, No. 2183, was a 4—4—0 which became No. 403 in 1907. When photographed it was in its original Johnson condition. Particular points to note are the 'Midland' fire doors, which comprised a top flap, seen in closed position and a bottom flap which is shown open. There is no evidence of fire in the firebox. In the forefront of the picture on the tender bulkhead, are the control handles which allow the water to go from the tender into the mixing valves of the injectors. The steam control valves are the lowest two mounted wheels on the boiler back or firebox back plate (both terms can be used), the left-hand wheel being by the elbow of the bowler-hatted fireman. The centre wheel beneath the regulator handle is the blower control and the fourth wheel, to the right of the regulator is the small vacuum ejector. Locomotive elegance notwithstanding, general footplate conditions are all too clearly of a spartan nature.

Authors' collection

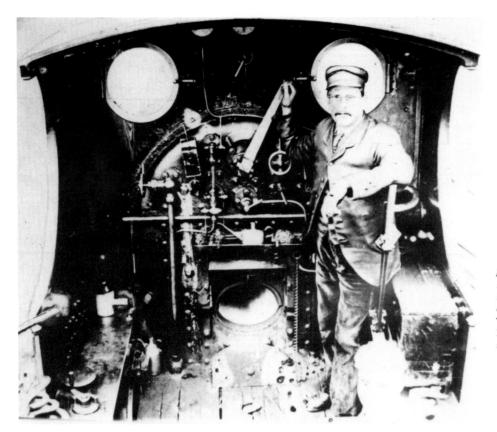

Plate 102. This footplate view is of a single frame class 2 goods No. 1591 and once again the spartan conditions on the footplate are very evident. This locomotive has a lever reverse. No. 1591 became No. 3089 in 1907 and was withdrawn in 1934.

Authors' collection

Plate 103. This picture of what is believed to be No. 20002 shows a storm sheet rolled up (not very neatly) and out of service.

Collection Roger Carpenter

B. LOCOMOTIVE CABS AND FOOTPLATES

GENERAL LAYOUT

As one author can testify from personal experience, the Midland Railway footplates varied from class to class. At best the 0—6—0 class '3F' with Belpaire boilers were very comfortable indeed, whereas at the other extreme, the old Johnson cab was truly a 'fair weather engine', a description not unknown at Saltley when describing the few 0—6—0s with this cab still in service at that depot c.1950. Whilst the passage of years tends to dim the memory, the presence of a large number of footplate views, many of which are featured in these volumes, does at least enable the authors to describe the principal controls, although in many respects the layout c.1911, the date when the majority of these pictures were taken, is, in a number of instances, somewhat different from that which one author knew from personal experience.

A number of footplate views are shown in this chapter in order to introduce the reader to the complexity of Midland cab layouts.

GAUGE GLASSES

The Johnson era saw the employment of only one gauge glass and this practice continued into the British Railways period for round-top boilers. The larger Deeley Belpaire boilers were equipped with two gauge glasses and it is believed that later (LMS) construction of 'G6' replacement

boilers also used two. The position of the gauge glass on the firebox back plate can clearly be seen in *Plate 104*.

LUBRICATORS

Many Midland locomotives when saturated were fitted with a Furness lubricator positioned each side of the locomotive at the base of the smokebox (see *Plate 100*). This device was removed by the LMS during the Stanier era. In addition, saturated boiler locomotives used a sight feed lubricator mounted on the fireman's side inside the cab (see *Plate 104*).

Mechanical lubricators, mounted on the framing, were to be found on superheated locomotives and this method was continued by the LMS for their standard locomotives (see *Plate 104*).

STORM SHEETS

Storm sheets were essential equipment for Midland locomotives with Johnson cabs. Each driver was issued with his own storm sheet which was kept in his personal locker at the shed and taken on the engine when required. When relieved he returned his sheet to the shed, leaving the fresh crew to attach their own.

In the Midland era locomotive sheets did not exist and it would seem that it was in the mid 1920s under LMS ownership that storm sheets began to be issued.

Plates 104, 105 & 106. These three pictures have been selected to introduce readers to the Midland locomotive footplate c.1911 and the various controls have been indicated. *Plate 104* shows 0–6–0 No. 3621 photographed in 1911 in 'ex works' condition. The locomotive has just been 'shopped' and the reader's attention is drawn to the painting style inside the cab. The lower half is in a dark colour, probably black, while the upper half is oak coloured. The inside of the roof is off white. The firebox back plate (commonly incorrectly referred to by enthusiasts as 'backhead') is also black. No. 3621 is fitted with an ejector and so can work vacuum braked trains. It carries a round-top 'B' class boiler. *Plates 105 & 106* illustrate class 2 goods engine No. 3438 and class 1 0–6–0T No. 1758. Whilst these pictures do not cover all the variations of fittings to be found on Midland locomotives, they do cover the majority of variations which were to be found. In Volumes 2 and 3 further footplate views will be featured and the same numbers used to identify the controls.

1 Steam regulator
2 Water gauge glass and protector
3 Water gauge steam cock
4 Water gauge water cock
5 Drain cock
6 Trial cock steam ⎤ Enable water/steam level in boiler to
7 Trial cock water ⎦ be established if gauge glass is broken.
8 Small steam ejector ⎤ Creates vacuum to enable automatic
9 Large steam ejector ⎦ vacuum brake system to work.
10 Combined automatic steam and vacuum brake valve
   (commonly referred to as the driver's brake handle)

11 Blower (on some locomotives the small ejector (8) and blower were combined)
12 Injector steam valves
13 Hydrostatic displacement feed lubricator
14 Vacuum brake gauge
15 Boiler steam pressure gauge
16 Whistle
17 Whistle shut off valve
18 Manual sand control
19 Damper control lever
20 Anti glare shield
21 Cylinder drain cocks control lever
22 Drip tray
23 Reversing lever safety catch
24 Reversing lever
25 Quadrant
26 Top firedoor flap
27 Top firedoor
28 Bottom firedoor
29 Bottom firedoor lifting chain
30 Steam sand valve
31 Top firedoor catch
32 Injector water valves
33 Screw reverser (see *Plate 101*)
34 Steam brake valve
35 Pocket to hold gauge glass lamp
36 Registered working pressure plate

Plates 107 & 108. 0–6–0T No. 1889 and 0–4–4T No. 1421 illustrate the sideways sliding cab roof used on the 'closed' Johnson tank engine cabs. No. 1889 was photographed at Kettering in 1923 in plain black, and No. 1421 carries early LMS Crimson Lake livery.

Collection Bernard Mathews

CAB ROOF VENTILATORS

Many Midland engines were fitted with cab roof ventilators of the double sliding type (see *Plate 107*) or the raised 'lifting' type, very familiar on the 'rounded eaves' Deeley cabs (see *Plate 109*). However, especially in the case of tender locomotives, not all engines were given a roof ventilator and since it is such an obvious feature, especially on a model, we have tried to analyse the situation in the absence of any recorded official policy, as far as we can determine.

Tank engine policy seems to have been constant. Closed cab locomotives with Johnson cabs had two sliding roof panels (see *Plate 108*) and this seems to have been a consistent feature of all closed cab tank engines in the pre-Deeley period. The two 'closed cab' Deeley tank engine designs were the 0–6–4Ts and 0–4–0Ts and these two classes seem to have had the type shown in *Plates 110 and 65* throughout their existence.

Open cab tank engines were never fitted with cab roof ventilators.

With tender engines, the position is a little more complicated but we believe the following analysis to be correct.

Firstly, roof ventilators were *never* fitted to tender engines with any form of Johnson cab. The feature was confined to the rounded eaves cab of Deeley pattern but *not* from the date of introduction of this type of cab. Photographic evidence tends to suggest that the 'H' boilered 0–6–0s commencing with No. 3815 (built 1908) were the first locomotives to receive this fitting. Thus, any engines built earlier with the full Deeley cab would be 'ventless'. These included the Deeley compound 4–4–0s, the first of the '990' class 4–4–0s (actually No. 999), the round-top 'H' boilered 4–4–0 rebuilds and *some* of the saturated Belpaire 4–4–0 rebuilds.

In this latter group, the 7 ft versions (*Plate 115*) seem to have all been in service before the introduction of cab ventilators but the 6' 6½" engines (the '378' type, *Plate 109*) came out *after* the roof ventilator had been adopted. The balance of the '990' class 4–4–0s (990-8) were built in

Plate 109. The cab roof ventilator is clearly seen on this picture of class '378' rebuilt 4–4–0 No. 382 photographed in plain black livery.

D. Ibbotson

Plate 110. 0—6—4T No. **2000** as new, clearly illustrates the cab roof ventilator. *Collection Bernard Mathews*

Plate 111. 0—6—0 No. 3815 in Works Grey livery clearly displays a cab roof ventilator and was probably the first new tender locomotive to be so equipped. In due course the locomotive was fitted with a 'G7' Belpaire boiler and lasted until withdrawal by British Railways in 1958 as 43815. *British Railways*

1909 but, presumably having been built to the 1907 drawings, had no roof ventilators; but when the original five Johnson 'Compounds' finally assumed the 'Deeley' configuration, they received the 'current' cab style, i.e. with roof ventilators. The original Deeley 'Compounds' frequently retained their 'ventless' cabs but some of them eventually sported the roof-vent version and we think this may well indicate the fitting of a totally *new* cab roof (probably, but not necessarily, at the time of superheating).

What does seem clear is that all *new* cabs built after c.1908-9 had roof ventilators, which automatically encom-

passes the '483' class superheated 4—4—0s, all the class '4' 0—6—0s and all the *Belpaire* boilered class '2' and class '3' 0—6—0s. However, if an engine did not *need* a new cab after 1908/9 (or, more accurately, a new cab *roof*) then it seems to have retained its 'ventless' roof for quite a long time, even though rebuilt and/or superheated (see *Plate 113*).

We go into this subject in more detail in the class sections of Volumes 2 and 3 but we conclude this section with a few pictures selected to illustrate the cab roof situation.

Plates 112 & 113. Compound variations are seen in these two pictures. Superheated No. 1002 in Midland livery c.1920 has a cab roof ventilator whereas No. 1021, photographed at Derby in April 1928, does not. The latter engine was not superheated until late 1927 and has retained its original plain cab roof dating from 1906, whereas No. 1002 got a new cab in 1919 when rebuilt from original Johnson state.

Collection Bernard Mathews

Plate 114. This picture of '483' class No. 477 has been included to illustrate the bogie brakes fitted to certain Midland Railway locomotives. This practice, originated by Fowler, was continued by the LMS but under the Stanier régime they were removed. No. 477 was renewed in 1922 and was withdrawn in 1951 as British Railways No. 40477.

Collection Bernard Mathews

C. BRAKES

STEAM BRAKES

The Midland Railway used steam brakes on their locomotives, a practice continued by both the LMS and British Railways. In addition a hand brake was fitted to all tank engines and to all tenders. Bogie brakes were fitted to some classes and this practice was later extended to some LMS standard classes. However, in the Stanier period, they were all removed (see *Plate 114*).

WESTINGHOUSE BRAKES

A number of Midland Railway locomotives were fitted with Westinghouse brakes and this extract from *The Locomotive* has been included to record which locomotives were so fitted.

> Originally the Midland Company fitted 57 engines with the Westinghouse brake, but 31 of these (marked in the accompanying list thus *) became too small for the Scotch trains, so their brakes were taken off and put on 31 larger engines. So 57 sets of gear were at various times on 88 engines.

Plate 115. Some of the Johnson 4—4—0s rebuilt with Belpaire boilers, but not as class '483' renewals, did not receive roof ventilators. These seem to have been from the 7 ft driving wheel series and this picture of 4—4—0 No. 349 has been included to illustrate the point. No. 349 was built in 1883 at Derby as No. 1658 and in 1907 it became No. 349 and received an 'H' boiler. Three years later in 1910 it was fitted with a Belpaire boiler with an extended smokebox, as illustrated; and of course received a new cab front, but it probably retained the original cab sides and roof which were fitted in 1907 when the Johnson cab was replaced and so predated the fitting of cab roof ventilators. If this part of the cab was retained, then this could help explain why no cab roof ventilators appeared on this series of locomotives, because the first rebuilding was done before cab roof ventilators became standard practice, and the subsequent Belpaire treatment did not involve a new cab roof.

Authors' collection

Most of the brakes on the '1' and '235' classes were put on the 812 to 829 engines, and the '900' brakes were mostly put on '1572' class.

The following is a list [published in 1907] of 88 engines, showing their [pre-] 1907 numbers which at various dates had the Westinghouse brake:—

1*	71*	238*	813	902*	1311
9*	73*	239*	814	903*	1572
10*	74*	800	815	904*	1573
13*	96*	801	816	905*	1574
22	101	802	817	906*	1575
40*	102	803	818	907*	1576
41*	134*	804	819	1302	1577
42*	146*	805	824	1303	1578
60	156*	806	826	1304	1579
62	165	807	829	1305	1580
63	166	808	894*	1306	1581
64	168	809	895*	1307	1675
65	235*	810	898*	1308	1677
66	236*	811	900*	1309	
70*	237*	812	901*	1310	

31 marked * changed to other engines.

Refer to Appendix 1 for details of their post 1907 numbers. In addition some 0–6–4Ts were Westinghouse fitted for service on the LT & SR section, and further details will be found in Volume 2 within the section dealing with this class of tank engines.

D. COUPLINGS

In the late 1880s many Midland locomotives did not have a drawbar hook, instead an arrangement similar to that shown in *Plate 96* was employed. It was usual to use a three link coupling on the tender drawbar and, whilst these arrangements are shown in the photographs, it would seem

Plate 116. 2–4–0 No. 824, seen here in Works Grey livery, was built in 1870 and in due course became No. 57. As such it did not survive to become LMS property, being withdrawn in 1922. This picture is particularly interesting in so far as it illustrates the Westinghouse brake fitted to a Midland locomotive, and a further example will be found in *Plate 45* illustrating 4–4–0 No. 1676.

Authors' collection

that the Midland practice for front couplings was altered in the early years of the century. See *Plates 127-129* for details of the tender coupling.

E. SANDING

The introduction of steam sanding enabled the Midland to reintroduce 'singles' for main line express work and steam sanding became the 'norm' on future construction. However, gravity sanding (which used much more sand) continued on older Midland locomotives until they were withdrawn by British Railways — as one of us can testify from personal experience.

Plate 117. 4–2–2 No. 26 was the second of the 'singles' which were built with steam sanding. On the original print it is possible to see that the steam pipes curled down to join the sand pipe at the end in a manner that is very different from later practice.

Collection Roger Carpenter

F. TENDERS

The earliest tenders which fall within the review period were of Kirtley design. Their springs were mounted above the framing and this style of tender is described in the relevant photograph captions (see *Plate 119*).

The Johnson designed tenders began with the construction of a similar design for both goods and passenger locomotives, these tenders having their springs mounted 'inside' the framing and so not visible (see *Plate 120*). This was altered to what could be considered to be a more conventional style with the springs mounted outside the framing (from c.1890), although it took many years from this date for them all to be altered.

The next change of design, used for goods locomotives only, was to go to a narrow tank with the springs mounted above the framing whilst the passenger locomotive tender design was changed from a tender with springs 'inside' the framing to one with springs outside the frames in a more conventional style.

The period prior to the introduction of water troughs saw the introduction of bogie 'water cart' tenders which, particularly in the case of the 'singles', dwarfed the locomotives. With the introduction of water troughs, these tenders were rebuilt with straight sides running on six wheel chassis and they generally remained associated with the same locomotives (class '3' Belpaires, Johnson 'Compounds', and 'Princess of Wales' type 'singles'). It is worth mentioning that when the 'singles' were scrapped, their tenders were used with the first LMS batch of 'Compounds', Nos. 1045-1054. The straight-sided tenders built new as such, had

Plate 118. No. 2627's tender. This close-up of the Kirtley goods engine tender shows the tender top in its final years.

Collection Bernard Mathews

Plate 119. Photographed in 1934, this 2,000 gallon Kirtley tender was coupled to 0−6−0 No. 22834. Note the distance between the end of the frames and the tank. These 'horse-shoe' tenders of Kirtley design varied somewhat in detail and gained their 'horse-shoe' nickname because of the shape (in plan) of the coal space.

R. E. Lacy

Fig. 13. The Kirtley 2,000 gallon horseshoe tank tender is shown in this drawing which was one of a series of diagrams issued by the Midland Railway Company. Although this style of tender is more commonly associated with the 0−6−0 goods engines, it was also found with passenger locomotives (see Plate 3). The preserved 2−4−0 No. 158A, part of the National Collection, is currently coupled to a tender of this type, but it did not run with a Kirtley tender when the locomotive was in the Deeley condition as preserved. One of the authors is rather sensitive on this point but does not quite know what can be done about it!

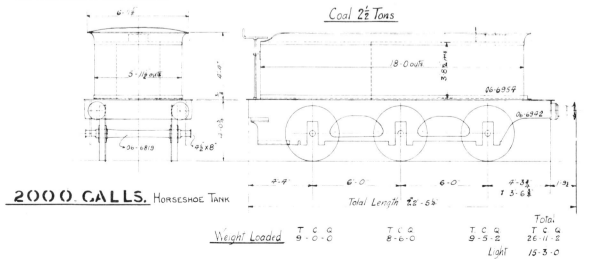

Coal 2½ Tons

2000 GALLS. HORSESHOE TANK

Total Length 22'-5½"

Weight Loaded	T C Q 9 - 0 - 0	T C Q 8 - 6 - 0	T C Q 9 - 5 - 2	Total T C Q 26 - 11 - 2
			Light	15 - 3 - 0

NOTE The 1600 & 2000 Gall Tenders vary considerably from one another, and the dimensions here given are only approximate

Plate 120. 0—6—0 No. 1234 was built in 1876 and became No. 3002 in 1907. It received a 'G6' boiler in 1918, was renumbered 23002 by the LMS before BR renumbered it 58175. Withdrawal was at the end of 1960. The photograph has been included to illustrate a tender with 'inside' springs. The locomotive is, of course, in green livery as built. *Authors' collection*

first appeared coupled to the Deeley 'Compounds' and '990s' and formed the basis of the LMS standard tender built steadily from 1923 to 1934, and occasionally later.

Two other straight-sided tenders should be noted. They were rebuilds of Johnson tenders coupled to 4—4—0 class '378' rebuilds. In 1911 these tenders went behind the two new 0—6—0s built that year, Nos. 3835/6.

Although the Deeley flat-sided tender had made its appearance, the Johnson style flared side tender of 3500 gallon capacity was built until the end of the Midland's existence and this type was coupled to class '2' 4—4—0s Nos. 523-562 and to the final series of class '3' 0—6—0s Nos. 3765-3834. Variations of this tender also appeared behind the class '4' 0—6—0s, built both by Armstrong Whitworth and the Midland Railway, these locomotives being numbered 3877-4026.

Plate 121. Tender No. 419 clearly illustrates the front end of a 3,250 gallon tender and shows a transverse and a lengthwise toolbox. *Collection David Tee*

Plate 122. Photographed c.1936, this picture of a Johnson axlebox and springs was part of a 3,250 gallon tender coupled to 0—6—0 class '2F' No. 3590.

G. Y. Hemingway

DESIGN DETAILS ANALYSED

Plate 123. This view of the rear end of a Johnson tender devoid of coal shows the small rear bulkhead which was not very good at restraining the coal — as one of us can personally testify. Note the fire irons. The centre one is the rake, but we cannot make out what the other two are. The round handle of the left-hand one should be that of a shovel, whilst the one on the right is probably the dart.   *R. E. Lacy*

Plate 124. No. 3157 is an 0—6—0 which was to become BR No. 58239. Originally No. 1765, this locomotive later received a Belpaire boiler before withdrawal in 1950. Taken in August 1939, this picture has been included to illustrate the top of a 3,250 gallon tender. Note the single tool box.   *A. E. West*

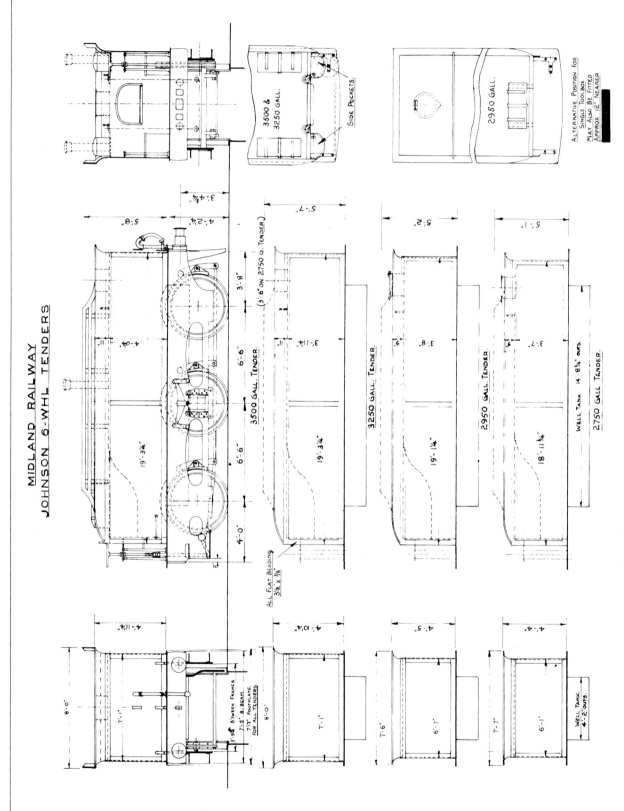

MIDLAND RAILWAY
JOHNSON 6-WHL TENDERS

3500 &
3250 GALL.

SIDE POCKETS.

2950 GALL.

ALTERNATIVE POSITION FOR
SINGLE TOOLBOX
MAY ALSO BE FITTED
APPROX 12" NEARER

3500 GALL. TENDER.

3250 GALL. TENDER.

2950 GALL. TENDER.

2750 GALL. TENDER.

ALL FLAT BEADING
3½ x ⅜

WELL TANK 14'-8¼" OUTS.

BETWEEN FRAMES.
FOOTPLATE
FOR ALL TENDERS.

WELL TANK
4'-2" OUTS.

*Fig. 14. Four Midland railway tenders of 3,500, 3,250, 2,950 and 2,750 gallon capacity are depicted in this drawing.
However, we believe that those to 2,950 gallon capacity did not, in some instances, have the bottom beading on the side
and the ends. (Drawings: K. C. Woodhead)*

Plate 125. No. 43356 is shown here with a 3,250 gallon tender with squared end coal rails, bulkhead, and tool box in front of the bulkhead. No. 43356 was originally No. 2079 built in 1891. It was fitted with an 'H' boiler in 1904 and received a 'G7' boiler in 1922, running as a class 3 until withdrawal in 1956. *Photomatic*

Plate 126. Compare this picture of a 3,500 gallon tender with the previous view which illustrates a 3,250 gallon capacity tender with detail differences. The tender coupled to No. 43356 is panelled, whereas the tender illustrated in this plate is of rivetted construction with edge beading only. This view also shows the squared end coal rails which are attached to the bulkhead. In front of this are the tool boxes. Readers will note that in this case there are three. The larger centre one was for clothes and personal equipment. The box behind the driver, which is the one on the left, held the oil cans; whilst the one behind the fireman was for tools. Note that this tender has a hand brake only and no water pick-up. The hand brake was the fireman's responsibility and was applied by turning the handle clockwise to apply the tender brakes. This was the normal method of securing a locomotive when standing, although at times the tender

brake was also used to assist controlling a train, in particular one which was loose coupled running down gradients.

Another point to observe is the tender tank water gauge, to the left of the oil can box. Although only one is visible, there were two water cocks for allowing the water to go from the tank to the mixing valve of the injectors. These cocks were just above the footplate to the left and right of the shovelling plate. This itself is of interest and again personal experience of one of the writers confirms how much easier it was to shovel off a plate some 9-12 inches above the footplate level than from the lower position.

The two rods with round knobs on the end were to secure the fire irons. Finally, the pipes coming from below the tender were to carry the water from the tender to the mixing valves of the injector.

Authors' collection

Fig. 14A. Water capacity plate as used by Midland locomotives (see Plates 108 & 252).

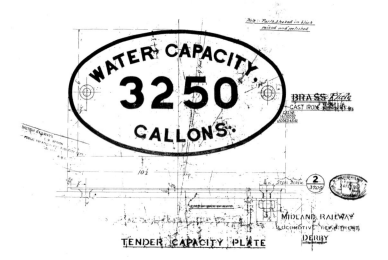

Plates 127 & 128. These two pictures have been selected to enable a comparison to be made between the same type of tender. *Plate 127* shows 4–4–0 'Compound' No. 1028 photographed just after the grouping. Note the locomotive number on the headlamps. Other points to note are that on 1028 there is a three-link coupling, whereas 1033 has a screw coupling and larger buffer heads.

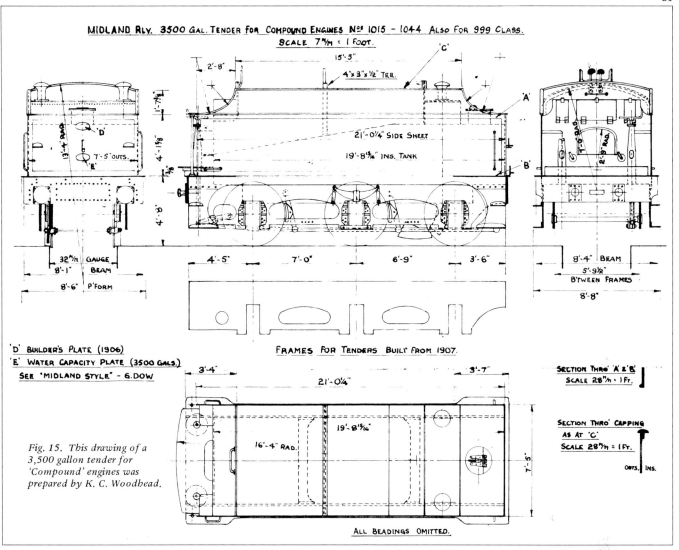

MIDLAND RLY. 3500 GAL. TENDER FOR COMPOUND ENGINES NOS 1015 - 1044 ALSO FOR 999 CLASS.

SCALE 7m/m = 1 FOOT.

15'-3"

2'-8"

4"x 3"x 1/2" TEE.

21'-0 1/4" SIDE SHEET

19'-8 15/16" INS. TANK

13'-4 RAD.

7'-5" OUTS.

'D'

'E'

'C'

'A'

'B'

1'-7 1/2"

4'-1 7/8"

4'-8"

32 m/m GAUGE

8'-1" BEAM

8'-6" P'FORM

4'-5"   7'-0"   6'-9"   3'-6"

8'-4" BEAM

5'-9 1/2" B'TWEEN FRAMES

8'-8"

'D' BUILDER'S PLATE (1906)

'E' WATER CAPACITY PLATE (3500 GALS.)

SEE 'MIDLAND STYLE' - G. DOW

FRAMES FOR TENDERS BUILT FROM 1907.

SECTION THRO' 'A' & 'B'

SCALE 28m/m = 1 FT.

SECTION THRO' CAPPING

AS AT 'C'

SCALE 28m/m = 1 FT.

OUTS. INS.

3'-4"   21'-0 1/4"   3'-7"

16'-4" RAD.   19'-8 15/16"   7'-5"

Fig. 15. This drawing of a 3,500 gallon tender for 'Compound' engines was prepared by K. C. Woodhead.

ALL BEADINGS OMITTED.

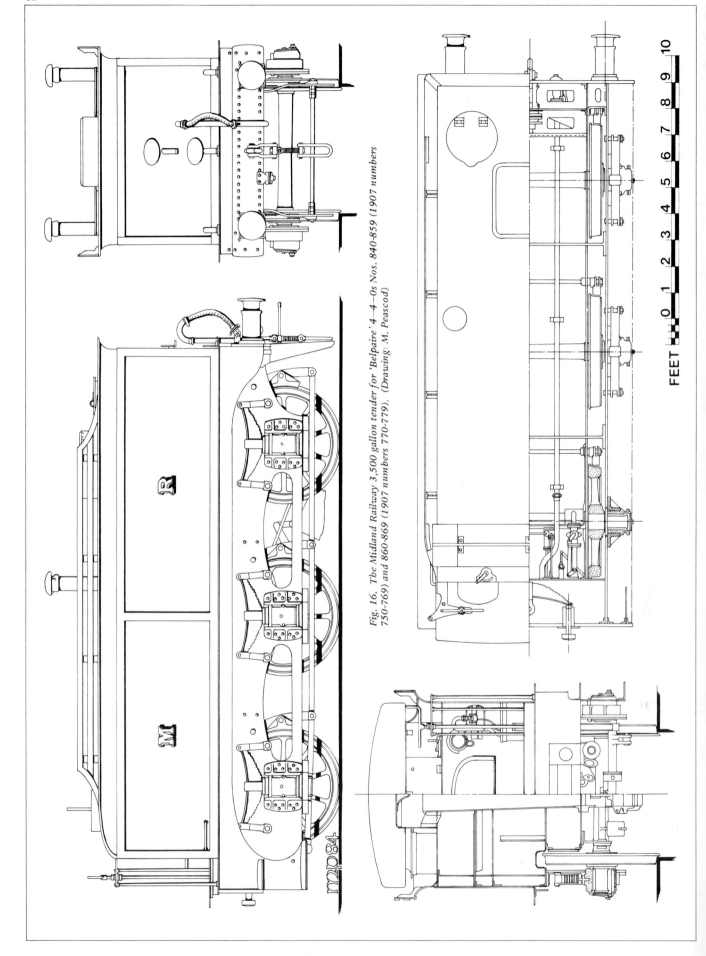

Fig. 16. The Midland Railway 3,500 gallon tender for 'Belpaire' 4–4–0s Nos. 840-859 (1907 numbers 750-769) and 860-869 (1907 numbers 770-779). (Drawing: M. Peascod)

FEET

COAL RAILS

Coal rails began to be fitted from about 1891 and, whilst almost all were on the sides of the tender only, a few tenders had their rails also round the rear (see *Plate 132*).

TOOL BOXES

Tool boxes were originally mounted at the rear of the tender but in 1904 instructions were issued to take them out of use or move them forward. This was not a totally new idea — some forward mounted tool boxes had been in use since c.1890 (see *Plate 141*). There could be either one or two tool boxes at the front of the tender and when there were two they could be both transverse, one transverse and one lengthwise, or both lengthwise.

Other Johnson tenders had squared end coal rails with a square tool box built in the front of the bulkhead and these variations are noted on the photo captions. Towards the end of the Midland period, orders were issued to rebuild many tenders in this form. The bogie tender rebuilds and the new flat-sided tenders produced a 'built in' arrangement with curved ends to the tool box.

TENDER CABS

In their earliest form tender cabs date from the late 19th century and were probably fitted to locomotives used with snow ploughs. Many temporary tender cabs were fitted during World War I and remained in use for a time after hostilities ceased.

WATER PICK-UPS

Water pick-up scoops were at first fitted to the tenders of all the large boiler passenger locomotives and then later to freight locomotive tenders; but even by the British Railways period not all locomotive tenders had been equipped with water pick-up apparatus.

Plate 129. This picture of No. 857 has been included principally to illustrate the tender number plate which can be seen just above the lamp. No. 857 was built in 1905 and became No. 767 in 1907. The locomotive is seen here in its original condition before rebuilding with a 'G8AS' boiler which took place in 1921. Withdrawal was in 1947. This picture displays many useful aspects. The roof is black on top and crimson up to the rainstrip. The reader can see the arrangement of the tender vent pipes and tank filter on the tender rear and the parts painted dull black. Note the fine chains and the multiple couplings but no hook! *National Railway Museum*

Plates 130 & 131. These have been selected to show differences between various types of tenders. *Plate 130* shows a 2,950 gallon tender coupled to No. 3229 with two toolboxes on the bulkhead whilst *Plate 131* illustrates 0—6—0 No. 3230 coupled to a 2,350 gallon tender with the springs above the running plate. The pictures were probably taken to illustrate the method of securing the storm sheets to the tender (see page 67).

British Railways

Plate 132. This picture of 0–6–0 No. 2948 has been included to illustrate the coal rails which extend 'all round' the rear of the tender. It is not known how many tenders were so equipped. This c.1927 photograph was taken within a few years of the end of this locomotive's existence. Built in 1875 by Dübs & Co. as No. 1180, it became No. 2948 in 1907 and was withdrawn in 1930.

Authors' collection

NUMBER PLATES

Tender numbers were not separately allocated in Midland days. The number plates on the rear of tenders (see *Plate 129*) actually carried the *engine* number and were discontinued from about the World War I period. They were reintroduced by the LMS from 1928 when tenders began to be numbered separately from engines.

Water tank capacity plates dated from c.1880 and were always found on the rear of the tender. On tank locomotives a similar plate was to be found on the rear of the bunker.

OIL BURNING

Coal strikes led to a number of British railways adopting oil firing in an attempt to conserve coal and the Midland Railway was one such. Pictures have been included to illustrate this aspect of the story, generally related to the period c.1921 when the Midland Railway converted a number of locomotives to oil burning.

Plate 133. 0–6–0 No. 1222 was built in 1876 by Neilson and became No. 2990 in 1907 and No. 58164 by British Railways before withdrawal in 1955. A 'G6' Belpaire boiler was fitted in 1919. The locomotive is seen here with a tender cab, snow plough and cabside doors. Note the locomotive's headlamps on the top of the snow plough. This picture was taken in the 'red for all types' period, but the locomotive displays no evidence of yellow lining whatsoever. The splasher beading seems to be of somewhat darker shade than the main colour, in which case it could be black and the locomotive itself in the 'Locomotive Brown' livery (see Chapter 5).
Authors' collection

Plates 134, 135 & 136. 4–4–0 No. 776 as equipped for oil burning. The footplate view shows the layout of the controls with the addition of the oil burning arrangement. *Plate 135* shows the 'tender front' little altered; the fuel supply can clearly be seen and the shovelling plate has been blocked off. No. 776 was later converted back to coal burning and finally withdrawn from service in 1936. *British Railways*

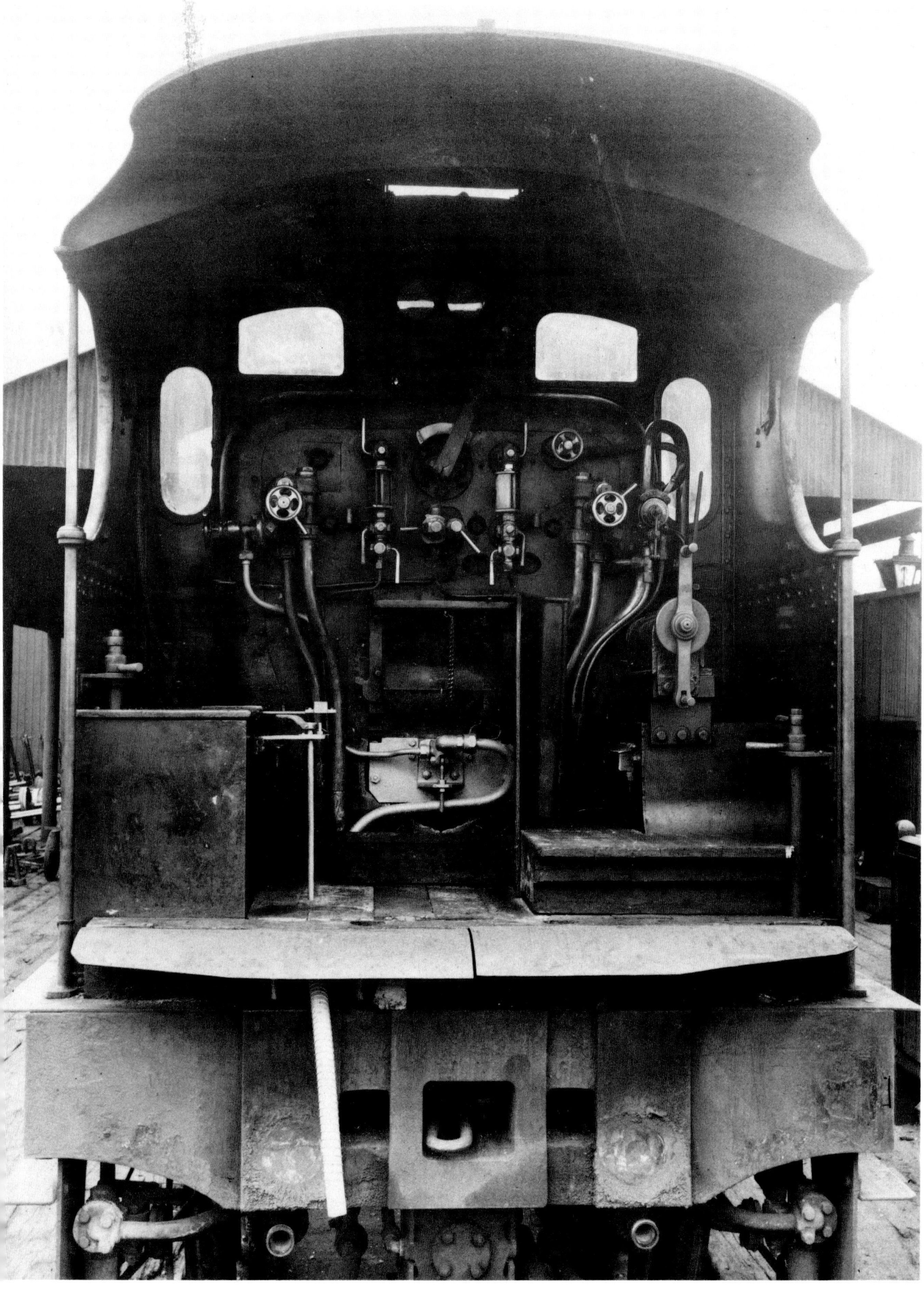

Plate 137. An alternative method of arranging oil tanks is shown in this picture of 4—4—0 No. 527. In due course No. 527 was converted back for coal burning and lasted until 1956 when it was withdrawn as BR No. 40527.   *W. L. Good*

Plate 138. This picture shows No. 504 in service in July 1921. The tender is a 3,250 gallon tender with two oil tanks fitted where the coal would normally be carried. No. 504, like all other oil burners, was converted back to coal burning and the locomotive survived to become British Railways No. 40504 and was withdrawn from service in 1961.   *Authors' collection*

Plate 139. 4—4—0 'Compound' No. 1005 is seen here being refuelled. It is just not possible to read the name on the oil tanks standing on the elevated road which is part of the coaling stage. No. 1005 was originally No. 1000, the first of the Deeley 'Compounds' and was super-heated in 1923 and is seen here in LMS pre-1928 passenger livery. As British Railways No. 41005, this locomotive was withdrawn from service in 1951.   *Authors' collection*

Plate 140. 4—4—0 No. 484 illustrates another method of securing the oil tanks into the tender. No. 484 was built at Derby in 1896 as No. 1668 and received an 'H' boiler in 1907, the year it became No. 484. Renewed to '483' class in 1913, it was to remain in service until 1953, spending its final years as British Railways No. 40484.   *Authors' collection*

Plate 141. This magnificent view of Derby paint shop in 1890 is worthy of careful study. Note the very clean condition of the shop. The only locomotives which can be identified are the two 'singles' on the centre row, Nos. 1862 and 1866, both entering traffic that year.

National Railway Museum

CHAPTER FOUR

LOCOMOTIVE LIVERIES
A GENERAL REVIEW 1883-1966

IN this and the next two chapters we attempt to unravel some of the mysteries of the Midland Railway locomotive livery. We say 'mysteries' advisedly because, contrary to popular belief, the story is not a simple one. Fortunately, some nine or ten years ago (in 1975), the Historical Model Railway Society published a book called *Midland Style* in which a valiant attempt was made to get to the bottom of some aspects of the story. We do not propose to repeat the substance of the HMRS survey here since we could, and no doubt would, be accused of plagiarism. We have, therefore, taken its findings as a valuable starting point in our story and would not only recommend the book to our readers as a basic guide to the general story, but we have made frequent references in this work to its conclusions.

At the same time, and given the much broader remit of the author of the HMRS work, it is not surprising that it falls short in the sort of precise detail which dedicated students might seek out — especially model makers who wish to be exact as possible in their reproduction of specific locomotives and periods. For one thing, it places considerable emphasis on narrative detail and this is frequently somewhat speculative. Secondly, and no doubt for economic reasons, it does not make anything like as much use of photographs as our publisher has permitted in this survey and of which we have, hopefully, taken full advantage. Moreover, the ever-increasing flow of information which has become available in the last ten years or so enables us to be a little more exact in certain areas. This has caused us to cast doubt on some of the findings in *Midland Style*,

although not its overall scholarship. Where there is a substantial difference of view, we draw it to our readers' attention. Of course, at this range in time, there can be few certainties, so we must leave matters to our readers to assess. All we can try to do is present the evidence on which we base our findings.

We have chosen to break the subject down into, hopefully, digestible elements. In consequence, this chapter concerns itself with a broad 'overview' of the story from c.1883 to 1966, whereas the next two chapters tackle the specifically Midland elements in more detail. However, regardless of the particular period, we have been conscious that locomotives were never at any time painted in accordance with the law of the Medes and Persians. There was nothing sacrosanct about painting an engine. The job was done to the direction of a foreman or charge-hand painter and he probably relied more often on his note-book and personal recollection than on the official specification which was, in any case, often somewhat imprecise (see, for example, page 97).

In consequence, engine painting was more art than science and frequently a personal business. Locomotives did not come off the production line like modern motor cars and one would naturally expect to find differences. Not surprisingly, therefore, in attempting to understand the paintshop procedures of the Midland Railway during the late Victorian era we must accept that we are, in the final analysis, in the hands of a man with a paint brush and paint pot. Furthermore, the Midland Railway did not have one central point where the entire stock of locomotives

Plates 142 and 143. The Midland Railway's first heraldic emblem of 'diamond shape' was introduced in the 1880s and was used on both coaches and locomotives although its use was not universal. They were not identical in colouring, the 'ribbon' surround being green for locomotives and blue for coaches. A full description is to be found in *Midland Style.* A second device was introduced in 1891 and was very similar to the 1880 version. However, in 1906 the final design of more conventional 'coat of arms' pattern (i.e. with 'crest' and 'supporters') was introduced, and this was used on most locomotives thereafter until the grouping of 1923. *British Railways*

was painted. In addition to Derby, locomotives were painted at Kentish Town, Bristol, Leeds, Manchester and Saltley. Furthermore, painters were employed at the other depots so it is inevitable that there were minor differences between locomotives outshopped from these various places. To this must be added the number of locomotives produced by various outside contractors. They often utilised further slight livery interpretations which added to the variety to be seen at any one time.

We must also include two further factors. The first is that the film used by the photographers during that period could not easily detect the difference between red and

to assume that, by September 1881 when the next change took place, the majority of the locomotives were running painted in a light green colour although there may have been a number in service still painted dark green. In September 1881, ten locomotives were painted in a new colour which has been described as Dull Red. Of these, one was a 2—4—0 No. 1500 but the numbers of the remainder are not known to us.

Following this experiment a Locomotive Committee minute dated 2nd November 1883 ordered that all Midland Railway locomotives were to be painted in a new colour, which we now know as Crimson Lake or Midland Red, but

Plate 144. The differentiation between green and red engines is not always easy in the early 1880s period, when the only evidence is a black and white picture. This view, however, certainly shows a green engine even though the locomotive itself is in the external configuration which it displayed at the start of our period of survey. Kirtley 0—6—0 No. 864 was built by Dübs in 1871 and remained as illustrated until 1885, well into the 'red' period. However, the somewhat florid lining, the 'three panel' treatment of the tender side and the concave corners to the panel lining all indicate the Kirtley pre-1876 dark green livery and it is quite likely that it remained thus until rebuilt. Given a second rebuild in 1901, this engine became No. 555 in 1905 and a year or so later was one of several sold to the Italian Railways when it became No. 3841. *British Railways*

black, so interpretation of old photographs is not easy, and finally we encounter the human element again. The drivers, in days of single manned locomotives, probably enlisted the services of various painters to add extra embellishments — and so we have a fleet of locomotives which were somewhat less than uniform in their livery styles.

In 1881, shortly before the commencement of the period reviewed in these volumes, all Midland Railway locomotives, however humble their duties, were almost certainly painted green and lined out. Sixty-seven years later, in the British Railways era, they were all black, mostly unlined. Interestingly, no such simple generalisations can be made for any part of the intervening period! Unfortunately, most published sources still persist in over-simplification and thus, popular opinion, nurtured over the years, assumes that all the Midland Railway locomotives were impeccably turned out in Crimson Lake but, as we have stated, this was not always so.

In Kirtley days Midland Railway locomotives had been painted in dark green, which was modified by Johnson to a lighter shade in 1876. It would therefore seem reasonable

which at that time and for many years later was referred to as 'Oxide of Iron and Lake'. It has been recorded that the change from green to red was made in order to find a more durable colour, the existing green being described as a fugitive colour that was also expensive to maintain. It was suggested that the red would last twice as long and, although it cost only slightly less to paint each engine red, the anticipated extra life between painting would produce considerable savings over the years. Therefore, from the end of 1883 the Midland Railway locomotive stock began to change into red; but several years would have elapsed before the entire stock was painted Crimson Lake. What is probably not appreciated is that the Midland, considered by many as a 'Total Red Engine' railway after 1883, was only such for a few years from c.1890 (by which date the last green locomotive had probably been repainted) until the turn of the century when the beginning of a further period of considerable livery change could be noted.

The new standard red livery was generally described as:- Boiler, frames, splashers, tanks, coal bunker and cab finished in red, picked out in black and fine lined with yellow. The

Plates 145 & 146. These two views of Kirtley 2–2–2 engines typify the difficulty in sorting out the green and red engines once Johnson had moved on the scene. Both engines exhibit Johnson modifications to the original Kirtley design (e.g. cabs/chimney) and, for all practical purposes, the arrangement of lining is identical. They represent the '30' class engines as running between 1881-92. No. 39, rebuilt in 1881, could have been photographed at any time during the 1881-92 period and may well be green. It became 39A in late 1892, which at least puts a last possible date to the view. However, 149 is certainly red. For one thing, it did not become 149 until 1885, two years after the start of the red livery, but it also carries the seriffed 'MR', the latter being an undoubted indication of red livery, not being seen on engines until c.1891. Since the engine became 149A in 1893, the photograph is almost certainly dateable as 1891/2.   *Collection Bernard Mathews*

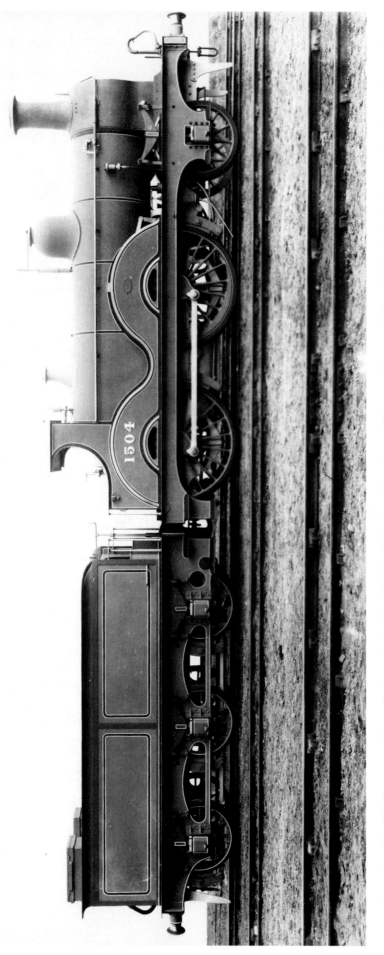

Plate 147. This official but undated view of Johnson 2—4—0 No. 1504 is in Works Grey livery but could be regarded as a typical 'model' for the early crimson style. There is a degree of lining below the footplate but the brake hangers, guard irons and other details (e.g. the springs) are unlined. The engine was built by Neilson in 1881 and is seen here with its original 'built-up' Johnson chimney (pre-1889) and absence of 'MR' (pre 1891). Moreover, the engine was rebuilt in 1890, so the lining style could well represent the final 'green' period. Having said this, however, the general characteristics of this view faithfully represent the 'red' period from c.1883-90. The lining at the base of the dome, the twin panels (with convex corners) on the tender, the polished brass splasher beading and the general treatment of all 'non-black' areas are highly characteristic. In later years, more lining of detail components would appear and the heraldic emblem would often be placed on the leading splasher, but this general style of painting could be said to be the basic 'Midland' layout for the twenty or more years until c.1905/6. The slightly darker grey of the tender springs and tender beading may be ignored — they were always crimson — but the single line below the tender 'flare' is interesting. Logically there ought, perhaps, to have been a line at the top edge of the horizontal upper beading, but this was something of a rarity. It did appear on some of the more elaborate liveries at a later date (see, for example, *Plate 149*). No. 1504 eventually became MR/1st LMS No. 244.

National Railway Museum

Plate 148. This view of Kirtley 2–4–0 No. 235A makes an interesting comparison with Johnson 2–4–0 No. 1504 in *Plate 147.* Even though the cab and chimney show the Johnson influence, the basic double-framed characteristics of the engine itself and the totally different visual lines of the tender meant that the 'standard' livery presented a different 'look' to the observer – note, for example, the tender lining treatment compared with No. 1504. This engine is undoubtedly red, carrying as it does 'MR' on the tender sides. There is also a certain amount of extra detail lining, for example, on the guard irons and brake hangers. This picture can be dated after 1895 since the engine (a rebuild of a Beyer-Peacock 2–4–0T of 1867) did not receive the 'A' number suffix until that year. However, there is no 'decorated' lining on wheels or springs so the picture can be taken as very typical of the full Crimson Lake livery (without embellishments) of the 1890s as applied to pre-Johnson engines. The engine was scrapped in 1904.

National Railway Museum

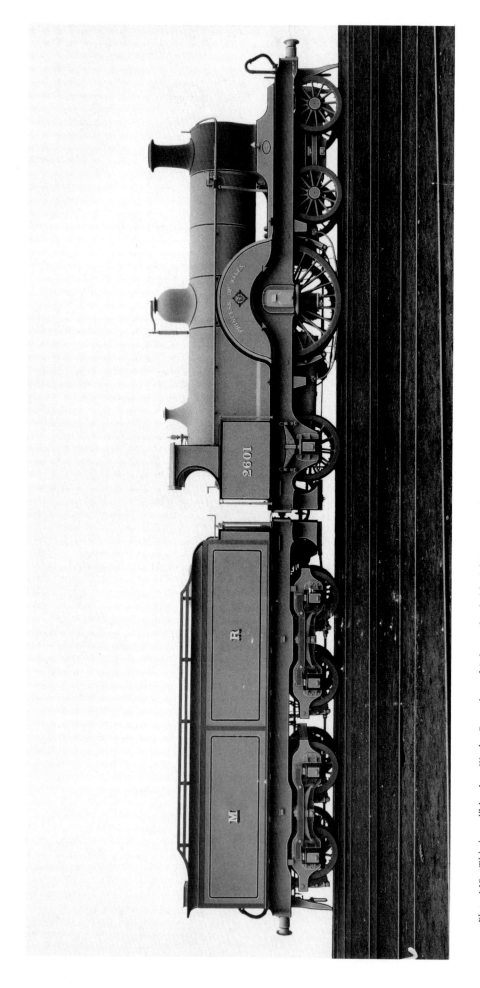

Plate 149. This incredibly clear Works Grey view of Johnson bogie 'single' No. 2601 *Princess of Wales*, taken in 1899 when the engine was brand new, shows what might be termed an 'official' interpretation of the full crimson livery at the turn of the century. It affords an interesting comparison with No. 21 (Chapter 5 *Plate 217*) in genuinely red livery and whilst No. 2601 does not carry, perhaps, a full array of all the 'local' embellishments, it does show quite an enhancement of lining compared with No. 1504, for instance, in *Plate 147*. An interesting point on this picture of *Princess of Wales* is the total absence of lining on the wheels – a feature not carried forward when the engine was given its proper red livery. The engine became No. 685 in 1907.

Authors' collection

Plate 150. At about the turn of the century, the Midland began to economise in its lining treatment on goods and shunting engines, and 0–6–0WT No. 2038A typifies the effect. We cannot positively confirm its colour but, since the picture must be dated between 1892 and 1906, the likelihood is plain crimson or 'brick red' or 'brown', depending on the preferred choice. We go into some detail on this subject in the next chapter, but this picture will serve to indicate the difficulty of resolving the issue from a black and white source.

Collection Bernard Mathews

outside of the frames, sandboxes and wheel guards were treated in a similar fashion with the inside of the frames in vermilion. In addition, the buffer planks were vermilion with the company's initials in gilt. The smokebox, firebox back within the cab, steps, platform, brake hangers and tyre rims were black. The cab interior had a light oak grained upper half and a lined red lower half. However, before proceeding further, it is also worth placing upon record a more detailed livery specification for 1900 as given to Neilson Reid & Co. in that year. Whilst very helpful, it unquestionably falls short of perfection in precise detail.

4–4–0 class 'T'. Built in 1901. MR original numbers 2591-2600. 1907 numbers 553-562.

PAINTING AND NUMBERS

SAMPLES. 1. Lead.
2. Oxide of Iron, called "Purple Brown".
3. Oxide of Iron and Lake, to be obtained from Messrs. Leech and Neal, Derby, or the Strathclyde Paint Co., Glasgow.
4. Vermilion.

The Boiler to receive two coats of Lead paint, No. 1 sample, before being lagged; and the Frames, Splashers and Cab two coats of Oxide of Iron Paint, No. 2 Sample.

Wheels to have one coat of Oxide of Iron Paint, No. 2 sample, then well stopped, rubbed down, then two more coats of No. 2, and finished with two coats of Oxide of Iron and Lake, No. 3 Sample, and three coats of Varnish – one of Carriage and two of best body Varnish.

The lagging of Boiler, the outside of Frames, Splashers and Cab to have one coat of Oxide of Iron Paint, No. 2 sample, then well stopped and filled up properly, and rubbed down; two coats of Oxide of Iron, No. 2 Sample, and sand-papered; two coats of Oxide of Iron and Lake, No. 3 Sample, picked out with black and fine lined with yellow, then three coats of Varnish – one of Carriage and two of best body Varnish.

Inside of Frames and the Axles to be finished with one coat of deep Vermilion Paint, No. 4 sample, and three coats of Varnish – one of Carriage and two of best body Varnish.

Buffer planks to be finished with one coat of deep Vermilion paint, No. 4 sample, with Company's Initials in Gilt on front Buffer Beam, and three coats of Varnish – one of Carriage and two of best body Varnish.

Smoke-box, Chimney, back of Fire-box, Platforms, Steps, Brake-hangers, &c., to have one coat of Black and one of Japan. Rims of Tyres to be finished with best Drop Black.

Two coats inside of Cab to be prepared similar to Boiler and Frame, and finished in Light Oak Graining, with three coats of Varnish – one of Carriage and two of best body Varnish.

Twelve hours must elapse between each coat of Varnish, and 24 hours after the last coat, before the Engine goes out of the paint shop.

BRASS NUMBERS to be supplied by the Midland Railway Company, and fitted by the Contractor.

By about 1902, some Kirtley locomotives were reported to be in Crimson Lake without lining.[1] At about the same period or slightly earlier, a considerable number of freight locomotives, not equipped with vacuum brakes, were reported as being painted a darkish brown with black boiler lagging bands, splasher tops and beading. Some contemporary records suggest this style continued until only the end of 1905 when it was again the policy to paint all freight locomotives in the current passenger engine livery. However, it was reported that possibly some locomotives remained in this brown livery until c.1909 running with their new post 1907 numbers.[2] We are inclined to favour this latter view.

At the same time it must be recorded that another style of livery appears to have been identified.[3] This was

1 *Midland Style*
2 *Midland Style*
3 P. C. Dewhurst Notes

Plate 151. Between the abandonment of what might be called the true 'Johnson' livery and the simplified Deeley style, there was a period of transition and some confusion. The full details are given in Chapter 6, but at this stage we offer a single typical view of the sort of thing which took place. Johnson 0–6–0 No. 3608 has received its new 1907 series number but retains 'MR' on the tender, and brass numbers.

Photographed at St. Pancras, it is employed upon empty stock working and is in immaculate simplified crimson livery with no lining on the footplate angle and only the boiler lagging bands adjacent to the smokebox and cab front lined. Note the 'flowerpot' chimney. Built by Neilson Reid in 1899 as Midland Railway No. 2469, this locomotive went on to receive an 'H' boiler in 1912, a 'G7' Belpaire boiler in 1923, and was withdrawn by British Railways as No. 43608 in 1962. Finally, the reader's attention is drawn to the red roof and lining on the tender spring brackets — a real hybrid livery if ever there was one!

probably a different description of the brown livery and was referred to by P. C. Dewhurst as the 'Brick Red' style, which he described as a variation of the current Derby Crimson Lake practice. This livery was for Johnson 0–6–0 (single frame) and Kirtley 0–6–0 (double frame), along with Johnson 0–6–0Ts and Kirtley double frame goods tank engines, and the style lasted until 1910 when black was introduced for all goods engines. The 'brown-cum-red' livery was described as a rather unpleasing Brick Red all over with the exception of black lagging bands on the boiler and upper edging of the splasher sides. No lining whatsoever was present. It was also suggested that this style commenced prior to 1904/5 with double frame locomotives being painted in Brick Red without any lining. It was also recorded that notwithstanding this drab style, fully lined Crimson Lake locomotives of the same classes were being turned out during the period. All told, therefore, one could have seen engines of the 0–6–0 type in full Crimson Lake (Derby practice), Dark Brown and/or Brick Red with some Black paintwork (splasher edging, splasher tops and boiler bands), and Brick Red or Crimson Lake unlined livery, together with Plain Black locomotives (see below).

In 1906 it was reported that 4–4–0T No. 204A was now in black livery.[4] It was also reported that some freight locomotives were painted plain black with vermilion buffer planks[5] and that 'later a revision to passenger livery was made'.[6] However, regardless of, or perhaps because of, these non standard livery variations, in June 1910 it was decided to paint all freight locomotives plain black with vermilion buffer casing and buffer beams, no lining whatsoever being employed. Gold number transfers and the heraldic emblem were to be used of the type introduced for red engines in 1906. A contemporary report said that 'quite a number of locomotives are already running in this livery

Plates 152 & 153. The following group of pictures (Plates 152-157) encompassing both the Johnson and Deeley livery periods, shows something of the variation to be seen in both the placing and style of the letters 'MR' during our period of survey. 0–4–4T No. 1273 shows the 'MR' on the rear of the bunker and lining on the cabside doors. Plate 153 gives another idea of the position of the lettering on the bunker back of an unidentified 0–4–4T. No. 1273 was built in 1875 by Neilson and became No. 1247 in 1907. Withdrawal, still carrying its LMS number, was at the end of 1949.

Collection Bernard Mathews
G. M. Perkins

4 F. H. Clarke's Note Book 8.8.1906
5 Locomotive Magazine 15th December 1906. p. 198.
6 Midland Style

Plates 154 & 155 have been selected to illustrate tender rear painting practice. No. 1930 illustrates the rear panel with the 'MR' just faintly visible on the buffer beam. No. 1930 was built in 1890 by Neilson. Receiving an 'H' boiler in 1904 and becoming No. 3257 in 1907, it received a 'G7' Belpaire boiler in 1925 and was withdrawn as British Railways 43257 in 1962. By contrast, 4–4–0 No. 1579 shows the simplified livery style on the tender but with all the boiler lagging bands lined and confirms that no use was made of initials on the back buffer beam after c.1905. Built in 1883 at Derby, it became No. 345 in 1907, having received an 'H' boiler in 1906. Withdrawal was in 1925. *Authors' collection*

which looks very good compared with the old badly kept unlined red'.[7]

During the entire period under review all passenger locomotives were painted in lined Crimson Lake but the method of lining varied and there were other detail variations which will be noted later in the livery chapters and on some of the photo captions contained within Volume 2.

From 1905 simplification of the lining began and then in 1906 the method of displaying the locomotive running number was altered with transferred gilt numerals being used instead of the brass numbers which had been used until that date.[8] In addition a new pattern of heraldic emblem — almost a true 'coat of arms' in fact — began to be displayed on some locomotives, usually where the brass numbers had been carried, and power classification figures for locomotives began to be added (see Chapter 6).

Apart from the wholesale renumbering in 1907, the Crimson Lake livery remained thus until the grouping in 1923 when, to all intents and purposes, Midland Railway livery was adopted by the LMS.

Throughout most of the Midland period with which we are concerned, company ownership was indicated frequently by the use of a heraldic emblem (especially on passenger tender engines) and always by the initials 'MR'. As stated above, the emblem came in two styles (see *Plates 142-143*), the change-over being in 1906, while the arrangement of the letters 'MR' was a little more complex to unravel. The buffer plank initials had always been there in some form, but the practice of displaying company ownership on the tender or tanks by using the seriffed initials 'MR' is believed to have commenced with the Sharp Stewart 4—4—0s built in 1892, (Nos. 2183-2202), and was extended to cover all tender locomotives owned by the company. However, it was not always applied after that date to all locomotives. The practice continued until 1906 when the locomotive number was moved to the tender side in the form of large transfer figures. On tank engines the letters 'MR' flanked the brass number on the tank side until 1906.

It was reported in *Midland Style* that the 0—6—0T series Nos. 1993-2012 built by Vulcan Foundry carried sans serif letters on the side tanks but these were replaced by serif initials in due course; neither was it unknown for sans serif letters to appear on tender sides. The actual position of the 'MR' is shown on the various plates but, apart from some Kirtley tenders where the rivet line caused the letters to be 'moved up', the 'M' and 'R' were normally each positioned centrally in the two side panels.

The initials 'MR' displayed to the front and rear of the locomotive were usually sans serif, initially on the buffer plank. In 1898, according to *Midland Style*, the practice of displaying 'MR' on the rear buffer plank of both tank engines and tenders ceased, and the letters, still in sans serif style, were transferred to the tender rear or bunker rear. However, by c.1905 this practice had also ceased and no

evidence of company ownership in transfer form appeared on the rear of tenders or bunkers at all, the 'MR' being used on the leading buffer planks from this point. An exception to this rule were the tank engines acquired when the LT & SR was taken over, these locomotives having 'MR' on the buffer planks at both ends (see Volume 2.).

By and large, whilst the tank/tender side letters were almost always serif, the buffer plank, tender/tank end lettering was usually sans serif. However, there were some exceptions in the end markings, with serif lettering being used — it is recorded in *Midland Style* that from 1899 until the end of the Johnson regime, a number of new and repainted locomotives received serif letters and this was revived c.1909-11 and again c.1920-22, and this serif style on the buffer plank will be seen in some plates in this volume.

By the end of the Midland period, therefore, only the front buffer planks carried the letters 'MR' and these vanished from 1923 onwards.

Plates 156 & 157 show 0—6—0s No. 2678 and 2593, both photographed in the spring of 1922 at King's Norton, display, respectively, serif (2678) and sans serif (2593) numbers on the front buffer planks.   *W. L. Good*

Plates 158 & 159. The final Deeley style of livery is given in these two views and, in view of the fact that it became the LMS standard in 1923 (apart from company markings), this style of painting was probably the most common and consistent of any of the Midland styles to be seen. It lasted, undiluted, until 1927/8 and many LMS engines (both ex-MR and others) retained it well into the 1930s. The first view shows the red livery on 'H' boilered rebuilt 4–4–0 No. 406 at Manchester Central. Originally No. 2186 and rebuilt in 1906, No. 406 was further rebuilt to the final '483' class type in 1914. The livery itself is absolutely standard for the time and the presence of the cabside 'tablet' (see Chapter 6) dates the view some time between 1911 and 1914. The second view shows Johnson 0–6–0 No. 3118 in plain black livery at Leicester West Bridge in June 1910 in a condition which demonstrates that the policy for vacuum piped goods engines was now plain black (see page 98). The locomotive was built in 1884 as Midland Railway No. 1620 by Beyer Peacock. In 1924 it received a 'G6' Belpaire boiler and lasted until 1958 when it was withdrawn by British Railways as No. 58225. When photographed it could have been just ex-works from Derby in the new black livery.   *Collection Bernard Mathews*

Plate 160. Photographed at Derby on 27th October 1923, this picture depicts a newly painted 4—4—0 without any evidence of company ownership. Built at Derby in 1894 as No. 191, this locomotive received an 'H' boiler in 1906 and was renumbered 450 in 1907. Renewal to '483' class was in 1923 and no doubt this picture was taken just after the rebuilding was completed. The locomotive remained in service until withdrawal in 1957 as BR No. 40450.
W. L. Good

Plate 161. For a short period, prior to the introduction of the LMS emblem, locomotives repainted during the first few months of 1923 did not, in many instances, carry any visible sign of identity. Some carried the letters 'LMS' on the cabside but others, like No. 138 illustrated here, were identified only by their locomotive number and smokebox numberplate, although it is possible that new works plates were cast. The engine was photographed at Kettering on 2nd November 1923.   *W. L. Good*

Plate 162. This view of 'straight framed' Kirtley 0—6—0 No. 2394 shows no evidence of ownership since it was taken in 1923 before the LMS ownership markings had been decided. It is also interesting for another reason, because it shows one of only a handful of ex-MR 0—6—0s which were renumbered by the LMS in 1923 to make room in the new enlarged LMS lists for absorbed engines from other companies — in this case the North Staffordshire Railway. No. 2394 was MR No. 2356 until 1923, having been No. 433 before 1907. The new 2XXX numbers allocated by the LMS in 1923 for this exercise were those of already withdrawn Kirtley 0—6—0s, but many engines were withdrawn before receiving them.
Collection Bernard Mathews

Plate 163. Kirtley 0–6–0 No. 2472 displays the very first LMS livery, adopted prior to the LMS panel used with black painted locomotives. This style was only applied for a short period in 1923 and then goods locomotives were liveried as illustrated in *Plate 105.* No. 2472 was built in 1865 as No. 249 and became No. 380 in 1903. It ran with an 'H' boiler between 1905 and 1923 when it was rebuilt as illustrated. Withdrawal was in 1932. *Collection Bernard Mathews*

Plate 164. The LMS pre-1928 livery on a red locomotive is seen in this picture of 4–4–0 No. 396. Built in 1891 at Derby and numbered 83, this locomotive received an 'H' boiler in 1905 and was renewed as a '483' class locomotive in 1923, running until 1961 when it was withdrawn as BR No. 40396.
Collection Bernard Mathews

Plate 165. Pre-1928 LMS black livery is seen here in a view of Johnson 0–6–0 No. 3175. Built in 1887 as No. 1783 at Derby, it became No. 3175 in 1907 and No. 58246 following nationalization. This locomotive was withdrawn in 1959. *Collection Bernard Matthews*

Plate 166. In 1928, following the decision to move locomotive numbers from the tender to the cabside, some locomotives, which were allocated the new intermediate passenger livery, retained Crimson Lake for a few years with their number in the new position — probably because they did not need repainting. 4–4–0 No. 369 with 10″ numerals was a case in point. Built in 1886 as No. 1749 and receiving an 'H' boiler and a new number in 1907, this locomotive was rebuilt as shown in 1910 and was withdrawn in 1940.   *Authors' collection*

In February 1928 the next change occurred with numbers moving to the cabside and 'LMS' in large letters on the tender (bunker and tankside respectively for most tank engines).

The number of classes entitled to red livery was reduced and, of the ex-Midland Railway stock, only the 45 'Compounds' qualified. All freight locomotives were to remain in unlined black and a new livery style, sometimes referred to as the Intermediate Passenger livery or Mixed Traffic livery, of black with red lining, was introduced. However, it is worth recording that the '990s', together with the remaining 'singles', both of which types were scrapped at about this time, remained in red livery until withdrawn. Apart from

these types, most, but not all, ex-Midland locomotives which had previously been painted red achieved the LMS Mixed Traffic livery.

The outbreak of World War II saw the 45 'Compounds' in Crimson Lake with most other passenger locomotives in the lined black livery and all freight locomotives in plain black. As the years progressed, the red locomotives were gradually repainted black, and we are not aware of any original *Midland* 'Compounds' remaining red at the time of Nationalization. The lined black locomotives, when repainted by the LMS at this time, emerged from the works without any lining.

Plate 167 and the following view (*Plate 168*) show the two larger sizes of LMS pattern cabside numerals — 12″ (1322) and 14″ (3127) — when applied to ex-Midland Railway locomotives during the post 1928 period. A variety of styles for numerals was to be seen: plain gold (actually black shaded transfers, but on a black locomotive this shading was not evident) on plain black engines and some lined ones; gold with red shading on most lined black engines and in the final years before the outbreak of the Second World War, chrome yellow with red shading on all repainted engines. During the war, plain yellow, hand-applied at the sheds, became increasingly common. 0–4–4T No. 1322 started life in 1886 at Derby as No. 1729. Receiving a Belpaire boiler in 1925, it survived to become No. 58228 following nationalization and was finally withdrawn in 1962.   *Collection Bernard Mathews*

Plate-168. The 14″ numerals shown on No. 3127 were of Midland pattern, noticeable by the larger 'loops' to the '9s' and '6s', whilst the 12″ and 10″ high numerals were to a new LMS standard design with a smaller loop on the '9' and '6'. The '5' was also slightly different and the study of these numbers reveals the principal difference between the Midland design of numeral and the later LMS version.   *Gordon Coltas*

Plate 169. In 1934 a number of old LMS locomotives were renumbered in order to allow all the new LMS standard locomotives to carry numbers below 10000 and those pre-group locomotives whose numbers were required for standard locomotives had 20000 added to their current numbers. It took a few years for all the stock to be renumbered and this picture illustrates LMS No. 22579 which started life in 1868 as No. 683, built at Derby. It displays the 12″ LMS numerals in plain gold (i.e. gold with 'invisible' black shading). Receiving an 'H' boiler in 1905, it became No. 2579 in 1907 and was rebuilt with a 'G6' Belpaire boiler in 1922. Renumbered in 1936, it survived until withdrawal in 1946.   *Collection Bernard Mathews*

Plate 170. A number of ex-Midland Railway locomotives carried the LMS 1936 livery, which was really a sans serif variation of the earlier 1928 style, and this picture of Kirtley 0−6−0 No. 22567 has been selected to illustrate this variation. The insignia are gold with black shading and 10″ figures. Built in 1868 as No. 649, the engine became No. 2567 in 1907 and ran with an 'H' boiler from 1905 until it was rebuilt with a 'G6' Belpaire boiler, as illustrated, in 1925. Renumbered 22567 in 1936, it lasted until withdrawal in 1946. The 1936 characters were almost certainly applied at the time of renumbering into the 2XXX series.   *Collection Bernard Mathews*

Plates 171-173. These views have been
chosen to illustrate many of the various
styles of livery used during the British
Railways era on ex-Midland Railway
locomotives. Following nationalization
in 1948 locomotives began to have 40000
added to their LMS numbers, but they
retained their former identity (e.g. Plate
171) which illustrates 4–4–0 No. 40362
photographed at Royston in 1949 in this
condition and utilizing LMS insignia.
However, prior to this happening, some
locomotives had an 'M' prefix added to
their running numbers and were lettered
'British Railways' in full. Plates 172 &
173 illustrate 'Compound' 4–4–0 No.
M1000 (Derby April 1948) and 0–6–0T
M7205 in this condition, the latter in
1948 at Cricklewood.

Authors' collection

Plate 174. A number of locomotives combined the full 'British Railways' with the new 4XXXX series numbers and Plates 174-177 have been selected to illustrate this style. Initially, the lettering etc. was a sort of creamy white and the figures basically of 1946 LMS pattern. 0−6−0T No. 41710 has a rather large tender size 'British Railways' on the tank side and was photographed at Derby in July 1948.   Authors' collection

Plate 175. 4−4−0 No. 40436 at Derby in October 1951 in plain black livery.
Authors' collection

Plate 176. 0−6−0T No. 41777 at Sheep-bridge. Note that the insignia are now pure Gill-sans in style and are rendered in 'cream' coloured transfers.
Authors' collection

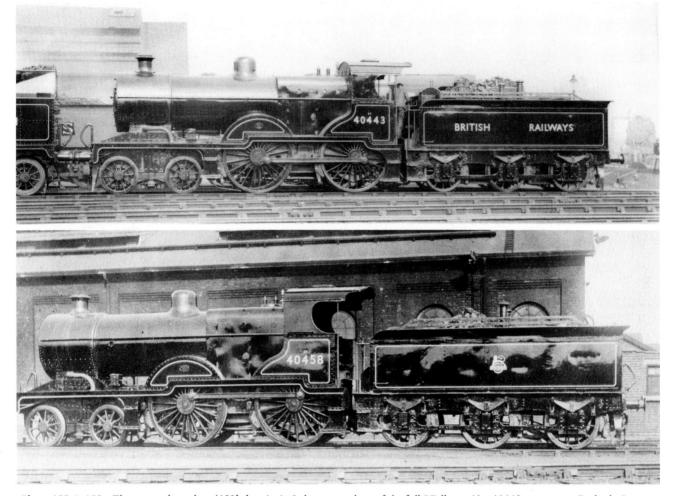

Plates 177 & 178. These two views show '483' class 4—4—0s in two versions of the full BR livery. No. 40443 was seen at Derby in September 1948 with 'British Railways' on the tender, whilst No. 40458, also at Derby (in September 1951), displays the first BR emblem.

Authors' collection

The change of ownership in 1948 saw many Midland locomotives repainted in what was the old LNWR livery of black lined with cream, red and grey, and this livery (plus plain black) became the final style for those Midland locomotives fully repainted by BR before scrapping. One class '3' Belpaire, most class '2P' 4—4—0s and many 0—4—4Ts received BR lined black livery.

For those modellers who wish to paint their locomotives in British Railways livery, the following information, reproduced from official records published in 1949[9], should be applied to Midland locomotives. The records refer to the first crest, which was changed to the more heraldic version in 1956, but it took a few years for the total change-over to be made. The lining details remained unchanged and were:

Passenger and mixed traffic steam (tender and tank) and mixed traffic electric locomotives. Black, lined red, cream and grey.

Freight steam (tender and tank) electric shunting and diesel shunting locomotives. Black (unlined).

General Details.

Locomotives.

The 'British Railways' crest to be placed centrally in the appropriate panels, one left-hand and one right-hand, so that the lion faces forward. Position can be varied slightly if necessary to avoid bolt or rivet heads.

All locomotives to carry the crest. Cab roofs and all handrails to be black. Buffer beams and casings to be signal red. Frame extensions, smoke-boxes, saddles, outside steam pipes and cylinder clothing to be black in all cases.

All parts below the platform angle to be black and unlined; this applies particularly to wheels, axle ends, etc., which have been previously painted otherwise. The motion to remain bright.

The exposed parts on tender tops to be black. No lining on rear of tender. All parts below the tender panel to be black and unlined. This applies particularly to wheels, frame cut-outs, etc., which may have been previously painted otherwise.

The position of the lining on tender sides varies slightly according to the type of tender.

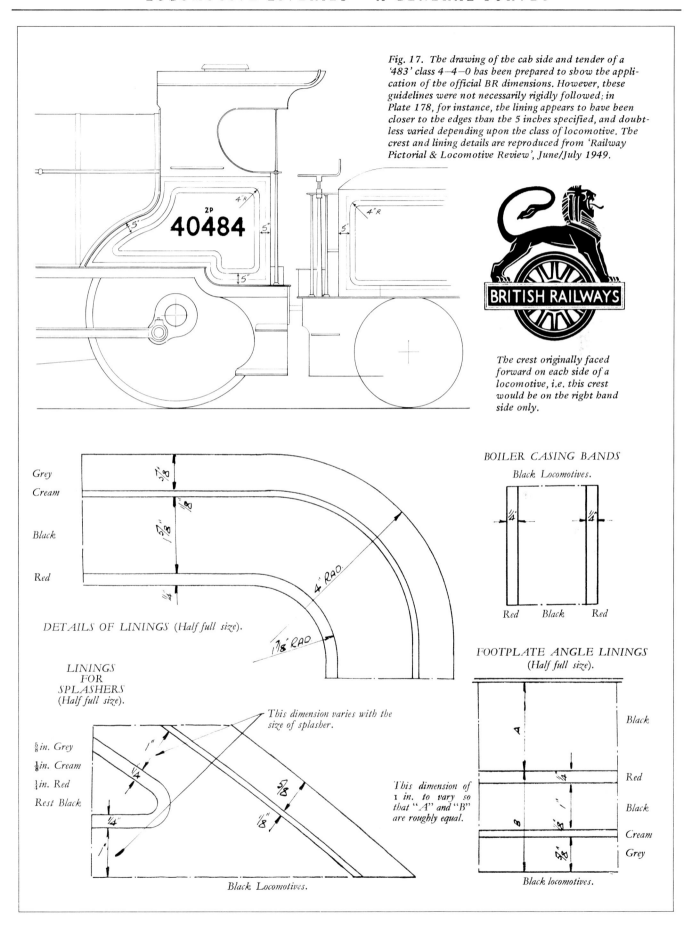

Fig. 17. The drawing of the cab side and tender of a '483' class 4–4–0 has been prepared to show the application of the official BR dimensions. However, these guidelines were not necessarily rigidly followed; in Plate 178, for instance, the lining appears to have been closer to the edges than the 5 inches specified, and doubtless varied depending upon the class of locomotive. The crest and lining details are reproduced from 'Railway Pictorial & Locomotive Review', June/July 1949.

The crest originally faced forward on each side of a locomotive, i.e. this crest would be on the right hand side only.

DETAILS OF LININGS (Half full size).

LININGS FOR SPLASHERS (Half full size).

⅝in. Grey
⅛in. Cream
¼in. Red
Rest Black

This dimension varies with the size of splasher.

Black Locomotives.

BOILER CASING BANDS
Black Locomotives.

Red   Black   Red

FOOTPLATE ANGLE LININGS (Half full size).

This dimension of 1 in. to vary so that "A" and "B" are roughly equal.

Black
Red
Black
Cream
Grey

Black locomotives.

Fig. 18.

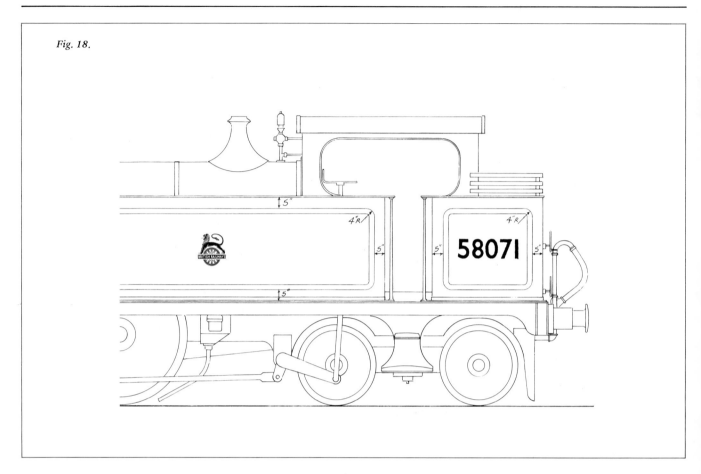

Plate 179. The lined out British Railways livery on 0—4—4T No. 58071 (previously No. 1377) at Derby in January 1951.

Authors' collection

Plate 180. Most 0—4—4Ts received the lined black livery but not all were so painted. This picture of No. 58066 (previously No. 1368) in plain black livery, photographed at Derby in November 1954, displays the more austere style. *Authors' collection*

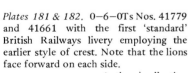

Plates 181 & 182. 0—6—0Ts Nos. 41779 and 41661 with the first 'standard' British Railways livery employing the earlier style of crest. Note that the lions face forward on each side.

Authors' collection

Plate 183. This typical view of the class '3F' 0−6−0 in BR days shows No. 43570 at Derby in August 1959. Note that the crest was always to the rear of the vertical centre beading.

Authors' collection

In 1956 the new crests also faced left and right for about a year, then the College of Heralds pointed out that the left facing lion was the approved version on the BR coat of arms and that a right facing lion was heraldically wrong for a device based upon a proper achievement of arms. Thereafter (again subject to the inevitable practical delay in application) the left facing lion was universal, regardless of which side of the engine it went.

Prior to this official policy there were transitional British Railways liveries and these are dealt with in *Plates 171-177.*

Whilst the foregoing, in our opinion, is an adequate review in an historical sense, particularly for the BR period, it is insufficient for the modeller who wishes to portray accurately his models in 'the correct livery' of earlier days, so the remainder of this and the next two chapters is devoted to the analysis of the Midland Railway locomotive livery from 1883 in some detail. It should, however, at the outset be stated that this is not, nor does it set out to be, the definitive answer to the subject of Midland locomotive livery. What it does attempt is to place upon record sufficient information, or to point the reader in the direction of such information so that models can be garbed in an accurate livery style for the Midland period.

Before commencing this task, one should perhaps review what is available and clarify why we have not chosen to go beyond the Midland period. We have already given the official BR livery specification, and in the mid 1960s we produced a work entitled *Locomotive Liveries of the LMS.* The general livery section of this work, slightly revised,

appeared in *An Illustrated History of LMS Locomotives Volume 1* published in 1981 by OPC, and the Midland engines appear in Volume 3 of that work. Readers and model-makers who are particularly concerned with the appearance of Midland locomotives in LMS livery should, therefore, refer to either of these books in the knowledge that we believe they contain sufficient information to enable them to find what they require for the post-1922 period − and so we return to the detailed analysis of

Plate 184. 0−6−0T No. 41708 is seen in this photograph with the final small size post-1956 crest.

Authors' collection

Midland livery in the period following the abandonment of the green scheme.

The earliest paint specification for Crimson Lake livery which has come to our attention is the one given below. It dates from 1891 and refers to a class of 4—4—0s built by Sharp Stewart. We quote it here rather than in the next chapter because it serves to draw attention to the problems of the whole 1883 onwards period.

Class 'L'. Original MR numbers 2183-2202. Built in 1892, they became Nos. 403-422 in 1907.

PAINTING AND NUMBERS

The Boiler to receive two coats of Lead Paint before being lagged, and the Frames, Splashers, Hand-rail, and Cab, two coats of Oxide of Iron Paint.

Wheels one coat Oxide of Iron Paint, then well stopped, rubbed down, then two coats of Oxide of Iron Paint, and finished with two coats of Oxide and Lake to sample supplied, and three coats of Varnish.

After lagging, the Boiler, Frames, Splashers, Hand-rail and Cab to have one coat of Lead colour, or Oxide; then well stopped, and filled up properly, rubbed down, two coats of Lead colour or Oxide, sand papered, two coats of Oxide and Lake to sample, picked out with Black and fine lined with Yellow, and three coats of Varnish. The outside of Frames, Sand Boxes, and Guards, &c., to be same as Boiler.

Inside of Frames and the Axles to be finished with one coat of Vermilion and two of Varnish.

Buffer Planks to be finished Vermilion, with Company's Initials in Gilt, and three coats of Varnish.

Smoke-box, Chimney, back of Fire-box, Platforms, Steps, Brake-hangers, &c., to be painted one coat of Black and one coat of Japan. Rim of Tyre to be Black.

Two coats inside of Cab to be prepared similar to Boiler and Frame, finished in Light Oak Graining, and three coats of Varnish.

NUMBERS to be supplied by the Company and fitted by the Contractor.

Pencilled on the original specification was the following: 'Transfer of Coat of Arms to be supplied from 18/12/91', which refers to the diamond-shaped heraldic emblem used until the fundamental insignia change of 1906.

TOOLS

Each Engine to be provided with a complete set of Screw-Keys and Gland-Keys (two Gland-Keys per set), to pattern, case-hardened and finished bright, and stamped with the Company's Initials and number of Engine; also special Spanner for Eccentric Bolts, Outside Rods, &c., to drawings.

One Heavy and one Small Hammer, one Lead Hammer, three Chisels, two Drifts, and three Pin Punches.

One Steel-pointed Crowbar, one Small Steel Pinch Bar, and one Screw Jack and Lever to pattern.

One Gallon Oil Bottle, one Half-Gallon Oil Bottle, one Large and one Small Oil Feeder.

One Shovel, one Coal Pick, one Hand Brush, two Galvanized Iron Buckets, together with all the necessary Fire Irons to pattern, Tube Cleaner, and Chain Carrier and Padlock to secure them to Tender.

One Fog Signal Case.

At first sight, like the previously quoted 1900 specification (page 97), this is a very comprehensive statement containing much useful detail of value to the historian. In addition to the paint specification, details of the tools which were to be supplied by the makers and carried upon the locomotive are also recorded. Readers will note that while basically it is the same specification as that already given for the Neilson Reid locomotives, the 1900 specification is more exact and refers to actual paint samples whereas the 1892 specification only describes the colours which were to be applied. Even so, both specifications do not detail certain parts of the locomotive and neither of them specifically state, even in basic detail, exactly where the lining is to appear. This is the root of the problem. At this point, therefore, we should perhaps pause to consider first the implication of this less than complete statement. When, in the 1960s, research for *Locomotive Liveries of the LMS* was being undertaken, it was possible to interview a paint shop foreman at Derby who had entered railway service in 1923 and we could, therefore, question him about various practices in use during the LMS period. However, we have not found anyone with first-hand experience of Midland paintshop practice and so, similar first-hand information for the Midland era has not been forthcoming. Furthermore, when we were researching LMS locomotives an enormous number of photographs were examined but regrettably the quantity of pictures available for these Midland Railway volumes was much less.

These two drawbacks, compared with our LMS period researches, therefore suggest to us that at this time a definitive story is not, and probably never will be, really possible. Therefore, unlike our LMS locomotive volumes already mentioned, these books will not attempt to give a generalised livery summary for each specific type of locomotive, or give lists of individual examples, other than to refer to them in the photo captions using the general terms listed on page 114.

It is also worth noting that the photographers who photographed Midland Railway locomotives of this period tended to concentrate upon the more glamorous, and the more unusual, and so, whilst the well-photographed exotic liveries applied, for example, by Robert Weatherburn of Kentish Town, are interesting, they are not, we feel, typical of Midland practice for the majority of the locomotive stock of the company during the period his influence existed.

In consequence of all this, we have had to resort to more purely detective work than we did with our LMS survey and this has its own limitations. However, what can be said, without fear of contradiction, is that whereas much variety existed for some twenty years after the change to red livery in 1883, there seems to us to have been a fundamental philosophical change in 1906 (during the Deeley period) which, at its most obvious, took the form of displaying the engine number in large transfer figures rather than the previous brass numerals. This was associated with a general simplification of the red livery (regardless of how engines had been decorated previously) and the development of a much more *consistent* lining treatment throughout the fleet. Only a year later, 1907, the stock was renumbered, and shortly afterwards all goods engines became black.

The 1906-10 period, therefore, represents to us a time when a clearly identifiable change in emphasis took place as far as Midland painting methods were concerned, so we have elected to split our detailed analysis into two periods, namely from 1883 to 1906 and from 1906 onwards. This two-fold division is the basis of the next two chapters, allowing for a little overlap to cover the confusing 1906-10 period. However, before dealing with this aspect of the subject, it will be useful at this stage to append a list of simplified general livery terms which we have adopted for reference purposes to cover the whole period of time when Midland engines were seen in traffic. We shall not make much further detailed reference in the text to LMS and/or BR liveries but concentrate on the various Midland practices in more detail in the next two chapters.

GENERAL LIVERY TERMS

MR Green — Pre-November 1883 livery. Could be either Kirtley Dark or Johnson Light Green.

Early Crimson Lake — Implies the pre c.1890 period when certain 'below the footplate' lining was not present.

Full and 'Decorated' Crimson Lake — Implies the period c.1890-1905 when additional lining was used below the footplate and elsewhere. While extra lining was universally used, the term 'decorated' is particularly appropriate when describing the ornate additional lining used by certain paintshops during the mid/late 1890s until after the turn of the century. This additional lining was most frequently applied to the more important passenger locomotives but was also placed on certain tank engines.

Simplified Crimson Lake or Deeley livery — Describes the simplified lining practices introduced by Deeley c.1905 which saw the level of lining gradually reduced over a 2-3 year period to less than that used during the Early Crimson Lake livery period. During this period black was introduced to replace the red used hitherto for wheels and the outside of the frames. This term also covers the LMS 1923-28.

Post 1928 Crimson Lake — This was almost identical to the pre-1928 style except that the locomotive running number was moved from the tender or tank side to the cab or bunker side. During this period there were variations in the shape and style of transfers used and the lining changed from pale cream to chrome yellow c.1936.

Locomotive Brown/Plain Crimson Lake/Brick Red — These descriptions apply to the various 'Utility Red' styles used for certain goods engines c.1900-1910 (see page 97).

Plain Black — MR/LMS/BR black without lining.

Intermediate Passenger Livery — This describes the black livery with red lining introduced in 1928 by the LMS for many locomotives which hitherto had been painted Crimson Lake.

Full BR Livery — Describes the lined black LNWR style livery adopted by British Railways and applied to certain ex-MR passenger locomotives (tender and tank).

CHAPTER FIVE

MIDLAND LIVERIES IN DETAIL

1883-1906

THE 1883-1906 period of the Midland Railway seems to us to have been the time at which the railway was both at its most elegant (especially around the turn of the century) but also at its most confusing in terms of consistency of decoration. There was a sort of conformity during the period but we have already offered enough pictures in preceding chapters to enable the perceptive reader to appreciate that precise detail treatment — especially of the lined-out crimson engines — tended to vary in many subtle ways which makes generalisation always difficult and, at times, impossible. However, we shall try in this and the next chapter to bring some order out of apparent chaos!

We have, in the previous chapter, considered the general trends and now we propose to tackle the detail. By so doing, we risk the dangers of some repetition but hope this might be more beneficial than irksome. So let us start by reviewing the story so far.

From the previous chapter readers will appreciate that six possible Midland Railway styles have been identified to some degree of authenticity.

At this point in time we cannot be certain exactly what did happen but we believe it is accurate to state that the body colours already described can be summarised as follows:-

1. Crimson Lake with black and yellow lining.
2. Crimson Lake without any lining.
3. Dark Brown with some black relief — boiler bands and splasher edges tops, axle ends.
4. Brick Red, otherwise as 3.
5. Brick Red without any lining.
6. Black (possibly?).

We think it reasonable to postulate that these six written descriptions actually identify four styles, viz.

(a) Crimson Lake with lining.
(b) A colour which has been variously described as Plain Crimson Lake/Brown/Brick Red with black relief as in 3 above.
(c) The same colour as (b) but without any black relief.
(d) Plain Black.

This in effect would give three principal 'body colours' of Crimson Lake, a utility reddish colour with or without black relief depending upon what actually happened in the various paint shops, and plain black.

Plate 185. Kirtley 0–6–0 No. 368A was built in 1855 by Sharp Stewart and went onto the duplicate list in 1894. In June 1902 it was restored to the capital list as No. 263, and in 1905 it was renumbered 665 and broken up the same year. Therefore we can date this picture as being between 1894 and 1902. The locomotive appears to be in Locomotive Brown. The boiler is clearly a lighter shade than the smokebox and there is black upper edging to the splashers and splasher tops. The outside of the frames appear to be the same colour but the line of rivets at the base of the firebox are probably black. The boiler lagging bands have not been painted black but the sections of the coupling rods have. In short, what at this period would have been Crimson Lake on a fully lined locomotive may well have been Locomotive Brown with very little black relief paintwork. *Authors' collection*

Plate 186. This view of a Kirtley 0−6−0 No. 681 in immaculate 'ex works' condition gives an excellent rendering of the utility goods livery. Built in 1868 at Derby, the locomotive was to become No. 2578 and was withdrawn in 1928. This picture can be dated before the numbering in 1907 and after the power classification was adopted in 1905. No. 681 is in Locomotive Brown with the boiler bands in black. The outside of the outside frame is also black, as indeed are the splasher tops and upper beading on the splashers. The outside cranks are vermilion while the axle centres and coupling rods, other than the area around the joints are also black. The wheels are black as indeed is the smokebox. The tender appears to be all in Locomotive Brown above the footplate but clearly has darker (black) side frames and wheels.

National Railway Museum

There should be no argument about lined Crimson Lake. This appears in written descriptions and specifications, whilst photographs confirm the presence of black and yellow lining; however, we submit this is as far as firm photographic evidence can be taken. The disposition of lining defies simple generalisation.

The real problems centre upon the various unlined red/brown schemes which are known to have existed, regardless of the precise colour shade used.

For example, *Plate 188* illustrates an 0−6−0T No. 1425. There is no visible evidence of any lining but what is the body colour? According to the various contemporary written descriptions it could be Brown, Brick Red, Crimson Lake without lining or plain black. We discount black if only because on the original print there is a slight visible variation in colour shade between the smokebox and the boiler, but if it is not black then what colour is the locomotive painted?

We believe that this is an example of a Crimson Lake livery without lining. No black relief paintwork can be identified on the various detail fittings, but it is possible to see that the black shading on the transferred 'MR' is of a

Plate 187. Kirtley 0−6−0 No. 769 is also in Locomotive Brown and should be compared with No. 681. All the locomotive and tender superstructure is painted Locomotive Brown and the only obvious black paintwork, other than the smokebox/chimney, appears to be on the axle centres and boiler lagging bands. The wheels appear to be black and the side frames could be either black or brown. No. 769 was built by Dübs in 1870 and became No. 2621 in 1907. Withdrawal was in 1932.

Collection Roger Carpenter

Plate 188. 0−6−0T No. 1425 is seen here in unlined livery − probably plain Crimson Lake. Built in 1879 at Derby, this locomotive became No. 1695 in 1907, received a Belpaire boiler in 1926 and was withdrawn by British Railways as No. 41695 in 1953.

Authors' collection

different colour from the tankside, which suggests a different body colour than, for example, the smokebox (always black).

Plate 189 is another picture which could be said to provide no 100 per cent answer to these puzzles. The locomotive is a Kirtley 0−6−0 No. 671 and on the original print it is clear that the locomotive is in unlined condition. However, it is just possible that the boiler bands, splasher tops and beading are a darker colour (black?). If one looks at the freshly painted tender, which is visible beyond the smokebox, then without doubt No. 671 is not the same colour; however, if one looks at the coach behind the locomotive then the difference in the colour shade is less notice-

able. Finally, the coach behind the tender displays yet another, fourth colour shade variation. Is the locomotive in a dirty unkempt Crimson Lake or is it Brick Red or Locomotive Brown? We believe that this locomotive is in the shade which has been variously described as Locomotive Brown with black relief − boiler lagging bands, splasher beading and splasher top, but it could be the same colour as an 0−6−0T No. 1425 (*Plate 188*).

One interesting fact is that Ahrons, writing in *Locomotive & Train Working in the Nineteenth Century* states that 'at the end of 1883 a brick red colour was adopted'. He was describing the change of colour by the Midland Railway for its locomotive stock, and the shade he calls 'brick red'

Plate 189. Kirtley 0−6−0 No. 671 in rebuilt Johnson condition, displays Locomotive Brown livery with 'black relief' somewhat similar to the two previous views at *Plates 186 & 187*. Built at Derby in 1868, this locomotive was to become No. 2568 in 1907 and it lasted until 1932 when it was withdrawn by the LMS. This picture is a very good example of the limitations of photographic evidence and is analysed in detail in the text.

Authors' collection

could only have been Crimson Lake at the time he described it.

What does seem clear is that after 1883 the constant body colour for Midland locomotives was a red which we now call Crimson Lake, Midland Red or Midland Lake, and that during the period c.1900-1910 a number of other colour schemes were employed upon certain freight locomotives. Of these, black is recorded as being in use prior to its general introduction for all freight locomotives in 1910,

engines were in the paint shops and for them to enter traffic in 'Unlined Crimson Lake'.

In fact, an article entitled 'English and American Locomotive Building' by C. Rous-Martin, which appeared in *Engineering* magazine for July 1899 said, 'A hasty coat of plain covering paint was all that time afforded to give them.' Regrettably, he did not say what the paint colour was.

It is also a fact that a Crimson Lake lined locomotive looks to be a different colour from a Crimson Lake unlined

Plate 190. Johnson 0-6-0 No. 1203 is a further example of the plain brown or plain Crimson Lake livery — there is no evidence of any black relief at all. Dated c.1904, this picture is of a locomotive built by Beyer-Peacock in 1876, which became No. 2971 in 1907, went on to receive a 'G6' Belpaire boiler in 1920, became LMS No. 22971 c.1934, and finally British Railways No. 58152, before withdrawal in 1955 at the ripe old age of 79! *National Railway Museum*

but at the time of writing we cannot identify with certainty any locomotive being in this colour from the photographs available — i.e. when carrying the old brass numbers and therefore photographed before 1908.

Therefore what is the most probable explanation for all these livery variations c.1900-1910 recorded by three contemporary observers and discernible on some photographs? We suggest that the explanation is really quite simple and begins c.1899. We know that at this time the Midland Railway, like other British railway companies, was short of motive power. We also know that the magnificent livery carried by Midland Railway locomotives took a long time to apply and while locomotives were standing in paint shops they could not be earning revenue in traffic. Furthermore, the Midland was primarily a freight line with the majority of its locomotives employed hauling goods and mineral trains. It is therefore not unlikely that at the time of the great locomotive shortage in 1899, ways and means of 'producing' more locomotives for freight trains were examined — and a relatively simple method of producing more motive power was to reduce the time when goods

locomotive and this in itself could well be the origin of the 'Brick Red' description used by several contemporary observers, possibly including Ahrons (above).

Therefore, the best that can be done is to try and find a genuine original sample of the colour in question. However, and this is where we *can* be certain, no matter what the base colour (red, green, blue, brown), the presence or absence of lining and even the *colour* of the lining can produce a visual 'change' in the perceived shade of the base colour as 'seen' by the observer. A plain red engine will actually seem to be a different and probably lighter colour than a locomotive painted the same shade but given lining.

Lest this fact be open to debate, let us digress for a moment. One of the authors, through his professional work at the National Railway Museum, has had numerous opportunities since 1975 of being put into the situation of having to help re-create old railway colour schemes. One thing that can be stated, beyond doubt, is the total inadequacy and unreliability of verbal description coupled with personal memory and recollection. No one, especially a member of the male species, is capable of retaining a mental image of

Plate 191. This picture of 0–6–0T No. 1100 shows another 0–6–0T locomotive in what we believe to be plain crimson. There is no sign of any black relief and there is, on the original print, a distinct difference in the shade between the smokebox and boiler. Built in 1885 at Derby, this locomotive became No. 1759 in 1907 and in due course it received a Belpaire boiler. Withdrawal was in 1948.
Collection Bernard Mathews

Plate 192. No. 2180, an 0–6–0 goods engine, was built in 1893 by Dübs. In 1904 the locomotive received an 'H' boiler as illustrated and this picture shows an immaculate locomotive in 'ex-works' condition displaying a very clear example of the Locomotive Brown or 'Brick Red' livery with black boiler lagging bands, splasher tops and beading and axle ends. Note the bright coupling rods. In addition, the lower beading strips of the splasher have also been picked out in black. Finally, the reader's attention is drawn to the bright work on the smokebox door and the flowerpot chimney. This locomotive was renumbered 3457 in 1907, became a class 3 'Belpaire' in 1921, and was withdrawn by British Railways in 1960 as No. 43457.
Authors' collection

Plate 193. This superb Works Grey picture of Kirtley 2—4—0 No. 192 serves as the ideal 'model' for the first version of the lined crimson livery. The engine itself was rebuilt in 1883 from a Beyer-Peacock built engine dating from 1867 and it is possible that the picture was taken to record both the rebuild and perhaps the new livery. It affords an interesting comparison with the similar engine shown in *Plate 148* (Chapter 4) in a somewhat more decorated style of painting. Note the lack of lining on spring, guard irons, brake hangers and tender top 'flare'. All these areas were to receive more decorative treatment as years went by, especially after c.1890. Note, however, that the wheel rims are shown lined — a by no means universal policy during the 1880s; although it has to be admitted that wheel lining is not always easy to spot on a black and white picture of an engine 'in service' and may in fact have been present even if not obviously so — see, for example, *Plate 196*. Apart from the added embellishments (and the adoption of tender-side 'MR') during the 1890s, this picture is entirely typical of the basic Midland lining layout until c.1905. The variations caused by the differing frame and body shapes of the locomotive fleet were no more than the inevitable consequence of applying the same principles to a variety of visual styles and the only really significantly obvious variation was the quite different style of lining applied to Johnson pattern tenders. No. 192 became 192A in 1894 and was withdrawn in 1898.

National Railway Museum

colour — this is a biological fact and it is undoubtedly also true that *women* 'hold' colours better than men — they rarely suffer colour-blindness, for example. But even women do not possess total colour recall.

Even the quantity and colour of lining can make a difference — the more and/or paler the lining is, the darker will seem the 'base' colour.

We therefore believe it possible that these various unlined reds, browns, etc. described at the time, may well have been Midland Red — or something very close to it.

At all events, having established that their goods engines worked just as well in unlined livery, the Midland directors may have suggested that further economies could be achieved if the final top coat of Crimson Lake was not applied at all! At this point we admit to being in the realm of pure conjecture, but it seems at least possible that either the Purple Brown undercoat or Purple Brown with something added could have been used as a top colour for goods engines and, if so, could well have been the 'Locomotive Brown' described and illustrated in *Midland Style* and mentioned elsewhere. Certainly the colour patch used in that volume is a purple red/brown and this colour, when varnished possibly became the standard for most goods locomotives *not* fitted with vacuum pipes. This latter point is significant. Readers should realise that the various 'utility' schemes described were for 'steam brake only' locomotives — in other words, goods locomotives which would *not* be used to work passenger trains.

So we have c.1899 a situation wherein the lining for certain red locomotives was discontinued, leading to the written description of the 'Brick Red' livery; and then a new finish is identified, almost certainly Varnished Purple Brown, possibly with something added to it, referred to as Locomotive Brown and sometimes used in conjunction with black boiler lagging bands, splasher tops and splasher beading and sometimes the outside of the frames and the axle ends as well.

And so we would conclude that if on a photograph there is evidence of yellow lining, then the body colour after 1900 must be Crimson Lake but, if there is no visible evidence of lining and the locomotive does not carry its post 1907 number, then the locomotive is probably in unlined Crimson Lake (which has also been referred to as Brick Red.) Additionally, if the locomotive has no yellow lining but displays black boiler lagging bands, splasher edges and tops, it would mean that the locomotive is, very probably, in Locomotive Brown. What we cannot state precisely is the difference in shade, if any, between the 'unlined Crimson Lake', 'Brick Red' and 'Locomotive Brown' colours.

These principles would seem to apply from c.1900, when the first changes were made from the fully lined Crimson Lake, until 1906 when it was reported that black was being used for some freight locomotives.

In summary, one has lined Crimson Lake with 'diamond' shaped emblem and brass numerals in continuous use for passenger locomotives from 1883 until the 1907 changes described in the next chapter, but the goods locomotive story is more complex. That the period from c.1900-1906

should have seen the use of unlined Crimson and Locomotive Brown is logical; but the absence of any 'steam brake only' goods engines positively identified by the authors in black with brass numerals during this period, suggests that possibly black for goods engines not equipped to work vacuum braked trains really did not become the practice until late 1906. With all the locomotive stock renumbered in 1907 mostly using large transfer numbers, this could be an explanation for the apparent absence of pictures of black locomotives with brass numbers. From 1907 until 1910 locomotives which can be classified as goods engines running in lined Crimson Lake livery appear to be those fitted with vacuum train pipes. However, there are exceptions and these could be locomotives which had been renumbered in 1907 and had not yet been repainted when photographed. However, hopefully, *Plates 248-250* will illustrate these points.

So far we have considered only the body colour which changed from green at the start of the period, through red and variations thereof, to black for some goods engines by the end of this period. It is now appropriate to consider the lining practice used on red locomotives and in order to do so we must return to c.1883.

Pictures of the early Crimson Lake livery period show that the use of lining below footplate level was quite modest, but that by the 1890s a more ornate style was being adopted. Under Robert Weatherburn and others these ornate styles were taken to the extreme as described below and illustrated later in this chapter.

As far as we can determine, the basic principles of the lining to be adopted with the new Crimson Lake livery in 1883 seem to have been an exact repeat (using black and *yellow*) of the lining style adopted by Johnson in black and *white* on the green livery from c.1876-83. This, of course, makes it extremely difficult and at times impossible to tell, from a photograph, whether the engine was green or red during the changeover period, say 1883-87. Even a dated picture cannot always help since both liveries could have been side by side at the time. If a locomotive is known to have been substantially modified after 1883 then it is a fair bet that after modification it would reappear in red but unrebuilt engines with a good paint job applied at the end of the 'green' period could well have run for several years before becoming red.

Notwithstanding these difficulties, a fair degree of consistency of lining treatment was to be seen and, rather than describe the lining in detail, we have chosen to offer a good selection of views which we believe to typify the period (*Plates 193-201*) and accompany them with extended and analytical captions in which we have tried to explain our reasoning.

What seems to have happened is that whilst there was a general set of principles laid down, the company does not seem to have worried too much if individual sheds (districts?) applied a few 'local' embellishments to the basic livery, provided the essential 'character' of the livery did not change. Thus it was that whilst the basic lining (exemplified, for example, by *Plate 193*), remained fairly consistent, individual additional lining was very much a personal

Plate 194. 2–4–0 No. 104 was built in 1867 and became No. 104A in 1879. It was renumbered 6 in 1907 and was withdrawn in 1932. Whilst it is not possible accurately to date the photograph, c.1900 would seem to be reasonable. It is an interesting photograph insofar that it provides a good view of the footplate arrangement of this class. However, the principal reason for including this picture was to provide a close-up of the brass numbers used until 1905.

Authors' collection

Plate 195. Although popular conception of Midland Railway locomotives was one of immaculate condition, this picture of 2–4–0 No. 44 disproves the theory. Built in 1874, it became No. 118 in 1907 and was withdrawn in 1925. The locomotive has a one-piece cast chimney and carries the first heraldic emblem on the leading splasher, the top of which appears to be red. Note the absence of any lining on the wheels or brake hangers. The base of the dome is lined, as indeed is the inside of the cab. The general style is very similar to No. 1504 (Chapter 4, *Plate 147*) and, with the one-piece chimney, cannot be earlier than 1890, thus reinforcing the view that from 1883 until the start of the 1890s lining of details below the footplate level was sparse compared with the policy at the end of the nineteenth and start of the twentieth century. The burning on the firebox and boiler, while extensive on No. 44, was not unusual and many photographs show this on Midland locomotives.

Collection Rogert Carpenter

Plate 196. 2–4–0 No. 86A was built in 1863 as a '50' class locomotive. The same year it was renumbered 59. In 1881 it was rebuilt, restored to the capital list as No. 86 and it is in this external form that it is pictured, having received the duplicate list 'A' in 1890. The locomotive was broken up in 1894 which enables an accurate date to be placed upon its livery condition. The unlined guard irons and brake hangers suggest a c.1890/1 date for the picture, but it is difficult to see whether the wheels are lined. *Authors' collection*

Plate 197. 2–4–0 No. 897 was built by Neilson & Co. in 1871 and was rebuilt in 1886 to the condition as shown in this picture. The reader's attention is drawn to the rebuilt works plate on the leading splasher which confirms this information. In 1907 the locomotive was renumbered 75 and withdrawn from service in 1928. It seems probable that this picture was taken c.1886 and so provides a good example of early Crimson Lake livery and in particular the lining. Readers will note that compared with the finish employed ten years later this locomotive received a less ornate style. For example, there is no lining on the guard irons, brake block hangers or sandboxes. The reader's attention is also drawn to the single line beneath the tender flare, but with no lining along the top edge of the beading. Finally, note that there is lining on the angle iron where the splashers join the boiler and that at this date the splasher tops would be red. *National Railway Museum*

matter. There is a sort of parallel here in the way the Caledonian Railway, for example, permitted its drivers to embellish the smokebox with decorated stars and other emblems.

As far as we can determine, this increase in decorative embellishment seems not to have become noticeable to any marked degree during the 1880s, but was confined, essentially, to the 'all red engine' period of the 1890s. By then the Crimson Lake colour was standard, and moreover, unique to the Midland. We do not think it surprising that, given the intense pride of the late Victorian railwaymen, many of the Midland men felt that they had such a lovely colour scheme to start with that it was well worth giving their principal locomotives that 'little bit extra' just to reinforce their sense of superiority over lesser systems! If this was the case, the company seems to have connived at the attitude because the treatment became even more elaborate towards the end of the century and, it must be said, went to such an extent in some places as to be applied to even the most humble of shunting engines.

Thus it was that while Derby works produced one style, a number of other paint shops at Bristol, Leeds and Manchester, and in particular Kentish Town, turned out locomotives in 'their' style. The best recorded photographically and in note form were from Kentish Town which, under the control of Robert Weatherburn, produced some very ornate styles.

It is recorded in *Midland Style* that a slightly deeper shade of Crimson Lake was employed at Kentish Town with cream lining replacing the yellow which was the usual colour. In addition the lining on the buffer beams was wider than the usual Derby practice. We are not altogether convinced that the base colour really was darker, in the absence of authentic evidence. The fact is that the undoubted change to cream lining (later called 'straw' — see page 156) and its application in more profusion would, for reasons explained on page 121, make the red seem darker. However, at this range in time we will let the matter rest — it is unlikely ever to be resolved without doubt.

On the so-called 'Weatherburn' liveries, the normal dome casing lining was used and in addition lining could be found around the base of the safety valve, on the boiler clothing. Additional lining could also often be found around the base of the chimney and actually around the smokebox itself on certain locomotives running with elaborate liveries (see *Plate 210*). The cab front was lined out around the window openings and, frequently, additional lining was applied to the outside edge of the heraldic emblem with the 'south east' side achieving a relief effect by using a double width line.

Some locomotives had the bottom of the boiler barrel painted cream with the object of reflecting the access of natural light to the motion — just how effective this was is open to speculation, but all the other points given are recorded in *Midland Style* and some of these variations are illustrated in the plates reproduced within this chapter. These livery variations, and others, are more fully detailed in the relevant photograph captions for the locomotives

concerned. We believe this is the best method to employ in order to illustrate these aspects of Weatherburn and similar special liveries.

At the same time we must also state that we are not at all convinced that the 'Weatherburn' livery for 0—6—0Ts as recorded in *Midland Style* is correct. This was a somewhat unusual instance of an elaborate livery being applied to some very humble engines. We do not know why — possibly they were in the public eye as station pilots — but the analysis previously published seems to fly in the face of all known paint shop practices of the late Victorian period. Our interpretation is given at *Plate 224* and we leave readers to decide. Once again, 'the only certainty is uncertainty!'

What might be termed the 'fully decorated' version of the lined-out Midland livery survived, just, into the 20th century, and was applied — modified to some extent by the very different shape of the engines — to the first of the 'Belpaires', 'Compounds' and 'H' boilered 4—4—0s, but it was not to last long. With the retirement of Johnson and the advent of Deeley, changes were soon forthcoming. We are disinclined to believe that these changes were solely explicable in terms of a 'new broom' at the head of the locomotive department. It seems much more likely that changed economic circumstances were filtering through to the locomotive side — one of the most expensive single departments of the railway — and that Deeley was, perforce, the instrument of these changes.

We have already described the 'economy' livery adopted after c.1899 on some goods engines and the next chapter will deal with the more profound visual changes in painting methods adopted after the middle of the Edwardian period in the interests of cutting costs still further. Meanwhile, we conclude this chapter with a comprehensive selection of views of the full and 'decorated' Midland period. We would also draw readers' attention to the fully detailed livery summary we have provided at the end of the next chapter in which we have attempted to draw all the many threads together and also to the note on headlamps (below).

LOCOMOTIVE HEADLAMPS

According to the *Locomotive Magazine* (Volume VII) of 1902, a change was made in the method of painting locomotive headlamps. The new style was to be:-

Passenger locomotive headlamps to be MR red, lined black and yellow with yellow lettering. Goods engines were to have black headlamps, unlined, with red lettering. The headlamps were to carry the engine number and the name of the district to which it was allocated.

Previous practice was to paint the driver's name and the name of the shed on the headlamp. What is not clear is if the colours and lining were unaltered from that used prior to 1902.

Plate 198. 2—4—0 No. 171, seen here at Ilkley, was built by Beyer-Peacock in 1867 and became 171A in 1893. Withdrawal was at the beginning of 1898. There is no lining on the guard irons but the brake hangers and spring buckles are lined. The engine looks fairly newly painted and the picture is probably c.1894/5, this being consistent with the increase in the elaboration of lining. The lining at the base of the tender side is horizontal and does not precisely follow the line of rivets. *Collection Bernard Mathews*

Plate 199. 2—4—0 No. 1519 displays the early Crimson Lake livery with apparently no lining on the cab front, brake hangers or guard irons, although the buckle on the springs behind the driving wheels is lined out. The spring over the leading wheel also has a lined buckle but the spring itself appears to be painted black, and there is no yellow lining. The built-up chimney suggests a late 1880s date for the picture. This locomotive was built by Neilson and Co. in 1881 and became No. 259 in 1907. In 1926 it received a Belpaire boiler and was withdrawn three years later in 1929. *Collection Bernard Mathews*

Plate 200. 0—4—4T No. 799 was built in 1870 by Dübs & Co., became No. 1225 in 1907, and was withdrawn at the end of 1931. This picture, taken at Kentish Town, shows No. 799 in its Johnson condition, carrying a slightly more elaborately lined livery, although there is no lining on the guard irons or brake hangers. There is, however, lining on the cab front around the spectacle plates, and the lining on the 'cabside' is interesting with a 'triangle' at the front and rear just below the cab roof. The springs have lining on the top leaf and bracket but not on the end supports. The tie bar between the driving wheel horn-guides is lined out and there is an extra line on the bogie wheel centres. This picture seems to represent the start of the so-called 'Weatherburn' treatment. *Collection Bernard Mathews*

Plate 201. Although in Works Grey, this picture of 0—6—0T No. 1413 does show very clearly one style of lining used on shunting loco-motives. Note the double yellow line around the base of the dome and the lined out brake hangers, but an absence of lining on the outside of the frames, guard irons and around the cab front windows. No. 1413 was built at Derby in 1880 and became No. 1203 in 1907. As such it lasted until withdrawal in 1932, and, as far as we know, it did not receive a Belpaire boiler. *British Railways*

FULL AND DECORATED CRIMSON LIVERY — 2—4—0 LOCOMOTIVES

Plate 202. This and the next view give a very clear impression of the full crimson livery in the 1900s on two typical 2—4—0s, neither of which has been given the more 'decorated' embellishments of, for example, Kentish Town. This view shows No. 822A of the famous Kirtley '800' class as running with Johnson tender and detail changes. The engine became 822A in 1903 and this is probably the date of the picture. In 1907 it was renumbered 55 and was withdrawn from service in 1922. It provides a very clear picture of the lining practice for the '800' class and other double-framed types. Points of interest are the lining on the back of the tender buffer plank, below the top flare of the tender only, and no lining on the spring hangers. The retention of the number on the boiler side and lack of heraldic emblem reflect the physical configuration of the engine. Unfortunately, the location cannot be identified, but the coal supply suggests that a heavy task was in prospect.   *National Railway Museum*

FULL AND DECORATED CRIMSON LIVERY — 4—4—0 LOCOMOTIVES

Plate 204. 4—4—0 No. 1562 was built at Derby in 1882 and became No. 328 in 1907, the year it received an 'H' boiler. Two years later it received a Belpaire boiler with an extended smokebox and in this condition it is illustrated in *Plate 328*. This is a particularly interesting picture, probably taken in or before 1893. The absence of 'MR' on the tender is noteworthy and, although instructions to place 'MR' on the tender appear on the 1891 livery specification (see page 113), it would seem that it took some time before all the locomotive stock was dealt with. Other points of interest are the additional circle on the axle ends, and the lining of the top and bottom of the driving wheel springs, which are themselves behind the wheels. The lining of the spring buckle is very clear. There is lining behind the tender buffer plank and there are two yellow lines around the base of the dome, separated by a black band. Photographs of locomotives in photographic grey show this feature but this is one of the clearest examples we have seen of a Crimson Lake painted locomotive with this feature. It is interesting to note that although tender springs, guard irons and brake hangers are all lined out, there is a lack of lining around the base of the safety valve, and the framing beneath the smokebox appears to be black. Finally, note the sandbox which is red with a horizontal black and yellow line at the base only. In all, this qualifies this locomotive as being perhaps an early example of the move towards increased embellishment before it had reached its final phase. It may even be one of Weatherburn's early efforts. *Collection Bernard Mathews*

Plate 203. 2—4—0 No. 130A affords an interesting comparison with No. 897 in *Plate 197*. No. 130A was built in 1874 and went onto the duplicate list in 1899, becoming No. 123 in 1907. The works plate above the leading wheel's axlebox reads 'Rebuilt Derby 1900', which is the probable date of this photograph. This works plate carries lining round the edge, unlike *Plate 202*. A forward toolbox has been fitted but the rear toolbox is still in place. Note also that, unlike 822A, the tender top lining is both along the top edge of the horizontal beading and beneath the flare of the tender. When also compared with 897, the lining around the locomotive footsteps is different. It is interesting to note that whilst two of the tender springs are lined the centre one appears to be an unlined replacement, as indeed does the leading spring above the locomotive platform. However, all spring hangers are lined on both engine and tender (unlike 822A) which suggests that all springs were originally lined on the top/bottom leaf. No. 130A is clearly not quite in ex-works livery condition.

National Railway Museum

Plates 205, 206 & 207. Depicting Johnson 4—4—0s Nos.1670, 2193 and 2196, these plates should be considered together and if they prove anything at all, it is that lining practice in the pre-1907 era was varied! The locomotive details are as below.

No. 1670 was built at Derby in 1884 (as noted on the works plate), and rebuilt in 1890; almost certainly this picture was therefore taken between these two dates. The locomotive was renewed in 1901 and emerged as a 'new' 1670 with a 6 inches longer driving wheel base. In 1907 this renewed locomotive became No. 486 and in 1908 it received an 'H' boiler. Four years later it was again renewed to class '483' and was finally withdrawn in 1957 as British Railways No. 40486. Nos. 2193 and 2196 were both of the '2183' class, built by Sharp Stewart in 1892 and became 413 and 416 respectively in 1907. They received 'H' boilers in 1907 and 1906, were again renewed as '483' class in 1918 and 1914, and withdrawn by British Railways in 1959 and 1957 respectively.

Turning now to the decorative details, much can be said, and we will do our best to explain. Firstly, it must be noted that if, as seems certain, No. 1670 was painted before 1890, it shows rather more elaboration than one would expect at this time. Wheel centres, brake hangers and bogie sideframes are all lined and the sandbox treatment is well nigh unique. At the same time, the lack of lining on tender springs and front guard-irons is fully in accordance with the late 1880s period. We therefore infer, largely from the totally non-standard treatment of the sandbox, that this engine may have been an early example of 'local' embellishment before the company itself adopted a more florid style as a matter of routine. All other details are as would be expected at this time.

Turning now to the Sharp Stewart engines, these, like No. 1670, have lining at the base of the dome, but also at the base of the safety valve casing and, in the case of No. 2193, around the chimney base as well. Both of them have extra lining at the wheel bosses (almost certainly with black axle ends inside the inner yellow circle) and have the heraldic emblem 'shaded' by extra lining on the 'SE' side. Springs are lined (except for the replacement leading tender spring on 2196) and sandboxes are lined all round. On No. 2193 this lining is also applied to the front and rear faces of the box as well as the outer face, but the shadow is too deep on 2196 to determine the issue. Nos. 2193 and 2196 also have the valance lining carried onto the rear faces of the drag beams, unlike No. 1670, where it is confined to the valance only. All engines have red splasher tops and lining next to the boiler.

Finally, on No. 2193, it is possible (under magnification) to confirm 'arrow heads' on the spoke ends which, together with its lined chimney base and other details, suggest the 'Weatherburn' style. These 'arrow heads' may also be present on No. 2196 which, interestingly, sported a coal railed tender without the letters 'MR' when the picture was taken in 1898. We cannot date the picture of No. 2193 but it was likely to have been at about the same time.

Collection Bernard Mathews
Collection David White

Plates 208 & 209. That the decorated livery of Nos. 2193 and 2196 (*Plates 206 & 207*) is likely to have been either by Weatherburn, or inspired by him, is clearly exemplified by these two views of possibly the most celebrated 4–4–0 owned by the Midland Railway No. 1757 *Beatrice*, and is known to have been finished in the 'Weatherburn' livery or 'London' style. Built at Derby in 1886, this locomotive was exhibited at the Royal Jubilee Exhibition at Saltaire in 1887 and was named after Princess Beatrice. The nameplate was made of brass and was curved to fit inside the perimeter of the splasher. The letters were incised into the brass and probably filled with black paint mixed with stopper. The name was retained until rebuilding with an 'H' boiler in 1907, the year it was renumbered 377. The locomotive was withdrawn in 1923. Both plates illustrate the locomotive in superb finish and many of the various aspects attributed to this 'London' style can be seen on the original prints. In the rear end view, the lining in the cab can be seen and of principal interest are the vees or arrowheads on the spokes at both the boss and rim ends. The double relief effect on the south-east side of the heraldic emblem can also be clearly seen but, interestingly, the chimney base of *Beatrice* carries no lining — unlike No. 2193 (*Plate 206*) which is otherwise all but identical in decoration embellishment. It is impossible to tell whether or not the top edge of the horizontal tender beading (below the 'flare') is lined — indeed this is the case with 2193 and 2196 as well — largely because this feature frequently displays a 'highlight' line caused by the effect of sunlight falling on the surface. This 'highlight' line can be confused with a genuine yellow one and often is.

National Railway Museum and collection Bernard Mathews

Plate 211. The full livery treatment was applied to the first five Johnson 'Compounds' of which No. 2634 (later to become No. 1003) is seen here, photographed in April 1904. Note the red lined panel on the splasher which is a principal reason for including this photograph (see *Plate 210* for a view of the front of the splasher). Finally, note lining around the washout plugs. In general, with these and other early 20th century designs (e.g. the 'Belpaires') the full and ornate livery was retained until the renumbering. It looked rather different to that on the slim-boilered Johnson engines but the basic principles governing where lining and decoration should go, still held good.   *J. H. Wright*

Plate 210. Johnson 'Compound' No. 2635, one of the second series with 'straight' footplate top over the cylinders, demonstrates that the full glory of MR livery was not confined to the late 19th century. Note the smokebox front lining (just to the rear of the rivets), the 'all round' cylinder lining, the splasher top 'panel', the additional cab roof panel (between vertical side sheet and rainstrip) and the horizontal lining just above the flat tender beading below the 'flare'. There is even lining round the rivets at the rear of the smokebox and on the slide bar support bracket. Oddly enough, the headlamps, although lined out, do not carry the locomotive number.
National Railway Museum

FULL AND DECORATED CRIMSON LIVERIES – JOHNSON 4–2–2 LOCOMOTIVES

Plate 212. The first of the Johnson bogie 'singles' did not appear until 1887, well into the 'red' period and close to the start of the more 'decorated' phase. In consequence, there are few pictures which show whether the earliest of the series ever received the 'basic' lined out crimson livery of the 1883-90 period. Most of them (probably all) sooner or later received one or other of the 'full livery' variations and the later examples did not appear, even for the first time, until well into the 1890s when MR livery was at its most exuberant. Such a group were the fourth series (the so called '115' class) of 1896 and of which No. 673 (ex-118) is now preserved at the National Railway Museum.

This picture displays the first of this class (No. 115, later 670) in what is believed to be the first Weatherburn experiment which was recorded as being somewhat shortened. Note the ornamental filigree-like decoration around the heraldic emblem on the driving wheel splasher, around the painted number panel and the extra-ordinary embellishment to the cab upper side sheet. It is not possible to see just what this is, perhaps fortunately. This experimental scheme is referred to in *Midland Style* in somewhat derogatory terms and we cannot but agree with the author of that survey. There is, indeed, a very fine line between good taste and vulgarity and we are not surprised that No. 115's livery was quickly suppressed!

Collection Bernard Mathews

Plate 214. Ornate livery styles were not confined to London as this picture of 4–2–2 No. 39 (No. 639 after 1907) will show. Photographed at Bristol, this picture shows a horizontal vee on the bogie sideframes but *not* the spoke ends, together with an elaborate treatment of the spring hangers of the trailing wheel. We cannot explain why, although the cab front (including spectacle glasses) is fully lined, the guard irons, sandboxes, brakes, etc. are in grey, unless the locomotive was in the process of being repainted. Finally, note the lining top and bottom of the valance and behind the front buffer plank and rear drag beam. There is also a double line round the dome base but no lining to the chimney base or safety valve casing.

Collection Roger Carpenter

Plate 213. By the late 1890s most Johnson 'singles' were fully arrayed in one or other of the fully decorated styles, and this picture of one of the first series (built 1887-9) shows 4–2–2 No. 1853 (later No. 608) at St. Pancras in the late 1890s showing the builder's plate and the plate commemorating the award of a gold medal at the Paris Exhibition of 1889. Note the lining around the base of the safety valve and chimney. Note also the vees on the spokes, the lining on the sides, front and presumably the rear of the sandbox, double relief on the heraldic emblem and lining on the cab front around the spectacle plates. Clearly this is the full 'Weatherburn' type treatment although the colour of the cab roof is a problem. We cannot quite decide if it is red or varnished black but favour the red choice. There is lining around the driving wheel axlebox, also on the driving wheel spring hangers. Finally, note the lining all round the valance, top and bottom, the former being distinctly unusual.

Collection Roger Carpenter

Plates 215 & 216. This utterly intriguing pair of pictures show Johnson 4–2–2 No. 1871 (No. 628 after 1907) at two different stages in its pre-1906 existence. The three-quarter rear view shows the earlier stage, probably taken in the mid-1890s (the engine was built in 1890). It shows quite a number of predictable livery details for this period – e.g. lined out brake hangers, guard-irons, wheel centres and tyres, sandbox bottom – but the principal point of interest is the tender panels which are square-cornered and this is the only example of this variation which has come to our attention. Note also that the tender beading seems to have been painted black, and the springs and hangers, but not the spring buckles, are still unlined. The engine is obviously not ex-works, so we would date the view at c.1893/4. Oddly enough, the unusual 'square-cornered' tender panelling seems in many ways rather more logical in relation to the tender shape than does the common round-cornered variety. The second view of No. 1871 is the very familiar picture of this engine, taken probably after re-boilering c.1900. Note the second 'works'

plate on the leading frames compared with the earlier view. The engine is now displaying a beautiful example of Weatherburn's livery. Note the vees at both ends of the spokes of the bogie wheels. These vees are also present on the other wheels although probably not so easily seen in this photograph. The picture also provides an example of the lining applied to the sides of the driving wheel axlebox. Other Weatherburn features are the crimson panel on the splasher front, which has been lined out, the lining on the cab front around the spectacle plates, and extra circles on the end of the bogie axles. In addition, there is lining around the base of the safety valve but not the chimney and below the running plate on the valances (top and bottom edges). The spring hangers have a small vee at the top with the centre buckle lined out. Finally, note the yellow painted area at the bottom of the boiler – intended to reflect light onto the motion – and the double relief effect on the south-east corner of the heraldic emblem. No. 1871, as No. 628, was withdrawn in 1926.

National Railway Museum

140

Plate 217. This picture displays an example of the fifth and final series of 'singles'. No. 21 was built in 1900, became No. 692 in 1907, was withdrawn in 1921, and is shown here in its original condition with a bogie tender. This tender was rebuilt with straight sides running on six wheels at some date after 1905. As an example of the official 'full' livery without decoration, it should be compared with *Plate 216*. The reader's attention is drawn to the lining of the sandboxes (side, front and rear) and the lining on the side of the driving axleboxes. The width of the lining on the boiler band in front of the safety valve was either thinner than that on the other boiler lagging bands or not present at all. Note the lack of lining around the spectacle glasses and upper edge of the side valances (compare with *Plate 216*). All told, we find it rather surprising that the 'ultimate singles' were not given the fully 'decorated' treatment.

National Railway Museum

FULL AND DECORATED CRIMSON LIVERIES — 0—4—4T LOCOMOTIVES

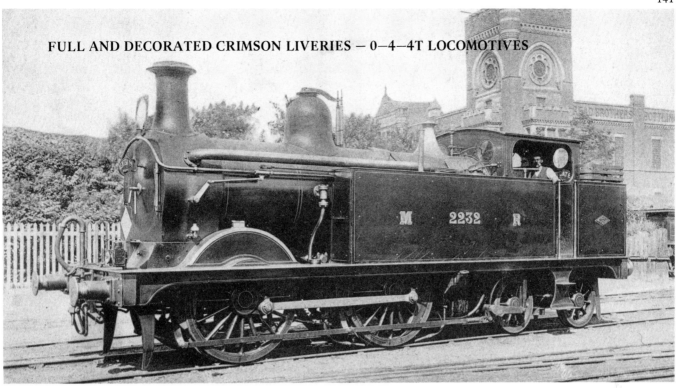

Plate 218. The Johnson 0—4—4Ts were built during both the 'green' and 'red' periods. This one, however, No. 2232, did not appear until 1895, well into the 'full crimson' period. The engine is a London area 'condensing' 0—4—4T and the picture is reproduced from a contemporary undated gravure postcard of MR origin. The lining is most peculiar in detail, although 'standard' in general layout. For example, the axle/wheel centre lining, cab spectacle plate lining and guard-irons are all as per 'Weatherburn', but there is no base lining to dome or safety valve, and the front frame extensions (above the footplate) and brake hangers seem to be black. The Dübs works plate and the boiler side 'clack' are both lined, as is the cab door and small coupling rod splasher. It seems almost like a 'decorated' livery not quite completed, but in general layout is highly typical of most of this group. No. 2232 became No. 1385 in 1907, was rebuilt in 1908 and just lasted into BR days, being scrapped in January 1948.   *Authors' collection*

Plate 219. As far as we know, the only significant variant in the 0—4—4T livery was that which is in *Midland Style* indicating that some of the condensing 0—4—4Ts received inner panels on the tank and bunker sides and tank end as seen in this picture of No. 1722. Although no pictures exist, as far as we know, to show the rear end of the coal bunker of locomotives painted in this style it seems probable that the backs of the bunkers were painted in similar style to the fronts of the side tanks. Other detail follows Weatherburn practice. No. 1722 was built at Derby in 1886 and became No. 1315 in 1907. It was fitted with a Belpaire boiler in 1926. Although allocated the number 58048 by British Railways, the locomotive was withdrawn in 1949 still carrying its LMS number.   *Collection Bernard Mathews*

FULL AND DECORATED CRIMSON LIVERIES — 0–6–0T LOCOMOTIVES

Plate 220. 0–6–0T No. 886A is seen here with cut-down boiler mountings working in the London area. This locomotive was built in 1871 by Beyer Peacock as No. 886 and went onto the duplicate list in 1890. Becoming No. 1616 in 1907, it was withdrawn in 1923. When compared with No. 885A in *Plate 224* it will be seen that 886A displays the simpler livery style of the early 1890s. The picture is probably c.1891/2 in view of the lack of 'MR' on the tank side. There is normal lining on the tank and bunker sides, together with the wheels, but no lining on the brake hangers, guard-irons or sandboxes. In addition there is no lining on the wheel splasher or springs. The toolbox is, however, lined out and we presume that similar lining was applied to the ends and the other side. Note the single line on the front boiler lagging band.
Collection Bernard Mathews

Plate 221. 0–6–0T No. 1390 was built in 1878 and this view seems to show the engine in a fairly early lined crimson style, but cannot be dated precisely except that it is before 1903. The 'MR' denotes post c.1891-2 and the early 1890s seems a likely date. Lining is quite modestly applied and there is none round the base of the dome. The lining at the front corner of the side tank is interesting, and the boiler band ahead of the dome was lined both sides where it is above the tank sides, but only at the chimney end where it is against the tank ends. The wheel centres are lined around the boss but the wheel tyres do not appear to be lined. There is no lining on the brake hangers or on the footsteps. No. 1390 was built at Derby and became No. 1673 in 1905. In 1912 it received a closed cab and was withdrawn in 1930.
Collection Roger Carpenter

Plate 222. Compared with No. 1390 (*Plate 221*) this picture of 0–6–0T No. 1387 poses some problems. It was taken between 1903 and 1907 and displays a locomotive which one would expect to see in full livery. However, apart from the tank and bunker sides, the rest of the loco-motive is somewhat dirty. At this date one would expect to see the brake hangers and guard-irons lined, and they may well be so — the lining is probably covered by dirt. Note that the sandboxes are lined across the top, the dome is lined, as is the cab front around the spectacle plate. This would all indicate 'full' crimson. Finally, note that compared with No. 1390, the tankside lining is taken around the tank front. No. 1387 was built at Derby in 1878 and became No. 1670 in 1907. In 1912 this open cab locomotive received a closed cab and as such lasted until withdrawal in 1938.

Collection Bernard Mathews

Plate 223. This picture shows one of the fairly new 'large' Johnson 0–6–0Ts, No. 2458, in lined red livery c.1903/4. Although hardly visible on the original print, it is possible to see that the brake hangers, outside of the frames, sandboxes and base of dome have been lined out. The locomotive is in the non-decorated 'full' livery. Built by the Vulcan Foundry in 1902, No. 2458 was renumbered 1937 in 1907 and received a Belpaire boiler in 1923. The LMS renumbered it 7237 c.1934 and British Railways added 40000 to make it 47237. With-drawal was in 1955.

Collection Roger Carpenter

Plate 224. In *Midland Style* it was stated that some of the London area 0–6–0Ts received a unique form of 'Weatherburn' finish with, and we quote: 'square-cornered black *inner* panels fine lined yellow, in addition to the usual lining out around the outer edges' (Authors' italics). The appended picture of No. 885A was offered in confirmation of this statement but we cannot in all honesty accept this interpretation. There is certainly an extra yellow line 'inboard' of the outer edge lining but we cannot believe that the whole of the tank side within this inner line (i.e. backing the 'MR' and number) was painted black — it would have looked most peculiar and quite un-Midlandlike.

The alternative explanation that the alleged 'black inner panel' was, in fact, the zone *between* the two rectangular yellow outlined areas also defies logic because this would make the colour sequence, reading from the tank top, as follows: black, yellow, black, yellow, red — such an unlikely occurrence as to be virtually ruled out. Moreover, on this particular type of engine, it would give a much broader black margin to the tank side than the bunker side. This would 'unbalance' the overall visual appearance and hardly seems compatible with the wish for enhanced appearance which the undoubted extra lining confirms. If there had been a black 'panel' feature, then it would surely have been double lined as, for example, on the cab side of certain 0–6–0s (e.g. *Plates 86, 230 & 231*), the conventional Johnson tender lining, particularly that with square corners (*Plate 215*), or on some 0–4–4Ts (*Plate 219*).

Therefore, we believe that the 'Weatherburn' 0–6–0Ts simply displayed an additional single yellow line on the *red* tank side panel some 2-3 inches inside the otherwise normally painted black/yellow edging to this feature. This would certainly be much more in line with Victorian/Edwardian paint shop practice and with the visual evidence of surviving pictures.

Engine No. 885A received its 'A' suffix in 1890 and became No. 1615 in 1907. What is interesting is that in spite of the embellishments clearly visible on this picture, the guard-irons, brake hangers and framing were unlined. The engine was scrapped in 1925.

Collection Bernard Mathews

Plates 225 & 226. By way of confirmation of our suggestions regarding the 'decorated' London area 0–6–0Ts, we offer these two views of Johnson engines of the 'open-cab' variety, both carrying heavily embellished lined red liveries. Firstly, compare No. 1382 with No. 1390 in *Plate 221*. Readers will note that there is an extra yellow line inside the outer yellow edging line on both the bunker side, end and tank side. On this locomotive the lining appears to be, reading from the outer edge of the tank, black edging, yellow lining, Crimson Lake and yellow lining. There can be no other logical explanation. On this locomotive the brake hangers are lined, as are the top of the sandboxes and the guard-irons, together with the top of the footsteps. This locomotive was built at Derby in 1878 and became No. 1665 in 1907. In 1912 it was fitted with a closed cab and was withdrawn at the end of 1937.

An almost identical version of the livery was applied to locomotive No. 1381 — only the somewhat poor quality of the picture prevents us from being more positive. There is, in fact, extra lining at the axle end compared with No. 1382, but the brake hangers and guard-irons are too scruffy to reveal (or deny) the presence of lining. No. 1381 was built in 1878, became No. 1664 in 1907, received a Belpaire boiler in 1925 and was scrapped as BR 41664 in 1953.

Quality apart, the picture of No. 1381 is additionally valuable in demonstrating the limitations of black and white photography. If one was to infer colour solely from the variable rendering of 'greys' on the picture then one could possibly envisage the zone between the two rectangular outlined areas on tank and bunker side as being somewhat darker than the main inner 'panels', black rather than red perhaps? If so, someone had better explain why the footplate valance, sidesteps and buffer plank ends were an even *darker* shade! We prefer our own interpretation but are happy to let others argue the issue.

Authors' collection

FULL AND DECORATED CRIMSON LIVERIES – 0–6–0 LOCOMOTIVES

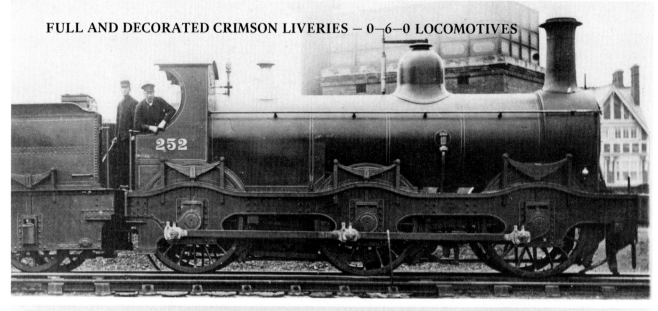

Plates 227 & 228. The double-framed Kirtley 0–6–0s were amongst several classes whose livery was derived by the move to plain crimson/brown/brick red (see page 118). However, many of them retained fully lined red livery and all had been that way in the 1880s/1890s. We give an example each of a steam braked only and vacuum braked engine in fully lined red livery.

Kirtley 0–6–0 No. 252 was built at Derby in 1871 and was renumbered 568 in 1903 and this picture enables us to give an example of full Crimson Lake livery of a steam braked Kirtley 0–6–0 goods engine c.1900 or a little earlier. The locomotive has the boiler lagging band lined (with a single line only on the front band), along with the base of the dome, splasher sides, and, where the centre and rear splashers adjoin the firebox, a further yellow line. The frame is lined around the cut-outs and axleboxes and along the bottom edge. However, there is no lining on the spring hangers or the springs themselves, except for the centre buckles. The brake hangers and guard-irons are not lined but the clack on the boiler side has been lined out. Finally, there is no evidence of lining on the driving wheels, but the coupling rods have been painted and the outside cranks lined out. In 1907 this locomotive was renumbered 2695 and was withdrawn from service in 1931.

Vacuum braked 0–6–0 No. 256 was built at Derby in 1864 and became No. 338 in 1904 and 2469 in 1907. Withdrawal was at the

end of 1930. The livery is interesting, the boiler lagging bands are lined out but not the angle at the cab front or the spectacle surrounds. None of the springs or spring buckles are lined, or the valance and buffer plank ends. The frames are edged black and lined yellow on the bottom and around the frame cut-outs but this is hard to see on the picture. There is no lining on the brake hangers, guard-irons or sandboxes. The base of the dome is lined and there is a line which extends along the top of the rear splasher and along the base of the firebox to the point where it meets the boiler lagging band. Finally, there does not appear to be any lining on the outside cranks.

The 'below footplate' lining is harder to see on this engine than that on the boiler and may well, therefore, have been applied to a narrower dimension. If so, it suggests that even before 1904 (when the engine was first renumbered) the MR had already adopted a principle of finer lining thickness below the footplate. This treatment became standard procedure for all engines during the Deeley and indeed the LMS period (see page 156) and tempts us to wonder whether No. 256 was perhaps painted at the time in the early part of the 20th century when the MR was beginning to move towards a more economical lining treatment. The absence of decoration on certain features would reinforce this speculation.

Authors' collection

Plate 229. This Works Grey picture of No. 2073 should be compared with *Plate 230,* No. 1451. On the tender, additional lining, which may have been done for the photograph, appears on the springs and on the inside edge of the tender beading panels. However, surprisingly, neither the tender nor locomotive brake hangers are lined. On the locomotive, extra lining (when compared with No. 1451) is evident around the footsteps. No. 2073 was built by Dübs & Co. in 1891 (note the distinctive Dübs works plate on the centre splasher) and became No. 3350 in 1907. In due course it received a 'G6' Belpaire boiler and was withdrawn in 1956 as British Railways No. 43350.

British Railways

Plate 230. 0−6−0 No. 1451 was built by Robert Stephenson & Co. (note large works plate on the centre splasher) in 1880. The existence of a one-piece chimney dates it after 1890, and the lack of tender initials suggests a date before 1893, but, of course, one cannot be 100 per cent certain of this assumption. The livery is very ornate and should be compared with *Plate 229,* No. 2073. Commencing with the tender, it is interesting to see that the guard-irons are black and not lined, but that the spring hangers and buckles are both lined out. Whilst the lining on No. 2073 around the tender panel and on the centre and lower leaf springs *may* have been done specifically for the photograph, on No. 1451 the top leaf only is lined. The lining on the top of the tender above the horizontal beading is identical to that shown on No. 2073 and there is a horizontal line above the top beading below the 'flare'. On the locomotive itself, the principle additional feature is the extra round-cornered panel 'inboard' of the edge lining. Note also the lining around the base of the dome, the cut-outs in the framing and the extra lining on axle ends. Only a single line is on the boiler lagging band next to the smokebox. There is no evidence of lining on the toolboxes or the upper edge of the framing beneath the smokebox. Finally, note that the handrails are in bright metal finish.

All in all, this is a highly mysterious picture. There is the sort of painting detail which one would expect in the late 1890s during the 'Weatherburn' period, yet there is no tender lettering. The extra 'panel' on the cab side is non-standard and somewhat reminiscent of the treatment given to 0−4−4Ts (see *Plate 219*). A possible explanation would be a contractor variation (see *Plate 231*) but if so, it could hardly still have been present some 10 years or so after building, or could it? Were it not for the Johnson one-piece chimney (1890 or later), we could believe this to be an ex-works engine in a highly embellished 'contractor' green livery c.1880/1, but, all in all, we think it more likely to be a mid- or late 1890s 'fancy' job in crimson. Just to cap it all, the engine is steam braked so could not work a passenger train − so what price the livery? Can any reader help?

Authors' collection

Plate 231. This picture of 0—6—0 No. 1597 poses almost as many queries as the last one (No. 1451), because it too seems to be unduly elaborate for the period in question, i.e. c.1883. In *Midland Style* it was recorded that the fifty 0—6—0 goods engines built by Beyer Peacock in 1882-84 did not have the usual vertical moulding in the middle of their 2,200 gallon tenders, and, consequentially, instead of being embellished with two panels with convex radiused corners, received one long panel as illustrated. However, later it would seem that two panels became the normal practice as illustrated by *Plate 233* which shows No. 1606. This picture of No. 1597 is undated but has been included to illustrate this tender feature. The locomotive was built in 1883 just before Crimson Lake became the official Midland Railway livery, but this picture could equally well illustrate No. 1597 when in Crimson Lake. The lack of lining on the guard-irons and brake hangers is typical of the early red period, but the axle ends have a circle around them as well as a line

around the wheel centres. The slots in the frames are lined but not the framing below the smokebox. However, what we do find intriguing is the extra 'panel' on the cab side and the appearance of two lines around the base of the dome, one on the dome and the other on the boiler clothing. These features, along with the fully lined springs (and buckles), are more reminiscent of the later 1890s than the 1880s yet the built-up chimney dates it before c.1889/90. Moreover, the single tender panel clearly implies a 'contractor' interpretation (i.e. c.1883). What we therefore conclude is that the lining style was probably a Beyer Peacock interpretation of the MR edicts and that this particular batch may well have been turned out in either green or red (depending on date of building) but with precisely the same (non-standard) lining layout regardless of basic colour. Once again, help from readers would be appreciated.

Collection Bernard Mathews

Plate 232. By contrast with the previous pair of 'maverick' 0—6—0s, this and the next view of Johnson goods engines show considerably more conventional treatment of the lined out crimson livery in the late 1890s. It may be noted that both of these are vacuum braked engines, not that this seems to have mattered. Locomotive No. 2268 was built by Sharp Stewart in 1897 and in due course became No. 3554, being withdrawn in 1947. This picture displays a 'contractor built' goods engine, after being repainted by the Midland Railway in quasi 'Weatherburn' style. The points to note are the lining on the cab front around the spectacle plates and the extra yellow line around works plate and boiler bands. The axle ends appear to be black. Finally, the reader's attention is drawn to the unlined toolbox on the tender top. All in all, these pictures of Johnson 0—6—0s well exemplify the difficulty of generalisation during the 'fully lined' MR period and point the need for modellers in particular to be very careful!

National Railway Museum

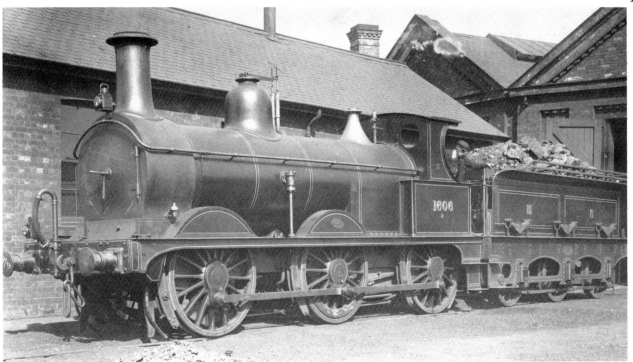

Plate 233. No. 1606 was built by Beyer Peacock in 1883 and became No. 3104 in 1907. A 'G6' Belpaire boiler was fitted in 1924 and the locomotive was withdrawn at the end of 1936. When compared with No. 2268, it will be seen that there are lining variations. On 1606 the framing below the smokebox is lined but the cab front around the spectacle windows is not. Note the shed identification on the buffer plank – 'SHE' is just visible, denoting Sheffield. According to *Midland Style* a few locomotives had either 'Sheffield' or 'Nottingham' painted onto the leading buffer plank. This style was short-lived. Guard irons, sandboxes, brake hangers and springs are all lined, so we place this firmly in the 'full livery' period of the 1890s but to the 'official' standard. Note the double 'panel' on the non standard Beyer Peacock tender (compare *Plate 231*) and the addition of 'all round' coal rails (see page 83). *Authors' collection*

Plate 234. This view of 'H' boilered rebuilt 0–6–0 No. 2117 was taken at Skipton c.1905/6 (note the power class figure below the running number) and is somewhat of a hybrid insofar as livery is concerned. The tender sides display Deeley simplified style but elsewhere there is lining on the guard-irons, framing beneath the smokebox, wheel centres, tender springs, sandbox sides and fronts, but not the brake hangers. No. 2117 was built by Sharp Stewart in 1892 and received its 'H' boiler in 1905. A Belpaire 'G7' boiler was fitted in 1922 and the locomotive, which had become No. 3394 in 1907, survived until 1961, being withdrawn as British Railways No. 43394. What is useful about this picture is that it confirms yet again that in 1905 goods engines, equipped with a train pipe which could enable them to work passenger trains, were still being outshopped in virtually full Crimson Lake livery. *Collection Bernard Mathews*

FULL CRIMSON LIVERY — 'AMERICAN' 2–6–0s

Plate 235. Clear photographs of the American 'Moguls' are rare, but this picture of a Baldwin 2–6–0 No. 2510 is very useful. Built in 1899, it became No. 2209 in 1907 and was withdrawn the following year. Seen here in Crimson Lake lined livery, the tender has a single large panel with convex corners. The end of the buffer plank is lined on all four edges. There is the usual lining on the guard-iron and all round the tender bogie side frames. Lining is evident along the bottom of the tender valance and around the steps, with the latter 'squared off' with a vertical line from the bottom of the valance to the top just below the tender handrail. What is not clear is if the lining which goes up the leading edge of the tender footstep support (and returns along the top of the footstep support) ends where the vertical line above mentioned meets it, or whether this line continues along the top of the tender valance.

On the locomotive there is lining around the windows and rear, bottom and front of the cab. There appears to be lining along the top edge of the cab side sheets but we cannot be certain. The wheel centres, guard-irons and sandboxes are lined, but the base of the real dome is unlined. There could, however, be a fine line round the base of the forward (sandbox) dome feature. The lining on the valance is on both the top and bottom and continues around the cab steps. The boiler lagging bands are lined, as indeed are the wheels. The casing of the two outside cylinders was painted Crimson Lake, and two vertical black bands, with yellow edging on each side were to be found here, positioned immediately below the squared casing above the cylinder. The ends of the cylinder covers were polished steel. Finally, it should be noted that a single oblong panel of black, edged yellow, was on the top of the cylinder casing. Further details of the 'Mogul' livery will be found in Volume 3.

Collection Bernard Mathews

Plate 236. The Schenectady built 2–6–0s were considerably more 'Anglicized' than the Baldwins as this view of No. 2516 confirms. The picture is copied from an original Midland publicity postcard and on close examination shows much the same detail as the Baldwin series. The tender was a close copy of the standard Johnson type (save for the lack of vertical centre beading) and the livery was standard but with one panel only. On the locomotive itself a commendable attempt was made to follow standard procedure. The dome base was lined out and the wheel bosses were double lined in the 'Weatherburn' fashion. We cannot detect how the cylinders were finished but they may possibly have followed the style of the Baldwins. No. 2516 was built in 1899, renumbered 2235 in 1907 and scrapped in 1914.

Authors' collection

CHAPTER SIX

MIDLAND LIVERIES IN DETAIL
1906 ONWARDS

FROM 1905/6 onwards, the locomotives of the Midland Railway began to assume a very different visual appearance. In part, this was anatomical, as described in Chapter 1, but it was considerably emphasised by the significant changes in painting methods adopted from this time, along with the renumbering of the fleet which took place in 1907. Like all changes, they did not happen overnight and the significant *visual* break more or less coincided with the great renumbering of 1907. However, there had been a sort of gradual build-up which must first be considered, and the real start seems to have been in or about 1905.

In this year it was decided to replace the brass numbers with large transferred numerals, yet whilst many locomotives carried their old (pre 1907) numbers using the new transfers, it was not unusual for locomotives to be renumbered in 1907 using the older brass numbers — very confusing to say the least! As far as can be ascertained, however, and with the exception of the old Kirtley 0—6—0 well tanks which carried their brass numbers until the end of their lives, brass numbers had been replaced by transferred numbers by c.1909.

During the early years of the century, as we have explained, considerable savings had already been effected by simplifying the freight engine livery for *steam brake only* engines. This eventually resulted in a plain black livery, officially confirmed as standard for all goods engines

(whether vacuum fitted or not) in 1910, by which time the insignia style had also changed and the locomotives had been renumbered. As usual, the change-over took time, additionally complicated by the fact that *vacuum braked* freight engines retained a lined crimson livery until possibly as late as 1909-10 in case they should be called on for passenger work.

When one considers that the majority of the Midland Railway's locomotives were goods engines not equipped with a train vacuum pipe, it is understandable that a few more years elapsed before it became necessary to make simplifications to the lined crimson livery, but c.1905 the Deeley simplified style began to be introduced, commencing with the simplification of the tender lining. This saw the replacement of the round-cornered tender panels used on the Johnson tenders, by the practice of painting the flat mouldings (which were on the tender sides and ends) black, with a yellow line usually separating the black from the Crimson Lake. Other changes were a gradual reduction in the number of boiler lagging bands which were lined, together with an end to the practice of lining the base of the dome and other boiler mountings. Lining of the guard irons and brake hangers also ceased and wheels became black with a simple yellow line at the tyre. This was accompanied by the adoption of black frames, save for some 4—4—0s (see *Plate 246*) and this simplified style for red locomotives remained Midland Railway practice until the

Plate 237. No. 105 was built at Derby in 1867 and went onto the duplicate list as 105A in 1879. The 'Boiler New' plate is dated 1892. In 1907 this locomotive was renumbered 7 and was withdrawn from service in 1925. The engine is shown here as it appeared at the start of the move towards simpler liveries in Deeley's time. The first change (as shown here) was to the tender only and took the form of eliminating the tender panels and spring lining and painting the flat beading black with fine yellow lining where the black met the red. Oddly enough, this so-called simplification seems in many ways a more logical way to line the tender than the former panel style. For a period this revised tender style was used with fully lined boiler lagging bands and other details as shown here. Later, all the boiler lagging bands, with the exception of those next to the cab front and smokebox, became unlined and with these only one yellow line was used. This went along with a gradual reduction of the ancillary lining on springs, guard-irons and so forth. *National Railway Museum*

Plates 238 & 239. These two pictures illustrate lined Crimson Lake locomotives renumbered in 1907 but using brass numbers to display the new 1907 numbers. Johnson 0–6–0 No. 3106 was photographed at Derby in 1908. Built by Beyer Peacock as No. 1608 in 1883, No. 3106 was withdrawn in 1925 as a class 2 locomotive. As far as can be seen, it is in the final simplified lining style. There is but one panel on the tender and the only boiler lagging bands which are lined are those adjacent to the smokebox and cab front.

The second view shows 0–6–0T No. 1844 displaying a very interesting livery. Note that the lining goes round the front of the tanks, forming a single panel as on No. 1387 (*Plate 222*) and that the black edging is very wide. Only the front boiler lagging band appears

to be lined and on the 'inside' edge only. The lining layout is essentially to the simplified Deeley style with a minimum of decoration below the footplate, save for the wheel rim lining. However, on this example, the footplate valance has retained lower edge lining — somewhat unusual for a red *tank* engine in and after the Deeley period.

Originally No. 2012, built in 1892 at Derby, this locomotive had probably just been renumbered 1844 using brass numerals. No. 1844 lasted until 1964 when it was withdrawn as 41844, having acquired a 'G5' Belpaire boiler in 1928.

Collection Bernard Mathews

Plate 240. 0—6—0 No. 3821 was built at Derby as a class 3 in 1908 and received a Belpaire boiler in 1921. In 1949 it became British Railways No. 43821 and was withdrawn in 1951. This undated photograph shows it as built with the new style markings but we are not entirely certain of its 'base' colour. Careful study suggests that it could well have been painted Locomotive Brown with some black relief. On the original print it is possible to see that the top edge beading on the leading and centre splashers is in a darker colour, as indeed is the splasher top. The axle ends also seem to be a darker colour, but the boiler lagging bands appear not to be painted a different colour to the boiler clothing. What cannot be established is whether the cab front colour continued onto the top of the rear splasher. Finally, it should be noted that the fluting in the coupling rods has been painted black. Whether it was brown or black, the overall style is typical of the Deeley livery for goods engines.

Collection Bernard Mathews

end of the company's existence when it was also adopted by the LMS. With the exception of the end of the practice of painting a yellow line on the locomotive wheels, it could be said that once black locomotive wheels and frames had been adopted from c.1906, this simplified Deeley livery had the longest life of any of the 'Red' locomotive styles and remained current until the last Midland locomotive was repainted black, just prior to nationalization. In fact, it re-appeared (in essence) on some London Midland Region 4—6—2s during 1957-64.

There were, of course, some variations. For example, the double-framed Kirtley passenger engines continued to have red frames and, although the yellow line on the wheels was eventually dropped by the LMS c.1928, Derby seems to have continued its use on at least some 'Compounds' until c.1938-9. But this is outside the Midland period.

What, perhaps, needs re-emphasising is that the simplified Deeley *livery* on red engines had, for all practical purposes, been adopted *before* the insignia changes and renumbering of 1906-7, although the latter events took place so soon afterwards as to somewhat confuse matters. It seems to us quite clear, however, that although there were many what might be called 'transitional' styles, most red painted Midland engines probably went directly from full or 'decorated' livery with pre-1907 numbers in brass figures, to the Deeley livery with post-1907 numbers in transfer figures, and it was this fact which was most obvious to the lineside observer.

The 'basic' pre-1906 lined out livery was with full lining, small brass locomotive numbers and diamond pattern

heraldic emblem on the splasher side of some tender engines. The essential post-1906 style was with simplified lining, new type heraldic emblem on the cab side of most tender engines and the new large transfer numerals. These differences were visible and obvious and, had they always coincided with the renumbering of the fleet in 1907, all would have been 'plain sailing' as it were. However, the transitional period saw quite a number of variations which we have tried to illustrate at *Plates 238, 239, 241 & 244.* Some of these can be itemised as follows:

(a) Simplified livery retaining old heraldic emblem and original brass numbers.

(b) Simplified livery with old emblem and new number but using original brass numbers.

(c) Simplified livery with old emblem, and *old* number in new style transfers.

(d) Simplified livery with new emblem but old number in *new* style transfers.

(e) *Partially* simplified livery with old number *and* heraldic emblem but employing new style transfers (e.g. the first 'Deeley' 'Compounds').

(f) Partially simplified livery with new emblem and new style transfers.

(g) Simplified livery with new emblem and new number in transfer form (the 'standard' version).

We do not believe that a 'fully decorated' red engine ever received the new style *transfers* with new emblem but it is possible that a fully lined red engine may well have received its new numbers in brass figures — and/or its new emblem

Plates 241 & 242. These three pictures (including *Plate 243*) illustrate the early use of the new style 18″ transfers on tender sides during the year or two before renumbering – in effect the *reverse* procedure to that shown in *Plates 238 & 239*. During this period, the heraldic emblem also changed and the lined red livery continued to get simplified. 'Belpaire' 4—4—0 No. 860, built at Derby in September 1905, is recorded as being the first *new* Midland locomotive to carry its number on the tender side, and the picture of No. 863 (completed the same month as part of the same batch) has been selected to illustrate the point. Note the wider than standard spacing of the numbers and lack of a central vertical beading strip on the tender side, thus enabling the '6' to be placed centrally. In 1907 this locomotive was renumbered 773 and in 1919 it received a 'G8AS' boiler. Withdrawal was in 1940. Finally, note that there is no lining on the lagging band on the firebox or on the top of the top horizon-

tal beading on the tender side – the first visible sign of a slight simplification – the rest of the engine continues to carry the full 'official' treatment. Like No. 863, 0—6—0 No. 1217 also displays the Johnson heraldic emblem but 2—4—0 No. 1497 (*Plate 243*) has been given the final device which came into general use in the later half of 1906. Both these engines received a much simpler version of the red livery and the number transfers are at the standard centre-to-centre spacing.

No. 1217 was built in 1876 by Beyer Peacock and in 1907 it was renumbered 2985. It carries 18″ figures on quite a 'shallow depth' tender – later on 14″ figures were more normal on this variant. Receiving a 'G6' Belpaire boiler in 1926, it was withdrawn in 1936.

Collection Bernard Mathews
National Railway Museum

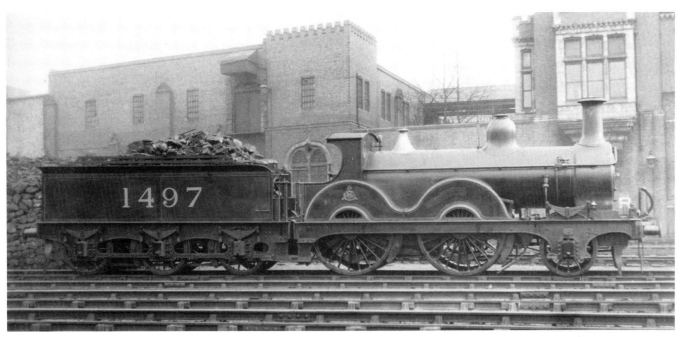

Plate 243. 2—4—0 No. 1497 was built at Derby in 1881. It became No. 277 in 1907 and was withdrawn at the end of 1924.

National Railway Museum

Plate 244. Johnson 'Belpaire' 4—4—0 No. 715 had originally been numbered 2786 when built in 1902 and originally carried the running number in brass numerals on the cab side. They were removed c.1905 and 18″ gilt transfers went onto the tender side. Finally in 1907 the locomotive was renumbered as illustrated, with the former location of the previous '2786' transfers clearly visible. There is no similarly obvious sign of a change of heraldic emblem on the cab side, but as 2786 it could well have sported the older version with the new livery. As shown here, it carries the new emblem and appears to be in standard post-1907 Deeley simplified livery throughout.   *Collection D. F. Tee*

without any simplification of lining. Neither do we believe that any engine received its *new* 1907 number in *transfer form* with the *old* emblem, since the change of heraldic device slightly preceded the renumbering. In general it seems that the new transfers were only applied to full repaints (even after renumbering).

We are tempted to advise modellers to steer clear of the 1905-8 period if they are not prepared to face up to this confusion but it does, at least, serve to emphasise the difficulty of generalisation!

Fortunately, by about 1910 things had settled down again with the universal adoption for red engines of the simplified livery style, new numbers, new transfers and new emblems, while on the freight side, plain black with new transfer numerals, new numbers and new emblem had at last been standardised. The new emblem, like its predecessor, was rarely applied to tank engines.

We should at this point state that the new transfer numerals were provided in two sizes, 18 ins and 14 ins high respectively, and the general principle was to use the larger size where they would fit. This applied to most tender classes (except those with the smaller height tenders) and to all tank classes save for the Deeley 0—6—4Ts. This latter group were somewhat exceptional in relation to the above summary because they always carried 18″ numerals *and* a bunker-side crest. They were, in effect, the 'exception which proved the rule'. In addition, all inside-framed red *tank* engines were devoid of any lining on or below the footplate angle iron.

The numeral transfers themselves were of a beautiful shape and, in spite of a statement to the contrary in *Midland Style*, were always applied in gilt with black shading to the right and below (see page 168). Suggestions that the MR occasionally applied them in yellow and/or sometimes with red shading have *no foundation in fact*. The LMS certainly adopted both of these options, but not until in and after 1929 for red shading and as late as 1937 in the case of yellow 'base' colour. Photographs purporting to indicate red shading, therefore, in the pre-1929 period are merely examples of a curious effect of light falling on a *black* shaded transfer applied to a *black* painted engine. During Midland times, these large transfer numerals were always gilt and also incorporated a fine white 'highlight' line — not always visible on photographs. The black shading was quite obvious on the red engines but on black engines did not always register on photographs which thus give the visual impression of a 'plain' figure.

With the simplified Deeley livery we are at last in the position to specify line thickness. It may have occurred to readers that so far we have 'skated round' this problem with the 'Johnson' livery — for no other reason than the lack of contemporary precision in defining what constituted a 'fine' line. We believe it to have been c.¼″ yellow but cannot verify this, and the MR, as far as we know, seems to have left matters to the judgement of its painters.

However, after 1906/7, the lining thickness was normally ½″ (above the footplate) and ³⁄₈″ below. In practice, it probably varied a little but at least it *was* defined. The black edging, where not determined by specific physical

Plate 245. This picture of No. 533, a class '483' rebuild, has been included simply to show the buffer plank lining and the unlined Crimson Lake zone between the top of the buffer plank and the running plate. Note the bright metalwork on the smokebox door.

Authors' collection

features like beadings, was ¾″-1″ (below footplate) and 2-2½″ (above footplate). These dimensions were carried through to the LMS period and even adopted by BR for the red 'Duchesses' in 1957-64! An interesting and well-recorded exception to this general principle was seen on the *rear* buffer plank of flat-sided Deeley tenders, where most of them received a wide (3-4″) black edging round a ³⁄₈″ yellow line.

Another interesting consequence of the wholesale adoption of new lining with the big transfer numerals in 1906/7 was the change in lining *colour* for the red engines. Until this time yellow lining was the usual practice, save at odd places like Kentish Town (see page 125). However, the new transfers, in gold leaf, had a much paler visual 'tone' than the previous brass numerals and this seems to have prompted the MR to adopt a new lining colour of pale 'creamy-yellow', often called 'straw', on the red engines to harmonise with the new transfers. The aim was to get as close as possible

Plates 246 & 247. We give here two excellent definitive views of the final and highly standardised simplified Deeley livery for red engines. They show opposite sides of that most characteristic of Midland passenger engines in the final pre-group years – the superheated '483' class 4–4–0. Note the bright steel 'dog ring' and hinges on the smokebox door – especially noticeable on No. 485. Note also the retention of sideframe lining above the bogies ahead of the footplate steps – a characteristic feature of most inside cylinder MR 4–4–0s at this period. This livery was adopted by the LMS in 1923, unchanged save for ownership markings. No. 485 was built at Derby in 1898 as No. 1669. It received an 'H' boiler in 1907 and was renewed to the '483' class in 1914. Withdrawal was in 1957 as BR No. 40485. No. 518 was built in 1899 as No. 2436, receiving an 'H' boiler in 1907 and renewed to '483' class in 1913. It became BR 40518 and was scrapped in 1956.

Collection Bernard Mathews & National Railway Museum

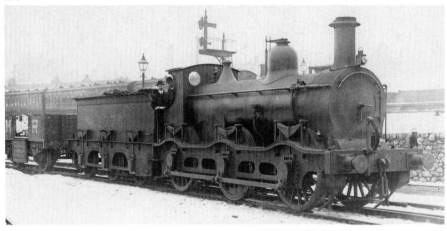

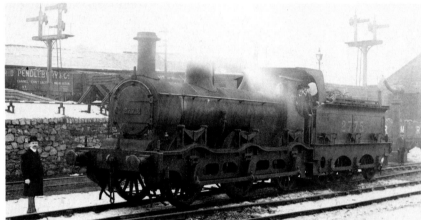

Plates 248, 249 & 250. These three pictures all show Kirtley 0–6–0 goods engines in lined red livery, albeit a bit scruffy in some instances, and carrying their new 1907 series numbers. This simply demonstrates that for a few years after the renumbering, many goods engines remained red. In theory these should have been the vacuum braked examples (see page 151), but clearly some 'steam brake only' examples, like No. 2775 illustrated, retained their red liveries for some considerable time, and in some instances (see *Plate 251*) continued to be repainted in crimson.

Engine No. 2776 was photographed at Buxton in lined Crimson Lake livery but regrettably it is not possible to place an exact date upon this picture, and the Johnson smokebox door and Deeley chimney further complicate matters. The lining is sparse and can only be seen on the tender side panels, cab side, splashers, spring centres, but nowhere else. Built by Neilson in 1871 as Midland Railway No. 916, this locomotive later served with the Railway Opera-

ting Division during the First World War and with No. 2775, returned to work until 1930 when it was withdrawn by the LMS.

Steam braked No. 2775 was also photographed at Buxton (c.1910). Built in 1871 by Neilson Reid as Midland Railway No. 915, this locomotive also served with the ROD during the First World War. In due course, it too returned to serve both the Midland and LMS Railway Company until 1930 when it was withdrawn. Note the tender cab.

Finally, No. 2585 at Leicester, was photographed on 9th April 1910, having arrived on the 2.40 p.m. from Birmingham. This clear example of a vacuum piped goods locomotive in full livery is undoubtedly the cleanest of this particular trio of engines – who said all MR locos were immaculate? Like the others, it does not carry the Midland emblem. No. 2585 was built by the Yorkshire Engine Co. in 1868 as Midland Railway No. 652 and was withdrawn in 1925.
A. G. Ellis & collection Bernard Mathews

Plate 251. We find it rather difficult to explain why this unidentified 'steam brake only' Kirtley goods engine was being repainted in lined crimson in Saltley in 1909. This year can be established exactly so it is clear that some places continued to paint some steam brake only locomotives in the older scheme well after official policy had changed. The lining is to the new simplified Deeley style, as far as can be judged, so it was not a question of this establishment working to outdated specifications. Perhaps they had a good supply of red paint to use up!

Collection Roger Carpenter

(in paint) to the 'pale-ish' colour of the new numbers and can be observed on the restored MR No. 1000 and No. 673 at the National Railway Museum. Interestingly, the LMS reverted to yellow lining in the mid 1930s when, for reasons of further economy, the transfers were changed from gold to chrome yellow. By this time, of course, the LMS had long since removed the numbers from the tender or tank side to the cab or bunker side (from 1928 in fact). However, with only the 'Compounds' remaining in red after 1928, these remarks hardly apply to ex-MR locomotives and in any case we have again gone beyond the purely MR period.

Midland Railway livery was complex. No simple set of rules apply. Instead it is hoped that sufficient pictures have been used within this section, together with the more detailed surveys in Volumes 2 and 3, for modellers either exactly to copy a particular locomotive or to interpret Midland practice for their favoured types. At the very least, this was somewhat variable between individual class members, to say nothing of the variations between different works or outside builders.

In conclusion, one can look at a model or picture of a locomotive and say, the style of painting suggests . . . . but unless a dated photograph actually exists it could be difficult to prove or disprove whether or not some of the interesting variations of the livery which have been described were ever applied to any locomotive other than those recorded photographically. It is likely that they were, but there seems no way of determining which specific engines were involved.

Notwithstanding all the problems which we have tried to identify, both in this running text and, hopefully, our

useful picture captions, we have still tried to rationalise the situation by providing at the end of this chapter a form of tabulated summary of what we feel to be the *basic* trends.

We can only apologise for its complexity and detail, but we do hope that those readers who find the subject as interesting as we do will be able to resolve at least the majority of their doubts. Needless to say, however, should any reader be able to add or indeed disprove our views, we would be pleased to hear from him (via the publisher) so as to be able to incorporate corrections/additions in the later volumes of this series.

We conclude this chapter by reviewing the question of power classification as it affected MR locomotive livery, along with the question of front numberplates and certain other specific details.

FRONT NUMBERPLATES

As part of the Motive Power Re-organisation of the 1905-7 period, already mentioned several times previously, the Midland Railway found it expedient to affix a front numberplate on the smokebox door of its locomotives from c.1906 onwards. This was essentially part of the new control procedures introduced by the company but imparted quite a change to the visual 'look' of the front end.

The numberplate took the form of a cast plate affixed to the smokebox door to enable locomotives to be more speedily identified 'on the road' and 'on shed'. It was most usually associated with the post 1906 'simplified' liveries (usually incorporating the new series numbers as well) but a number of locomotives carried smokebox door plates with pre 1907 numbers, but exceptions did occur. The style

Plates 252 & 253. The fact that some three years elapsed between the 1907 renumbering and the decision to paint *all* goods engines black, meant a considerable number of *vacuum* braked goods locomotives were given the official simplified red livery with the new transfer figures. By this time, the 14″ height numerals were also beginning to appear and in this pair of pictures we give one example each of the two sizes of figures.

The rear view of 0—6—0 No. 3674 carrying 14″ figures is a particularly good picture of the Deeley Crimson Lake livery, and also shows the locomotive number carried on the top plate on the rear of the tender. Note also the 'out of service' toolbox carried across the full width of the tender. Although they are not visible on the picture, by this date toolboxes would probably be on the front of the tender as well — probably in the style of *Plate 121* (page 76). Note also that the spring buckles on the tender springs are lined — a little unusual at this time. There is also a total absence of lining below the running plate on both the locomotive and tender. This poses the question whether the tender frames and engine valance were painted black or red. We believe them to be black with black wheels. No. 3674 was built in 1901 by Kitson & Co. as Midland Railway No. 2645. In 1914 it was to receive an 'H' boiler and ten years later it received a 'G7' Belpaire boiler. It was in this condition that it entered British Railways service and lasted until withdrawal in 1959.

Whilst it has no connection with this story, one of us cannot but have a 'soft spot' for this locomotive. In its Belpaire condition

it was the first class '3F' he ever fired, spending his first week on its footplate working as a bank pilot in the Birmingham area.

The 18″ figures were used on 0—6—0 No. 3809 in lined Crimson Lake livery. Built at Derby in 1906 as No. 279, this picture proves that the 'H' boilered 'Johnson cab' class 3 goods engines, which in 1907 became 3805-3814, were turned out in lined Crimson Lake, thus confirming the reports by contemporary observers mentioned on page 98. Like No. 3674, there is no evidence of lining on the engine valances, and footsteps, or the tender underframes, and we wonder whether this area was all black on goods engines. In 1906 a change in wheel colour from red to black was made and under a glass the wheels on the locomotive appear to be black with no evidence of any yellow line. It is not possible to say what colour the outside of the frames are painted, but in our view it is unlikely to have been other than black. The yellow lining is sparse. It can be seen on the upper and lower cab side panels, cab front, splasher sides and end of the buffer casing, but not on the boiler. This is likely to have been lined front and rear in Deeley style even though it is not possible to see it on the picture. The faintly discernible lining on the tender front and below the top flare suggests that although the locomotive was in a shabby condition when photographed, normal lining for the post 1906 period was employed in all 'above the footplate' areas. No. 3809 received a Belpaire boiler in 1922 and was withdrawn as BR No. 43809 in 1961.

Collection Bernard Mathews

Plates 254 & 255. We conclude the picture survey in this chapter with views showing the definitive versions of the black goods livery adopted after 1910 and again featuring both numeral sizes.

The first view shows class 4 0−6−0 No. 3848, built at Derby in 1917, paired with a Johnson pattern tender bearing 18″ numerals. This picture demonstrates excellently the point made about black shading on black engines on page 156. The first '8' (ahead of the vertical beading) can more clearly be seen to be shaded than any of the other figures, most of which seem quite plain. Seen on its own, this figure might well suggest a lighter tone for the shading, but in company with the other figures which are reflecting the light 'normally', it can be seen to be 'playing tricks'. All four figures, in fact, carried black shading to the right and below. No. 3848 was withdrawn in 1962 as No. 43848.

Class 3 0−6−0T No. 1936 displays the plain black Midland Railway livery with 14″ figures and there would be no evidence of ownership other than on the buffer plank. Under LMS ownership in the pre-1928 period, the LMS freight emblem was placed on the bunker side which caused the removal of the Vulcan Foundry works plate which was in the way. Built in 1902 as No. 2757 and renumbered No. 1936 in 1907, this locomotive received a Belpaire boiler in 1924, and became No. 7236 as part of the 1934 renumbering scheme. Nationalization saw it running as No. 47236 until withdrawal in 1964. Note that as depicted, it carried no visible indication of its power class on the cab side. This feature did not appear on *tank* engines until well into the LMS period.   *W. L. Good*
Collection Bernard Mathews

Plates 256 & 257. The evidence on the colour of cab roofs in the Deeley period is confusing and we are less sure of this aspect that we would like to be. The pictures reproduced here illustrate 4—4—0 'Compound' No. 1021, photographed in 1920, and 4—4—0 No. 365 c.1923, and both appear to confirm that the area between the rainstrips was painted black on the Deeley cab. In *Midland Style* it is recorded that the original Deeley 'Compounds' Nos. 1000-1009 (later 1005-1014) when built had red roofs but that the next series, together with the '990s', had black roofs as indicated in these pictures. However, a further picture of 4—2—2 No. 600 (not included here), which had a Deeley cab, clearly shows this was Crimson Lake all over, and when we enquired at Derby works as long ago as 1965, one of the ex-Midland men was positive that Midland cab roofs were 'always red'. The restored MR 'Compound' has a red roof but No. 673 (4—2—2), although red at the time of writing, is shortly to have a black roof.

Collection David Tee and collection Bernard Mathews

was carried through to the LMS period in 1923 and the figure style was clearly based on the old brass cabside numerals (*Plate 194* and *Fig. 20*).

The basic idea, albeit with a new shaped figure, was adopted by BR in 1948 for all its engines, and Midland enthusiasts can smile benignly at the thought of 'Castles', 'A4s' and Bulleid 'Spam Cans' all carrying emblems inspired by Derby during the Edwardian period!

POWER CLASSIFICATION

Although there were various 19th century schemes for passenger locomotives only, the power classification system adopted in 1905 by the Midland Railway, was to number, in ascending order of power, the freight tender locomotives from 1-3. The arrival in 1911 of 0—6—0s Nos. 3835/6 saw the prototypes of what was to become power class 4 enter traffic, but these two locomotives were at first classified as power class 3 and were still running in June 1913 with this code. It is not known when they were upgraded. This power classification was displayed on the cabside sheets by means of a small brass figure, at first below the brass locomotive running number, but when the locomotives were renumbered in 1907 and the locomotive number moved to the tender side in transfer form, the position of the power

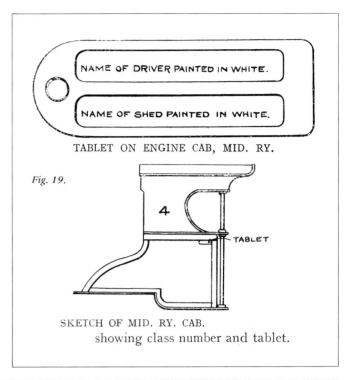

TABLET ON ENGINE CAB, MID. RY.

Fig. 19.

SKETCH OF MID. RY. CAB.
showing class number and tablet.

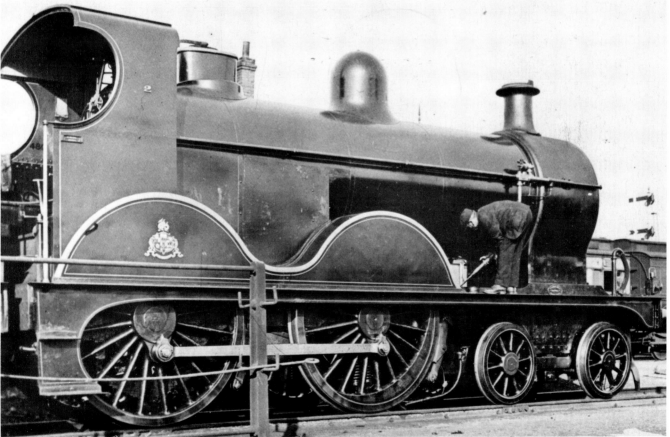

Plate 258. The *Locomotive Magazine*, Volume 20, recorded that it was now Midland Railway practice to attach a small tablet to the cab side containing information required by the guard for making up his journal. It was reported that this practice was introduced by Fowler shortly after his appointment as Chief Mechanical Engineer. We give here a drawing (*Fig. 19*) to show the tablet details, and a picture of an 'H' boilered 4—4—0 No. 480 showing it attached to the cab side. No. 480 was built in 1900 by Beyer Peacock as No. 2588 and received its 'H' boiler in 1905. It remained in this condition until renewal as a '483' class locomotive in 1922 and was finally withdrawn as British Railways No. 40480 in 1954. *Collection Roger Carpenter*

classification number was moved to the upper cab side sheets to leave space for the heraldic emblem.

In 1905 the passenger classification was 1-5 but this was not displayed upon the locomotives and appeared only in the loading books.

In 1906 the previous power classification scheme for passenger locomotives was altered and they were brought into line with the freight classes and numbered 1-3, with the power classification numerals being displayed for the first time upon the upper cab side sheets. The power class 4 was introduced c.1908 for the 'Compounds' and '990' class and this system remained in vogue until the end of the Midland Railway's separate existence. Like the goods engines, the power class was displayed by means of a small brass figure.

Photographic and other evidence suggests that only tender locomotives carried this visible evidence of power classification during the Midland period and it was only during the LMS era that tank locomotives were so numbered. Finally, it should be noted that no locomotive carried the '0' power classification even though this classification could be found in the post grouping loading books.

The MR system was adopted by the LMS and in 1928 the 'P' and 'F' suffix (for passenger and freight) was added and this survived until Nationalization whereupon British Railways adopted this system, with modifications, for all BR locomotives. *En passant*, there was always a visible indication of some sort on the cabside, so it could be said that Midland influence lasted until the very end of steam.

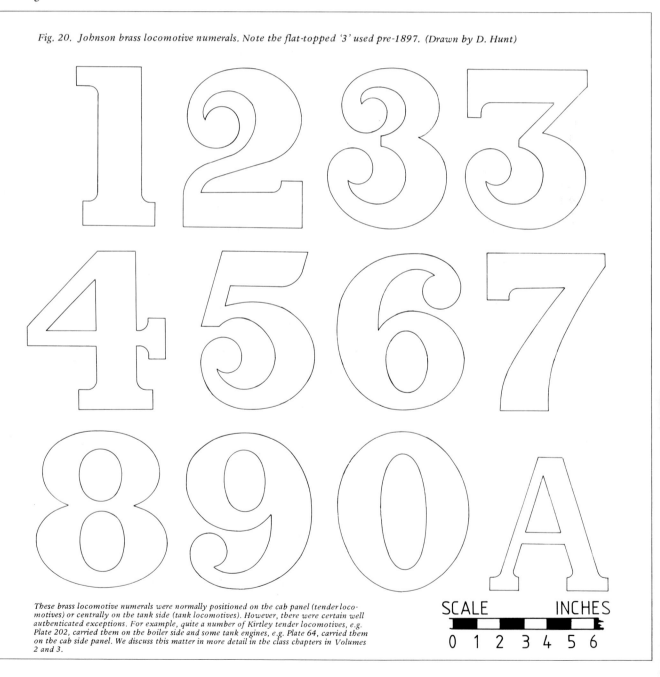

Fig. 20. Johnson brass locomotive numerals. Note the flat-topped '3' used pre-1897. (Drawn by D. Hunt)

These brass locomotive numerals were normally positioned on the cab panel (tender locomotives) or centrally on the tank side (tank locomotives). However, there were certain well authenticated exceptions. For example, quite a number of Kirtley tender locomotives, e.g. Plate 202, carried them on the boiler side and some tank engines, e.g. Plate 64, carried them on the cab side panel. We discuss this matter in more detail in the class chapters in Volumes 2 and 3.

SCALE   INCHES

0 1 2 3 4 5 6

SUMMARY TABLES

NOTES TO BE USED WITH THE SUMMARY TABLES

In Chapters 4-6 we have discussed the various decorative styles to be found on Midland locomotives and these summaries attempt to relate MR Red as a body colour to the most likely arrangement of lining to be found during the various livery style periods. Naturally, there was no lining on black locomotives, and the various photo captions themselves describe what is known of the practices employed when engines were painted in Locomotive Brown/Brick Red (see page 118).

The MR red era commenced in 1883 for all locomotives and continued until 1928, after which only the 'Compounds' retained what was, in effect, the final MR red livery style.

The careful study of pictures suggests that this 45 year period can be divided into the three distinct phases already described:

1883-c.1892   Early Crimson Lake period — essentially the 'green' lining applied to 'red' engines.

c.1892-1905   Full Crimson Lake or 'decorated' period (includes Weatherburn and other variations).

1905-1928   Deeley simplified (including LMS continuation).

The early period was noteworthy for the lack of lining on guard irons, sandboxes, brake hangers etc. The 'decorated' period saw lining applied to areas which hitherto had not been lined and which, in the next livery period, again became unlined: guard irons, sandboxes, framing beneath the smokebox, extra lining on springs, axle ends, etc.

The final style reverted to something approaching the first style but was even less ornate. Fewer boiler lagging bands were lined, and black (on wheels and outsides of frames, etc.) was applied to many parts of the locomotive which hitherto had been red. There is, however, one exception to the 'black frames post-1906' generalisation, and it applies to the inside cylinder 4-4-0s. The use of red to paint the outside of the frame forward of the sandbox was normal practice on these engines and the bottom edge of the frame was edged black and lined yellow.

There is another point where a clear difference exists and this concerns the brake hangers. The various specifications state black, yet pictures show that during the full livery period they were frequently lined out. One can only assume that whilst in the early and simplified period, when they were not lined, they were painted black, but when lined during the full livery period they were red.

Finally, it should be noted that undoubtedly there are exceptions to the details given in these summaries and wherever possible these variations are noted in Volumes 2 and 3.

NOTE: More than one name has been used for certain parts of the locomotive, e.g. footplate. Technically this refers to the floor of the cab area where the crew stand but the term is often used to refer to the 'platform' which is sometimes called the 'running plate'. These three separate descriptions all refer to the flat area in front of the cab alongside the boiler. We hope that readers will realise that we have tried to avoid being over pedantic and have used more than one name where these different terms are clear in context.

SUMMARY TABLE 1 — LINED CRIMSON LAKE TENDER LOCOMOTIVES (ENGINES ONLY)

Boiler and firebox	Crimson Lake. All boiler lagging bands black, fine lined yellow on both sides. There was a short-lived intermediate stage c.1904/5 which saw four boiler bands only double-lined, see No. 863 (*Plate 241*, Chapter 6). Commencing with the 'Compounds' 1010-1019 built in 1906, only the boiler lagging band next to the smokebox and the cab were painted black, lined yellow on one side only. This practice was then applied to all new construction and repaints. The yellow line on the band next to the smokebox was on the side adjacent to the Lake. The angle iron at cab front was black, fine lined yellow on both edges. From 1906 the angle iron was only fine lined on the smokebox side.
Cab side and cab front	Crimson Lake. Edged black, fine yellow line separating black from crimson. Cab sides and cab front were, in the early and full Crimson Lake periods, treated as three separate panels, but in the simplified era this was not so, and the vertical lining on the front corner of the cab was omitted. Fronts of cabs with rounded eaves were unlined at *all* times.
Cab roof	Rounded eaves cabs — Crimson Lake up to rainstrips, black between rainstrips. Some could have been red all over. Earlier style Johnson cabs usually had black roofs but some were crimson. (See captions)
Footplate angle (sometimes called platform angle) and/or outside of outside frames	Crimson Lake edged black on lower edge. Fine yellow line separating black from crimson. Not applied during simplified era to goods engines which retained lined Crimson Lake livery. Some 4-2-2s had lining on top and bottom of the outside frame. Frame cut-out slots were edged black, fine lined yellow around the edges of the cut-outs.

166

Plate 259. This general view of Derby works paint shops shows a mixture of locomotives and tenders being repaired.

National Railway Museum

Splasher side	Crimson Lake edged black. Fine yellow line separating black from crimson. Pre c.1906 many had polished brass beading. From March 1906 beading was often overpainted black, but locomotives with brass beading were evident for many years thereafter. With polished brass treatment black/yellow edging was located 'inside' the beading on the splasher side itself.
Splasher top	Crimson Lake until c.1898. Post 1898 black. Some locomotives, 4–2–2 and 'Compounds', had red panel edged black, fine lined yellow c.1898-1905. (See *Plate 216* Chapter 5)
Footstep supports	Crimson Lake. Edged black with fine yellow line separating black from crimson.
Footsteps	Black.
Outside cylinders	Crimson Lake. End covers polished steel with a black band at each end of the cylinder side. Later a yellow line was used between black and MR Red. First Johnson 'Compounds' had a 'rectangular' lined panel on cylinder cover rather than front/rear lining.
Smokebox	Black. Some locomotives with drum head smokeboxes had a fine yellow line on the smokebox top, around the base of the chimney, and also on a few, a yellow circumferential line about one inch or so back from the smokebox front. Smokebox saddle '990' class only – Black.
Footplate or platform top	Black.
Outside of inside frames	Crimson Lake edged black, fine lined yellow. Treatment variable but generally on the bottom edge of the frames sometimes around the cut-outs. Discontinued during the Deeley simplified period when painted plain black other than inside cylinder 4–4–0s which retained lined red frames forward of the leading sand-box until the 1928 livery changes.
Inside of inside frames	Vermilion.
Axlebox faces	4–2–2s' driving wheels bright metal finish. Others Crimson Lake, edged black, fine lined yellow.
Axlebox guides	Black.
Wheels	Crimson Lake. Tyres black, fine yellow line separating black and crimson. C.1906 wheels began to be painted black with yellow line on the inside of each tyre. Single yellow line on axle end during full livery period with black axle ends.
Bogie frames	Crimson Lake edged black, fine lined yellow.
Coupling and connecting rods	Polished steel. Fluting, if present, usually painted black. Exceptions occurred especially during post Deeley period.
Outside cranks	Vermilion edged black, fine lined yellow*.
Buffer planks	Vermilion edged black, fine lined yellow. The initials 'MR' appeared in either serif or sans serif at all times.
Buffer casing	Vermilion. Rim black with fine yellow line separating black/vermilion.
Chimney	Black.
Dome	Crimson Lake. Pre 1905 the base of the dome casing was fine lined yellow with black below the yellow line to the edge of the casing. Very infrequently two yellow lines separated by a black band were used.
Safety valve casing	Polished brass. However, some were painted from 1906 onwards, depending on type (see class chapters). Some locomotives had lining on the firebox around the base of the safety valve casing during the pre 1905 period.
Hand rails	Varied. Frequently polished steel but at times painted.
Cab interior	Top half grained oak edged black/yellow. Roof cream. Bottom half crimson, frequently edged black, fine lined yellow. Post c.1907 (goods locomotives only) bottom half of the cab black, no lining. Passenger tender classes had upper half of cab edged black and lined yellow. Number painted (tender locomotives only) in black inside the upper half of the cab side sheets. Exact position varied.
Brakework	Brake hangers. Full Crimson Lake period frequently crimson edged black, fine lined yellow. During early Crimson Lake probably black without lining and then black again during Deeley simplified period. Remainder black.
Springs above platform	Crimson Lake. Frequently top leaf was black with fine yellow line. Often the bottom leaf was black, also lined yellow. At times no lining appeared at all. During the post 1906 period springs were usually all black.
Spring buckle	Pre 1906 – usually red, edged black, fine lined yellow; post 1906 – black.
Spring pillar	Pre 1906 – often red, edged black and fine lined yellow; post 1906 – black.
Sandbox	Crimson Lake and c.1890-1905 edged black and fine lined yellow on three faces (front, outer and rear) or just on the outside face. Pre c.1890 and post c.1905 probably not lined at all. Plain red or black pre 1890, probably black only post 1905. Style of lining varied considerably.

Fig. 21 shows two styles of 'MR' and the 14 inch (excluding shading) numeral transfers, introduced in 1905, and reproduced here at a scale of 1 inch to 1 foot. Shading colours on the 'MR were to the left (shown dotted) blue with white highlights, and to the right (shown as horizontal lines) black. The numeral transfers were always gilt with fine white highlights and black shading. Based on Derby original drawings and drawn by Peter Chatham.

Guard-irons	Full Crimson Lake period — Crimson Lake, usually edged black, fine lined yellow on outer face, black on inner face. Some locomotives lined on both faces. Pre c.1890 plain red or black. Post c.1905 unlined plain red then black.
Axles	Vermilion. Axle outer ends, where visible, black, frequently lined yellow around end of axle itself during the full livery period additional to normal wheel centre lining.
Firebox back plate	Black. Valve wheels and cock handles polished brass. Reversing screw or lever polished steel. Regulator handle polished steel. Pipework generally polished metal, copper and/or brass.
Whistle	Polished brass.
Smokebox door	Black. Hinges sometimes polished steel. Locking handle — sometimes polished steel.
Maker's plate	Pre 1909 background Vermilion. Post 1909 MR Red. Sometimes a yellow line was outside of the edge of the plate (Weatherburn practice).
RHS of locomotive only	On the right-hand side of locomotives equipped to work vacuum fitted trains there is a large ejector. The pipe which runs horizontally from the cab could be painted Crimson Lake or could be polished steel. The vertical pipe from the platform to the base of the ejector could be polished copper or painted crimson. The large ejector was made of brass and was sometimes left in an unpainted condition. This apparatus was used to 'eject' the air from the train pipes in order to create a vacuum and make the brakes come off.
End train pipe (metal parts only)	Crimson Lake.

Midland Style records that pre 1895 white lining was used on outside cranks but the authors are not entirely certain this is correct.

SUMMARY TABLE 2 — LINED CRIMSON LAKE TENDERS

Kirtley tenders
Sides and back

From the early Crimson Lake period Kirtley tenders were lined black and yellow below the top and above the bottom rows of horizontal rivets and this style of lining was apparently not altered during the entire period when these tenders were painted Crimson Lake. In addition the top beading was edged black with a fine yellow line adjacent to the Crimson Lake. At both ends of the tender vertical black lines edged yellow joined the horizontal lines. These vertical lines at the rear were usually on the corner of the tender and so provided the division between the side and rear panels. It should be noted that the style of construction and position of rivets on these tenders varied considerably and *Plate 148* provides a good example of the lining treatment for a Kirtley tender. It also shows the position of 'MR' when applied from c.1892 onwards.

Johnson Tenders
Tender side

Crimson Lake. Pre 1905 there were inside the flat side beading normally two round cornered painted 'panels' (one *only* on some 0–6–0 locomotives), marked by a black band, fine lined yellow on both sides. However, there is evidence to suggest that at least one passenger locomotive had the flat beading additionally painted black, but this practice did not become widespread until after c.1904 when the 'panels' were abolished, and instead the beading itself was always painted black normally with a yellow line where the adjacent colour was Crimson Lake. Extreme top edge beading was black with a fine yellow line below, and in the pre 1905 period a fine yellow line was sometimes placed above the top of the horizontal beading on the flat part of the tender side where the 'flare' met the vertical side panelling (see *Plate 203*). It would appear that during the full livery period the lower half of the bottom horizontal beading adjacent to the platform was painted black and fine lined yellow to balance the similar line under the flare (again see *Plate 203*). This line was continued around the back of the tender and along the other side. On some tenders the front vertical edge of the side panel was black edged, fine lined yellow. Some, e.g. 2950 gallon tenders, did not have a lower horizontal side and end beading, and a black band was painted where the beading would have been. Commencing with the Sharp Stewart built 4–4–0s, Nos. 2183-2202 of 1892, the practice of placing 'MR' on the tender tank sides began. Each letter was placed centrally in the two tender side panels. The letters were almost always serif and this practice continued until c.1905 when the brass cabside numerals began to be removed and the locomotive number was displayed on the tender by using nominally 18″ or 14″ gold shaded black transfers. Where the vertical beading was present in the centre of the side, any running number with an odd number of digits was always placed with the extra figure to the rear of the beading in such a way that the beading was midway between the figures on either side of it. Single digit numbers were always placed to the rear of the beading. The horizontal spacing between the figures when the 18″ height was used was as follows: Between the centres of any two '1's — 16″; between the centre of '1' and any other figure — 20″; between the centres of any other two figures — 24″. With 14″ high figures the spacing was: centre of any two '1's — 13″; between '1' and any other figure — 15″; between any other figures — 19″. *Plate 147* provides a good example of lining treatment for Johnson tenders.

Tender back   Crimson Lake. One normally round cornered 'panel' formed by a black band, fine lined by yellow both sides. Post 1904 the beading itself was painted black with a fine yellow line adjacent to the Crimson Lake and the 'panel' was suppressed. The extreme top beading was painted black with a fine yellow line and below adjacent to the Crimson Lake. In some cases, the top of the horizontal flat beading at the junction of 'flare' and vertical panel was fine lined yellow, but not always.

Straight-sided tenders   These tenders did not appear until the simplified livery period and post 1905 were red with the beading painted black, fine lined yellow in a single rectangular shaped panel on each side and also on the rear. Upper side panels were separated from main rectangular portion. The locomotive number was displayed on the tender side using 18″ numbers central top to bottom and left to right.

Footplate or platform angle   Crimson Lake. Edged black on lower edge. Fine yellow line separating black from crimson. Not applied during simplified era to the goods engines which retained Crimson Lake lined livery.

Outside of tender frames   Crimson Lake. Edged black with fine yellow line separating black from Crimson Lake. Frame cut-out slots were similar to locomotives.

Plate 259A. Photographed in 1905, this picture should be compared with *Plate 129* which illustrates the other end of the same tender. While the photograph was undoubtedly taken to illustrate 'maximum coaling', it also affords a very good view of livery practice of the period, together with the front 'end' of the tender detail. One of the authors clearly recalls firing locomotives coupled to this style of tender and cursed them because he could not get back into the coal space without climbing up and so becoming 'out of gauge'.

National Railway Museum

Spring above and below the footplate	
Buffer plank	As tender locomotives.
Buffer casing	
Handrails	
Tender top	Black.
Tender front	Pre 1905 Crimson Lake edged black, fine lined yellow. Post 1905 frequently as pre 1905. This scheme applied to all tenders including those with built in tool-boxes.
Toolbox	Pre 1905 when on the tender rear they were probably painted black. When on the tender front some were crimson, edged black and fine lined yellow. During the simplified livery period separate toolboxes were almost certainly black.
Inside of frames	
Wheels	
Brakework	
Guard irons	As tender locomotives.
Axles	
Footstep support	
Coal rails	Black.
Axlebox guides	Black.
Axlebox face	Crimson Lake edged black. Fine yellow line separating black/Crimson Lake. Polished brass lids. Deeley simplified livery era the axlebox face, guides, springs and spring pillars were black.
Capacity number and works plates	As tender locomotives.
End train pipe	
'MR' on tender back and buffer plank	Prior to c.1898 the initials 'MR' appeared in sans serif on the rear buffer planks but from that date they were transferred to the back of the tender tank. This practice lasted until c.1905 when it was discontinued, and 'MR' appeared only on the leading buffer plank of locomotives.

SUMMARY TABLE 3 — LINED CRIMSON LAKE TANK LOCOMOTIVES

Tank engines were generally painted as tender locomotives except where the obvious configuration of the locomotive differed. These differences are noted below.

Boiler and firebox	As tender locomotives apart from intermediate stage. From c.1906 not every tank locomotive had the angle iron next to the cab front lined.
Cab side and cab front	As tender locomotives except for 0—6—4Ts which had lining right round the cab fronts adjacent to the roof and cab sides but not adjacent to the firebox and tanks.
Cab rear	Crimson Lake edged black, fine yellow line separating black from Crimson Lake. In the simplified period the separate back panel was omitted from 'closed cab' locomotives and the lining was carried round under the roof only.
Footplate or platform angle	As tender locomotives until 1906. Thereafter unlined. Unlined footplate angle was a notable feature of red Midland tank locos in both MR post 1906 and the LMS period.
Tank top	Black.
Tank sides	Crimson Lake edged black, fine yellow line separating black/crimson. Brass locomotive number flanked by gilt 'MR'. From 1907 renumbering, brass number replaced by gold shaded black numbers and 'MR' omitted.
Bunker side	Crimson Lake edged black, fine yellow line separating black/Crimson Lake.
Bunker rear/tank front	Crimson Lake edged black. Fine yellow line separating black/Crimson Lake.
Coal rails	Black.
Condenser pipes	Crimson Lake.
'MR' on bunker rear	Prior to c.1898 the initials 'MR' appeared in sans serif on the rear of the bunker but from that date they were transferred to the rear buffer plank until c.1905 when this practice was discontinued. From 1912 the absorbed ex-LTSR locomotives were lettered at both ends of the locomotive. (See Volume 2)

Plate 260. There was a need to regularly wash out the boilers of steam locomotives in order to remove the sludge, etc., which accumulated in them. This picture illustrates 4—4—0 No. 1043 being washed out at an unknown location. An interesting livery point is the fully burnished side and connecting rods. Normally with the Deeley livery, the recessed 'flutes' were painted black.

National Railway Museum

CHAPTER SEVEN

WORKING ON MIDLAND LOCOMOTIVES

BY R.J. ESSERY

MODERNISATION of Midland Railway engine sheds did not really commence until the mid 1930s when, under the LMS, mechanical coaling and ash handling plants began to be installed, together with water softening plants and improved shed yard layouts. Notwithstanding these improvements, it is probably true to state that a fireman from the 1950s and 1960s would be very much 'at home' in an Edwardian Midland Railway environment and would almost certainly find some aspects of his work easier in the earlier period. For example, all the tools would have been locked upon the locomotive and he would not encounter the problems experienced by firemen in the early British Railways era when there was a considerable shortage of vital equipment. Furthermore, unrepaired war damage, including sheds without roofs, did not exist. Nevertheless, not all old Midland Railway engine sheds were modernised by the LMS or British Railways, and it is probably true to say that the 'engine servicing conditions' on many of the preserved lines closely approximate those which existed in the 'good old days' of hand coaling and primitive engine disposal facilities.

Preparation and disposal, collectively called servicing, occupied a considerable amount of time, and no doubt this practice did not alter overmuch. However, during my footplate service I did not ask as many questions of old Midland men as I would if the opportunity arose again. Therefore many aspects of Midland Railway arrangements and workings are unknown to me. One firm recollection is the remark made by an old Midland driver, who started firing in 1912. His first driver took a piece of chalk from his pocket, drew a line down the centre of the footplate, and told him 'This is my half and that's your half'. Having made this statement on the first occasion that they came together, he never spoke to the fireman again! Certainly my impression was that, by and large, 'North Western' drivers were better 'mates' than those who came from the old Midland Railway.

Plate 261. Another view of No. 1043 on the same occasion but this time with the water being fed through the firebox washout plugs.

National Railway Museum

Plate 262. 4–4–0 No. 2587 being prepared. Note the bowler-hatted driver using a long feeder while oiling the inside slide bars and associated oil cups. The locomotive has been fully coaled. Note the piles of ash from smokebox and fireboxes of previously serviced locomotives. No. 2587 was built in 1900 by Beyer Peacock, reboilered in 1905 with an 'H' boiler, and two years later became No. 479, being renewed to the '483' class in 1917.   *National Railway Museum*

It would perhaps be of interest to readers to outline the sequence of daily servicing operations back in time at a Midland shed. The first job for any crew was to 'book on' and then to read the notices which were displayed within the 'lobby'. This area contained the enginemen's rosters which gave details of their work, notices of engineering work, new or temporary speed restrictions, etc. In addition, they might receive a 'job card' which was a metal backed wallet containing a thick piece of paper upon which was printed the details of their work. Moving out into the shed area, they would find the engine arrangements board which gave details of the locomotives allocated to the various jobs and, in large sheds, their location.

Preparation of a locomotive is a straightforward affair. In the Midland era all the engine tools were locked upon the locomotive and one presumes that the key was drawn from the stores. Many of the tools had the locomotive number stamped upon them and on page 113 a full list is given. Having found his locomotive, the fireman's first concern was to test the water gauge and establish that there was sufficient water in the boiler. Many Midland locomotives only had one gauge glass, supplemented by trial cocks (see page 68). He would then check the boiler and smokebox for any leaks by examining the firebox seams, tubeplates, fusible plugs, washout plugs, etc. While the engine was left standing in the shed the fire was banked up

under the firebox door, and, assuming all was well, this had to be spread across the grate. This would be done by using one of the fire-irons which were carried on the tender or on top of the side-tanks. The rake was the usual choice although the back of the clinker shovel was a useful alternative. The build-up of the fire depended upon the job and, of course, the class of locomotive, but regardless of these factors other tasks were to ensure that the sandboxes were filled and the sand was running freely, that the smokebox door was closed securely and the water gauge lamp and headlamps were filled and trimmed. Another of the fireman's responsibilities was to fill the 'sight feed' lubricator whose correct name was 'hydrostatic displacement feed lubricator', which was mounted on the fireman's side of the cab. Other tasks included clearing all the char from the platform to avoid ash blowing back into the crew's eyes while they were on the road, cleaning the windows, 'trimming' the coal, and generally cleaning up the footplate using the slaking pipe if fitted. The final task before leaving the shed was to top up the water in the tender or tanks. While all this was being done and the steam pressure was rising, the driver oiled and examined the locomotive for faults.

The opposite of preparation was 'disposal'. When returning with the locomotive to the shed, the crew tried to run the fire down to ease their task and avoid unnecessary waste of fuel. There was an art in arriving with such a

Plates 263 & 264. 2—4—0 No. 203 is seen taking water in these two pictures. From personal experience one author can testify that it did not make good sense to allow 'the bag' to droop when full of water — it caused a big splash when the bag was dropped. Note the water control lever. This was frequently located in a separate unit at ground level. One other aspect associated with water columns is not evident in these pictures. This was the frost fire, a brazier which was kept alight during cold weather to prevent the water from freezing.

National Railway Museum

Plate 265. 0–6–0 No. 2359 being coaled at Toton in July 1922. Here coal was loaded into the tubs which were tipped into the tender below. As the coal piled into the tender it was trimmed by the crew. *Collection Bernard Mathews*

Plate 266. 0–6–0 No. 2435 at Peterborough in August 1930. In this picture the fireman is on top of the tender levelling the coal. 'Trimming' was the normal term employed for this. *Collection Ken Nunn*

minimal fire and yet with the water level in the boiler and steam pressure high. The sequence of disposal generally was to top up the tank (but only if the level was low, since it would be done prior to departing from the depot for the next turn of duty), coal, clean the fire, rake out the ashpan and empty the smokebox.

Coaling in Midland days would have taken more time than with the aid of mechanical coaling stages. The coal was shovelled by shedmen and coalmen from the wagon into tubs, and tipped from tubs onto the tenders (see *Plates 265-267*) and 'trimmed'. With the coaling complete, the fire would either be cleaned or dropped. Cleaning the fire involved carefully searching through it with fire-irons to find any clinker which had formed. Depending on the coal and conditions, this frequently clogged the firebars, sometimes all across the grate, thus preventing the passage of air through the fire and seriously impairing combustion. This was a long wearisome task, particularly at the end of a duty, but clinker was far easier to remove while it was still hot. There were two ways to do this. One method was to shovel out all the ash and clinker, throwing it onto the ground in piles alongside (see *Plate 262*) or alternatively three or four firebars could be pulled up in order to leave a space through which you could push all the unwanted fire, ash and clinker into the ashpan, which then had to be emptied quickly before any distortion took place with the heat. The firebars would be replaced by a 'bar boy' who would use a tool which was like a large pair of tongs to grip

Plate 267. 0–6–0 No. 23011 being coaled at Kettering in July 1948. Note the 'weather protection' for the coalmen in this picture when compared with the earlier views. *H. C. Casserley*

them. This task was completed at some time prior to the crew arriving to prepare the locomotive for its next term of duty.

Having cleaned the fire, the ashpan was cleaned by raking it out. Standing in a pit, armed with a long handled rake, this was a dirty and miserable job, particularly if the wind was blowing the wrong way.

The final job was to clean out the smokebox and this was done by opening the door and shovelling it out (see *Plate 268*).

Plate 268. The task of cleaning out the smokebox was one which the author frequently carried out during his railway service. 4–4–0 No. 2425 is seen at Leeds c.1902. In 1912 it became No. 507, was given an 'H' boiler, and, of course, renewed to '483' class.

Authors' collection

Plate 269. This view shows 'Compound' No. 1036 at Kentish Town in March 1934. Judging by the depleted coal supply on the tender, the authors assume that it is in the process of being 'put away' and the driver is walking around the framing carrying out an inspection before 'booking off'.

Collection Bernard Mathews

Having completed these tasks, the locomotive could be stabled in the shed or in the yard as directed by the shed foreman. At large sheds a set of marshalling men shunted locomotives as required.

My railway career began in the summer of 1947 just before Nationalization. When I was a child, my family had lived within sight and sound of the GWR's North Warwickshire line from Tyseley Junction to Stratford-upon-Avon. Many happy hours were spent 'sitting on the fence watching the trains go by', and later, when we moved closer to the centre of Birmingham to Small Heath, the temptation to spend summer evenings on the bridge at Small Heath & Sparkbrook station overlooking Bordesley sidings was too great, and so these actions helped to produce, by virtue of lack of attention to homework, a poor academic result when I left school.

With this strong GWR background, it was not surprising that, having decided upon a footplate career, my steps should take me to Tyseley. However, during my train-watching period I had not been 100 per cent faithful to the GWR. Several Saturday visits during 1941-44 to Tamworth, where the old LNWR main line was crossed by the 'Midland' Derby-Birmingham railway, are never to be forgotten, with the seemingly endless procession of trains passing through. In addition, there were visits to Saltley shed, but in the end it was Tyseley where I started and where the disappointments began.

In retrospect, Tyseley was everything I should have expected from the GWR — orderly and timeless. Two shifts

of cleaners worked week and week about under the charge of a foreman cleaner and the engines remained in the shed long enough for them to be cleaned. If I recall correctly, the 4—6—0 'Halls' and 'Grange' classes were 12-hour engines, whilst the 2—6—2Ts of the '51XX' class were 8-hour engines. This meant that a gang of four cleaners was allowed 3 or 2 hours respectively to clean a locomotive using oil and cotton waste. We engaged in the usual tricks that cleaners have done since railways began, and eagerly awaited the time when we would go out firing — but there was a snag. Down in the Welsh Valleys there was a never ending supply of cleaners, all senior to the local Birmingham men at Tyseley, and every time there was a vacancy for a fireman, along came yet another Welshman to fill the need. This, of course, led to discontent. Then the stories began to circulate around the shed. Saltley did not have a supply of Welshmen, just a shortage of firemen, so the story went — after four weeks' cleaning you were 'on the road'.

Deciding that a life on the footplate was more important than my affection for the GWR, I went to Saltley to inquire if these stories were true, and was told that if I gave in my notice at Tyseley and cared to report on Monday week at 8.00 a.m. I could start as a cleaner. So, in the summer of 1947, I began again as an engine cleaner at Saltley — thus was born my love for Midland Railway locomotives.

The four week story was true. It took just that amount of time for me to become passed for firing and those four weeks flew by. I think I spent two days 'cleaning locomotives' and even so my 'gang' never finished one because the crew always arrived to prepare it for its next turn of duty. This was the essential difference between Tyseley and Saltley. Although it is nearer forty than thirty years ago, the memory of my arrival at Saltley is firmly impressed upon my mind. Walking up the slope to the shed at Duddeston Road, pushing my bicycle a little before 8.00 a.m., I was amazed by the scene of activity. Smoke, steam, noise, and engines, engines, engines, always coming and going. Tyseley was a big shed but nowhere as active as Saltley and, whilst it is probably unjust to the GWR, my impression was that whereas at Tyseley the locomotives spent hours doing nothing between turns of duty, at Saltley there were never sufficient locomotives to go around or enough space to stable them on a Sunday afternoon.

People see railways through many different eyes, but to me they spell out one single theme — industry, noise, smoke, steam, multiple tracks, yards and freight — but then, that was the Midland Railway in Birmingham.

As far as I recall, after the first week, which was either trying to clean locomotives, mostly the numbers only, or labouring in the yard around the coal hopper, collecting spilled coal and moving ashes, the second and third weeks were spent 'in the stores'. These two weeks were one of days and one of nights issuing materials and supplies. This in itself was interesting and helpful in understanding the procedures at the shed. For example, the prized possession of LMS footplate men was 'a new white cloth'. Whereas the GWR men used cotton waste, at Saltley we were issued with three new cloths and three 'washed cloths' per week. It is interesting to recall a very experienced engineman who came from one of 'the other British railways' condemn cotton waste as being a prime cause of problems because strands of it could prevent clacks seating correctly, for instance. I have only heard this from one source, but he was a very experienced engineman. Monday, Wednesday and Friday were 'new cloth' days, and Tuesday, Thursday, Saturday, and, of course, Sunday, were 'washed cloth' days. Soft and white, a new cloth was prized. As the men handed in their old cloths and received the day's issue, I ticked their paycheck number in my register, a duty performed between supplying various oils, firing shovels, lamps, spanners, etc. When a locomotive came onto the shed, the idea was that the slaking pipe, coal pick, fire irons, clinker shovel, dart, rake and oil cans remained on the locomotive, whilst the bucket, firing shovel, four spanners, tin of detonators and headlamps were taken to the stores. At this time, c.1950, the hand brush was the fireman's personal property! No doubt the theory was that since every locomotive was not in service at the same time, the railway could run with less sets of tools than there were locomotives — but the theory didn't work! By midday Monday the stores would be out of stock of so many items that firemen preparing locomotives would stand close to the bridge at Duddeston Road ready to leap aboard locomotives (coming onto the shed to be disposed) so as to be able to take what they needed. This search could at times include not only the tools, which should have been in the stores, but all the above mentioned items that should have been on the locomotive. One other 'tool' was also in urgent demand — a 'seat', preferably more

than one. Class '3' and '4' locomotives would leave Derby works with wooden tops to the lockers inside the cab, two on the class '3s' and one on the class '4s', but within a short period of arriving at Saltley (or any other shed), steamraisers would smash the seats to provide kindling wood for steam raising — so from that point until the next trip to works, 'seats' were needed for the locomotive crew. I often wondered why the works did not provide a metal top to the lockers with a piece of wood attached to it. At least this way steamraisers would probably have left it alone.

My fourth week was spent at school. Actually it was only during the mornings and 'school' was a room at Saltley station, where for the first four days we were instructed by one of the two 'firing instructors' at Saltley. They were also locomotive inspectors and our class of about twenty cleaners was given a basic course on railway work and firing duties. As the only member of the class who had not come 'off the street' and who therefore knew something about railways, I revelled in that week. At a real school my performance would probably have been rated an E grade, but at Saltley I was 'top of the class' and for a few brief hours tasted the sweet smell of success which had, until that time, eluded me in the classroom. After all, who else in that class could tell, let alone explain, the difference between stop and distant signals, ground and calling on signals, and explain what the various headlamp codes were?

The final day was 'practical'. It took place in Lawley Street goods yard and comprised every member of the class coupling up and uncoupling screw couplings, connecting vacuum hoses and then moving onto a locomotive to work the injectors, test water gauge glasses, etc. What we were not allowed to do was to put coal onto the fire. Twenty of us doing that would have been much too much for the class '2' goods engine's firebox to hold without 'blowing off' for hours once the coal started to burn through. When the practical tests were over, we trooped over the shedmaster's office and one by one were taken in to see the 'Great Man'. A few brief words of introduction were followed by two questions, one on 'Rule 55', the other, in my case, concerned protecting the train with detonators. A brief word of congratulation and I, along with the others, became a passed cleaner — i.e. engine cleaners who were passed to act as firemen.

In theory we only went out firing if there was work until having completed, I think, 313 firing turns, when we became registered firemen and could then always draw firemen's pay regardless of what we did. As cleaners our pay was £4 12s 0d per week, whereas a fireman's pay started at £5 3s 0d. As passed cleaners we received firemen's rates only when actually firing but, in actual fact, I never did anything other than firing turns for the remainder of my career on the footplate. For the record, the top rate fireman's basic pay was £5 17s 0d and the driver's pay started at £6 and went up to £6 12s 0d. Overtime was on top of these rates and it varied according to the time of day. Night rate was duty between 10.00 pm and 6.00 am and was worth 'time and a quarter'. Sunday rate was worth 'time and three-quarters' regardless of the number of hours worked. Day rate was paid for duty between 6.00 am and

10.00 pm and we worked a guaranteed eight hours a day. Overtime during day rate hours paid 'time and a quarter', and overtime on night rate paid 'time and a half', with all Sunday work at 'time and three-quarters'. With eight hours work guaranteed from booking on time (and overtime paid at the relevant rates when applicable), there was in addition, a mileage rate. This was based upon the rule that 130 miles constituted a day's work and one received an hour's pay for each additional 15 miles worked. So, for example, on the Carlisle run (which was about 220 miles) you could get $90 \div 15 = 6$ hours extra pay, but if you 'lost your path' and did four hours overtime then you lost two-thirds of your mileage bonus and it wasn't so profitable. However, mileage jobs were only in the top links. The rates were altered during the early 1950s, and you even received a bonus for booking on during a Saturday afternoon. Whilst the latter rates are not so clear in my memory, the c.1948 figures given above are deeply impressed, never to be forgotten. Finally, there were rest days. You were booked to work two Sundays in twelve weeks, plus six days one week and five days the next (5½ day week).

Because this chapter deals with my experiences with Midland locomotives and I have taken this to cover locomotives of Midland Railway origin or design, I will not dwell too deeply on my first trip which was with a class '8F' 2-8-0 No. 8010. This was a shunting and trip job at Washwood Heath. My outstanding memory of that trip was the run down to the 'up' sidings at Washwood Heath, the bewildering array of signals and the feeling that I would never learn what they all meant. My second day was with a Midland design locomotive, a standard class '4F' No. 4525. At first Fred Aish, my driver, refused to take me with him 'on the main line' and whilst, at the time, I resented this attitude, I can understand his feelings. Not only was I green, I was *very* green. However, he relented and we went to Landor Street Junction to relieve the Gloucester men who were on the Westerleigh (Bristol) to Water Orton express goods. Actually, it wasn't too bad. The Gloucester men had built up a fire which not only took us to Water Orton but also back to Saltley without my touching the firing shovel. Putting water into the boiler was easy. The exhaust injector worked beautifully and we reached the shed in good order. Fred cleaned the fire — I lacked the skill or knowledge — but he made sure that I cleaned out the smokebox and raked out the ash pan. These were very filthy jobs that remained with most steam locomotives until the end.

However, the run to Water Orton introduced me to the class '4' goods engine. Love them or hate them, you couldn't as a Midland Division man, ignore them — there were too many in service for that, at first, and for a long time I hated them. They were difficult to fire, or rather to maintain with a good head of steam, and I just couldn't get the hang of them. No wonder they were disliked by the majority of non Midland LMS locomotive crews. Mind you, I could claim that it wasn't all my fault. Once I went onto the main line, my first driver was Charlie Smith, and his idea of driving was to run with the locomotive 'wound back'. This in itself reduced the exhaust draw on the fire and that didn't help

since usually I had too thick a fire. Nevertheless, we sometimes had good trips with class '4s'. Another mate, Charlie R. . . . , was reputed to be the worst fireman Saltley had ever produced, so I didn't exactly gain much from my year with him — but then, with a new mate, Arthur Thorpe, it all came together.

During our first week, we relieved a set of Gloucester men at Bromsgrove with a Bristol-Washwood Heath through freight. I climbed aboard and the Gloucester fireman said, "She's a good 'un" — and that was it. I opened the firedoors and some of the fire fell onto the footplate. The locomotive was No. 43940 and it was fitted with the Midland type of firedoors. I had never seen a class 4's fire made up like this. It rose up and I couldn't see the top of it. It was a mountain of hot burned through fire. I now know that there was virtually nothing at the front, with the fire sloping down from the apex, which left space between the fire and the bottom of the brick arch as well as leaving sufficient space to clear the deflector plate. Naturally, the back corners were well packed up.

While I was trying to grasp all this, the signals came off and whistling up we were away. Discarding the inclination to 'put some fire on' (note the expression — not 'put some coal on'), I 'boxed her up' (closed the firehole doors), left a little space for 'top air' (secondary air), and decided to see what happened. I adjusted the injector and as we went up the bank the needle stayed 'on the red line', so much so that I tapped the boiler pressure gauge just because I didn't believe it, and somehow formed the theory that the needle was stuck. 'Glued to the red line' was a common expression but not with a class '4' — impossible! Impossible or not, it was actually happening and, whilst the remainder of that journey is somewhat blurred in my memory, I do recall breasting the summit of Blackwell and, as my mate eased up, the safety valves lifted. Fortunately we went main line to King's Norton and I didn't touch the fire. We were not checked and went straight down the bank from King's Norton, making our first halt at Landor Street Junction. Here we were held up a few minutes and then released to go down to Duddeston Road, then across 'the main' into the Lawley Street goods lines, from which we rolled down to Washwood Heath. Arriving on the goods lines, we were soon at the top of the bank and, being uncoupled from our train, ran light engine to Saltley. During this entire period all I did was to spread the fire with the rake, I never touched the firing shovel. We disposed of the locomotive and went home. It all made me think. Maybe this was the way to fire the class '4'.

A few weeks later we came round to our prize job. It was the 3.55 (. means a.m., and / means p.m. in footplate language) express freight from Washwood Heath to Bristol. We normally worked it to Gloucester and were booked to return with an empty wagon train. At this time, 1951, this job was booked to be worked by a class '4F' 0-6-0. Booking on time was 2.40, 'ring off' the shed at 3.25, light engine to Washwood Heath West End and depart at 3.55.

A beautiful June morning saw me arrive at Saltley to book on a few minutes after 2.0. Frank, the foreman's assistant, probably raised an eyebrow at the sight of one of these 'young firemen' giving 'the company' so much time, but I doubt if I saw it. If I was to leave Washwood Heath with my fire 'Gloucester' fashion, I needed time and the 45 minutes allowed to prepare a class '4' locomotive was not sufficient.

Signing my card 2.40, I glanced at the notices and saw nothing to delay me. Round to the engine diagram board and a quick glance told me all I needed to know. 438XX was in No. 2 shed. This was the locomotive allocated for the 3.55 'Maltese' to Bristol. I should perhaps pause to explain the term 'Maltese'. Certain express freight trains were described in the WTT (Working Time Table) with a Maltese cross, which meant that the first four vehicles that were coupled to the locomotive were to be equipped with automatic vacuum brakes. This brake power, additional to that available on the locomotive, meant that we could run at speeds faster than ordinary express goods and, as such, claimed a higher priority from the signalman's point of view.

My next move was to the stores. Being a Tuesday morning (the train didn't run on a Monday — that was our booked rest day) there was a good possibility that not all the tools would be available, but I was lucky. As I approached the stores, a set of men were handing theirs in, so I claimed them. At the same time I drew the oil for the locomotive and, fully burdened, turned round to find the locomotive. There wasn't far to go, the stores were in the corner of No. 2 shed and I climbed upon the footplate and took stock.

The usual filthy sight greeted me — a trickle of smoke from the chimney, 80 lbs on the clock and the water 'out of sight' up the glass. Stowing my haversack in the locker, I checked both gauge glasses — yes, the boiler was full. At this time I used my torch, since I hadn't lit the gauge glass lamp. This was to be my next action. But first I opened the fire-doors, and surveyed the scene. There was some clinker still in the firebox but there was a 'good back on' which was burning through nicely. With the rake, I knocked the clinker and ash through the firebars and at the same time noted that they were all in good condition. A quick glance at the brick arch revealed that all was in order, and the tube plate did not show any signs of leaks or furring up. (A trip with a class '4' with a furred up tube plate saw me 'down the nick' and we were travelling 'light engine', until some nifty work with the clinker shovel opened up the tube ends and thus transformed the steaming properties).

With everything in order, I spread the fire over most of the firebars, but kept it away from the front of the box. A quick trip to the corner of No. 2 shed provided some firebrick which I scattered over the fire. If any clinker was going to form, it would be around these bricks and not on the firebars. Then, satisfied that the base of the fire was in order, I started to build up the fire in the rear half of the firebox, using selected pieces of good quality coal.

This build-up of the fire was something which was done gradually. A few shovels, leave it, do something else, come back and, as the coal was burning through, add a few shovelsful more. This build-up of the fire continued while I tightened the smokebox door, filled and trimmed the locomotive headlamps, and water gauge lamp, made sure I had a red shade, checked the fire irons — clinker shovel, dart and rake. You could tell which was which by the shape of the handle. This was very useful in the dark, particularly when they were in the fire-iron tunnel of a Stanier tender. I climbed onto the tender to ensure that the coal was safely trimmed — no lumps had to fall off onto the heads of other railwaymen. I looked at the sandboxes and made sure the sand was dry, they were full, or at least nearly so, and the sand was running. Sometimes wet sand at the base would cause the sand to clog and it had to be cleared away.

The locomotive was almost ready by the time my mate arrived, and I had already tested both injectors. We had two live steam injectors on this locomotive. It was not unusual to have one live steam and one exhaust injector on a class '4'.

While Arthur oiled and inspected the locomotive I cleaned the windows and tidied up the footplate. Setting the turntable, Arthur drove her forward and then we pushed the table round to line up with the shed exit road. With headlamps set, red on the smokebox, white on the tender, we ran up the yard and set back onto the exit roads. Our tea had already been 'mashed' and we stopped for water. The fireman's duty was to put 'the bag' in, the driver's to turn the water supply on and off.

With the tank filled, my mate went to 'ring off'. This, in effect, was to tell the outside foreman that we were ready and he, in turn, telephoned the signalman at Duddeston Road signal box which controlled the entrance and exit roads from Saltley shed. It was quite remarkable that for such a large depot there was but a single road used for both purposes.

'Right away', off came the signal, and we ran light engine down the Camp Hill goods lines to the Washwood Heath West End sidings. Running past the bank pilot sidings, I noticed a single pilot there. 'Get her hot' was the usual cry to the waiting fireman on the class '3F' 0—6—0.

Being one of the most important trains to depart from this part of Washwood Heath, our arrival was greeted by three sets of gleaming handlamps held by the yard inspector, shunter and guard. The inspector was 'in charge'. The shunter 'set the road' by pulling over the point hand levers and coupled up the train, while the guard climbed onto the footplate and told Arthur that our load was 43 goods with four fitted. For my part, I removed the white light on the tender, took out the red shade and set the correct headlamp code for 'Maltese'.

By now I had a big fire in the back which, hopefully, was burning through well. So far I had avoided closing the dampers, although we were not blowing off and, with the boiler full, I decided to drop the damper door for a few minutes until we departed. With the firedoors open, I put a quick eight shovelsful of coal up the front and so, hopefully, filled up the hole in the front of the firegrate; I couldn't see it. My fire had been built up 'Gloucester fashion'.

Then it all happened, the pegs (signals) were off, a green light held steady and the shout rang out, 'Right away'. The whistle was popped and we were off, *en route* west.

I opened the damper, set the doors to admit secondary air and looked at my exhaust; yes, it was tinged grey, so there was no hole in the firebed. The safety valves were lifting as we headed out of the yard towards the Camp Hill goods lines.

As we cleared the sidings I exchanged signals with the guard. There were a variety of ways to do this but by night it was usually done by the guard swinging his handlamp while the crew sounded the locomotive whistle. Daytime often saw the guard wave a rolled-up newspaper up and down. When the bank pilot came behind the brake van, the guard would remove his tail lamp, but the brake van side lamps would remain in place. If on the goods line, the rear of the train would show a red tail lamp on the rear of the bank pilot, a red side light on the brake van on the side farthest away from the main line, while a white side light would be displayed on the side adjacent to the main line. This enabled any train approaching from the rear to know which line the train in front was on and to be aware that we were on the goods lines. Three red lights would indicate that we were on the main lines. Of course, the brake van side lamps displayed two white lights to the front, and so enabled the train crew to know that their train was intact. With a loose-coupled train, the absence of brake van lights showing forward at night could only mean that either the lamps were out or the train had parted in two!

Passing the pilot sidings, we whistled up for a pilot as we kept going towards Duddeston Mill signal box. We were held there for a few minutes and then came the 'right away'. The sight of these signals going to clear with the 'back'uns' (distants) off is a sight which I will never forget. Pairs of green lights up the bank through Landor Street, Brickyards Crossing, St. Andrew's Junction and then past Bordesley Junction, over the GWR, and on to Camp Hill, where the pilot would be dropped. However, heavy westbound trains or trains in trouble could keep the pilot and run with this assistance past Moseley to King's Heath. Then you were on your own through Hazelwell and Lifford to King's Norton, where the main line through New Street, which had diverged away at Landor Street Junction, rejoined again.

Our departure from Duddeston Mill was rapid, Arthur opened her up to full first valve and wound her back to about 40 per cent cut off. My thoughts were, 'Have I got it right?', I watched the exhaust, was it clear? The boiler pressure gauge, what did it read, and the water level in the gauge glass? When the regulator was opened, this lifted the level of the water in the boiler which, together with the fact that we were climbing the bank, tended to give a false reading. As we stormed past Brickyards Crossing there was no sign of any drop in the boiler pressure so I decided to start firing and then kept adding a few shovelsful every few minutes. By now I had the injector on, the water level was showing in the top of the glass, but, even so, there was no falling off in boiler pressure. The needle was glued to the red line.

By the time we crossed the GWR at Bordesley, I had begun to relax and then, as if to proclaim her superiority to the world, the engine's safety valves lifted, and I countered this by opening the doors and putting more coal onto the fire, which was white hot.

We had no need of the pilot from Camp Hill and so we made no signal to the 'Bobby' (signalman) as we passed the signal box. When the pilot dropped behind, I exchanged signals with the guard. This told all concerned that the train was intact, and so we hammered away past Brighton Road and began the climb towards Moseley Tunnel.

By now I was cock-a-hoop. Here I was on a class '4' with 43 on. The water was just visible in the top of the glass and the needle was on the mark. What more could I want? There was time to relax, take a drink of tea from the can which was on the drip tray, wipe my hands on the cloth — a washed one (it was the one I had drawn the previous Saturday!) and even reflect that the world was a wonderful place if you were young, keen, and on the footplate of a class '4' that was performing like it should do but which, until that time, you had never succeeded in achieving!

Everything was in our favour that morning — no crawling up the goods line for us, a welcome respite if you were 'down the nick'. We were going main line and away we went. To our right there were the goods lines with the inevitable empty wagon train heading north. To our left were the carriage sidings and then the small yard at King's Norton, where certain westbound coal trains originated. It was designed to relieve the congestion at Washwood Heath in the days when coal was the staple traffic of the Midland Division and it travelled by rail.

On through Northfield we went, past Halesowen Junction, where the line to the Austin Motor Works diverged, and up to Barnt Green, past the junction for the Redditch and Evesham line and onto Blackwell, where we halted to pin down a few wagon brakes before descending the Lickey incline. On the run up to Blackwell I had let the water level drop so that I could fill the boiler while we stopped at Blackwell to avoid blowing off. Down the bank we rolled, pulling the train at first, and then, with the regulator shut and tender handbrake on, letting the weight of the train do the work! Arthur made a good stop for water and we quickly filled the tank. Then we were off again, heading past Stoke Works Junction for Gloucester.

I've always enjoyed the west road out of Birmingham and this morning was no exception. The needle remained constant between 165-175 lbs, the water remained in the top three-quarters of the glass and our speed through Ashchurch was the highest I had achieved at that point to date with a freight train.

All too soon we were through Cheltenham Lansdown, and close to Gloucester. We were on time; the question was would Gloucester men relieve us or would we be able to take the train on through ourselves? There was no such luck. I would have to wait a little longer before I was able to work a freight train from Birmingham to Bristol and then it was to be on a class '5' 4—6—0.

As they climbed aboard, we exchanged greetings with the Gloucester men, of whom even the younger (the fireman) was probably twice my age. Like all firemen, his quick glance around took in the coal. A good quantity had been used but there was no problem — he had more than sufficient to get to Bristol, but he would need to get some forward while they took water. His glance at the water gauge glass showed it to be three-quarters full and steam pressure was just below the mark. All this was observed without comment by either him or me — but it was his remarks after looking at the fire that I have never forgotten. Speaking in that Gloucestershire accent it meant, 'Here was a young fireman from Saltley who had actually got the correct fire formed for the job'. Praise indeed.

The remainder of the day was spent working an empty wagon train with a class '3F' 0–6–0 to Bromsgrove where we were relieved and then rode home passenger to Saltley.

This trip marked a new beginning for me with the class '4Fs' and, whilst it would be untrue to say that never again was I in trouble with them, at least I understood them and my successful runs by far outnumbered the 'rough trips' of the past.

In retrospect, it is worth reflecting about this controversial class of locomotives. Writers have often remarked about how unpopular they were when, in the early years of the grouping, class '4Fs' went onto the Western and Central divisions.

Almost certainly this was because the old LNWR and LYR men had no idea how to fire them. The LNWR didn't have an 0–6–0 anything like the '4F' in size or power and Midland men, who worked on ex-LYR 0–6–0s, equally didn't speak very highly of the Aspinall design, so perhaps it has something to do with the inbuilt conservatism of engine men together with a lack of knowledge in handling different types. I also believe that many writers have tended to enlarge upon the shortcomings of the '4Fs' — but whilst they were far from perfect, they were not as bad as some people would make out.

In my view the problem with a '4' lay in the fact that once you got into trouble there was no easy way out. With steam pressure dropping, you could on most locomotives mortgage the boiler level in order to get more 'lbs per square inch on the clock', but this didn't seem to work on a '4F'. The fact was that once the needle started to go back it would continue to do so. Nevertheless, they would continue to run and I have worked between Burton and Birmingham, hauling a coal train with a class '4F' with less than 100 lbs on the clock and with the water in the bottom nut! We didn't keep time but we kept going.

One thing about the class '4s', which I cannot explain, was the fact that by and large the old Midland locomotives were generally better machines than the LMS standard locomotives, and the Derby built standard engines were superior to any of the others built post-1923. There was, however, one notable exception, in my own experience. My memories of No. 44190, a St. Rollox built locomotive, suggest that she should have been rated class '4½F' and it is perhaps fitting that she was my final firing turn in May 1954.

Before finally leaving the '4s' perhaps a word about tenders would not be out of place.

The straight side Fowler tenders fitted to the standard locomotives and then to the old ex-Midland engines during the early 1950s, were, in my humble opinion, not the best. With a fixed bulkhead they could be well coaled, as seen in certain illustrations used in this volume, but this took time and was difficult to do at a busy shed using a mechanical coaling plant. Once the forward supply had been used and the remaining stock was well back in the tender, it had to

be brought forward. To do this on the move was not easy and most drivers didn't like the idea of the fireman climbing up to get into the tenders. Bridges, etc., could be dangerous for a fireman who would, as he clambered over the tender bulkhead, be 'out of gauge'. On the other hand, this style of tender, when equipped with coal doors (and sometimes coal rails), was very good indeed. It was not in the same class as a Stanier tender but was a tremendous improvement on the fixed bulkhead type.

The old Midland flared top tenders coupled to Midland class '4s' suffered the same problem as the Fowler tender, having a solid bulkhead which made it difficult to bring coal forward while on the move.

By the time I started at Saltley, the most important work for class '4F' 0–6–0s was the Bristol express goods trains, and even so, by the early 1950s they were being replaced by the Ivatt class '4MT' 2–6–0s, commonly known as 'Doodlebugs'. The majority of the class '4F' work in the Saltley area was on through mineral, empty wagon and freight trains, together with many local trip jobs. However, one of my mates, Charlie Smith, used to speak of the class '4' work on the London link, pre-war, when as a fireman, he lodged in London. They ran via Wigston and so the route must have been all of 130 miles. I remember he said that he used to fill up the rear of the firebox before running under the coaling stage and bribing the coalman with a packet of Woodbine cigarettes, to 'fill up the hole'. The idea was to ensure they started with the maximum amount of coal at the front of the tender and so reduce the amount of coal which was required to be brought forward.

Charlie said that they stood in Somers' Town yard and 'as the tail lamp of the first express went by, the pegs came off and we were away — fast line to Kettering'. At this point they were booked to go onto the slow lines because, by now, hard on their heels was another express out of St. Pancras heading north. I could relate this story from my own experiences with the class '4s' — maybe not seventy miles with an express closing on my tail, but more than fifty miles before handing over our train. This was railway work, in my estimation and without wishing to denegrate in any way the magnificent efforts of the preservationists, there is no way by which they can recapture the true railway scene other than that portrayed on a small branch line which, as I have already stated, is not, in my humble opinion, what railways are all about.

Nevertheless, the class '4s' are still with us, one in the national collection and another on the Keighley and Worth Valley where the distinctive Derby exhaust can be heard. They have the gradients to test her; I often wonder how they fire her.

We should now turn to what I consider to be the most typical of the 'Midland' locomotives I ever fired, the class '3F' 0–6–0s. They were everyone's favourite. Introduced in their Belpaire boiler form in 1916, they were in essence the Belpaire boiler version of the 'H' boilered locomotives built by Johnson and dating from 1903. However one considers their origins one could not ignore them. In 1950 there were quite a few in service and they seemed apparently indestructible.

Two of my favourites were No. 3674, the first class '3F' I ever fired during my first week on the bank pilots, and No. 43284, the first locomotive I drove on the main line from Bromsgrove to Washwood Heath and, with a gagged regulator, nearly ran past the home signal for Camp Hill — but that is another story. The one I have chosen to represent this class is a locomotive whose full number I do not remember beyond the fact that it was in the 33XX series. We will call it 433XX. The story begins when I was 'spare', our regular job was cancelled and my mate was on holiday. My driver for the week was Fred Wilkinson and we were on an 8.40 shift. In the morning, it was a Friday, we had worked a Gloucester-Toton empty wagon train to Burton Leicester Junction, we had been relieved and were now on 433XX at the head of a through freight train *en route* for Washwood Heath West End sidings. The time was around 3/10 and both Fred and I were worried. He was in a darts match final and I had a date with a girl I had met the previous weekend. The problem was that if we didn't get the road soon we would have had it. From a little after 4.0 p.m. the main line would be occupied by passenger trains with little chance of a through run.

Consulting the WTT and the point to point timings, I calculated that if we didn't go soon we wouldn't go until after 6.0 p.m., but if we did get the road we could be at Washwood Heath without stopping anything. I therefore told Fred that I proposed to consult control and, leaving the engine, walked to the signal box and asked the 'Bobby' if I could phone control. On receiving his consent I lifted the instrument and was soon speaking to control. The conversation went like this: 'Control, this is Fireman Essery on 433XX at Leicester Junction. We are working the XYZ from Derby to Washwood Heath.'

'Yes, Fireman', said control, 'What do you want?'

'Well, control it's like this. My mate is Fred Wilkinson and he is playing in a darts final tonight and I've got a date with this girl and if you don't give us the road we won't get there. I've looked at the WTT and point to point timings and if you give us the road we want we won't stop anything.'

'Wait, fireman', said the voice of control, and I waited. After a few moments control replied, 'Fireman, we will give you the road, but don't you dare stop the passenger.'

I ran back to the engine, opened the damper and began to pile in coal.

'What on earth are you doing?' asked Fred.

'We've got the road to Washwood Heath' was my reply.

'Fat chance!' said Fred.

'You'll see — he said so', was my reply. As I spoke, there was the sound of the points being set, and off came the pegs.

'Come on, Fred — I said we would go like hell and not stop the passenger.'

Fred just looked and muttered something to the effect that we would go like hell if he got the road and in which case I'd better be prepared for some hard work. Well, we had the road, and control kept their word with 'back 'uns' (distants) all the way to Washwood Heath.

We kept ours, Fred had her onto the second valve with the lever about halfway between full and mid gear. I kept

the top flap open, it was a Midland type door and I bailed (another firing expression) the coal in over the top of the bottom door. 'Hammered' is probably the best description of the way Fred drove this '3F'. What a run, with forty or so goods on our tail, we roared west towards Birmingham and as we went through Elford there was even a fitted 'inside'. Every goods line and layby was full and more than one startled crew leaned out of their cabs to see what was happening and who was causing the racket as we hurtled west. I picked up water just north of Tamworth, but most of the time I kept tipping coal into the rear of the firebox. As far as I recall, the injector was on all of the time and most of the time the needle stayed on the mark.

I stopped firing at Kingsbury and we ran fast line to Water Orton and main line to Washwood Heath. We probably had a little too much fire on, and between Water Orton and Castle Bromwich Fred dropped her down a nick in an attempt to remove some of it through the chimney!

Turning onto the goods arrival line at Washwood Heath Junction, we found that within minutes of arriving, we had been relieved, and so were able to make our way to the shed and book off.

Fred lost in the darts final and I don't even remember the girl's name, but what I'll never forget is that run, made in 1953, one autumn afternoon when an old class '3F' showed me just what you could do with a goods engine.

To my everlasting regret I never fired either a class '4F' or '3F' on a passenger train, even though they were to be found on these workings almost to the end of their respective careers in certain parts of the country. All of my class '3F' work was on mineral, empty wagon and through freights interspersed with local freight, bank pilot and shunting work.

The smallest of the ex-Midland Railway goods engines which I fired were some of the handful of old Johnson class '2Fs' at Saltley. To the best of my knowledge, they were all of the small Johnson cab variety. When in the 'trip link', booked with Freddy Robinson, we had, I think, some three weeks work in twelve with these locomotives and I wish I had known more about their history when I fired them.

To me they were very small; you could almost fire them with a teaspoon and yet it was their small size that fascinated me. 'They used to go all over with these engines', old drivers told me. I couldn't even imagine going to London or Leeds with a class '4F' — to my mind that kind of job was more suited to either a 'Crab' 2–6–0 or class '5' 4–6–0, but to travel that distance in this little goods engine was something I couldn't comprehend and yet it was done.

An old driver told me, 'Any fool can fire a big engine. All you need is a strong back — a little engine requires skill, the safety margin on a small locomotive is minute indeed.' This was certainly true of the class '2Fs'. Two or three well placed shovelsful of coal could soon bring them round, but equally a few minutes inattention would see the boiler pressure drop 40 lbs and the water level in the glass drop a long way.

The closest I ever came to main line work with a class '2' was a midday run from Lawley Street to Water Orton conveying traffic for the northbound 'fitteds' starting from those sidings during the late afternoon. This fast main line run, albeit for a few miles, gave me an insight into the capability of these goods engines which, in their late Victorian heyday, handled most of the fast goods trains on the Midland Railway.

It is a great pity that one was never preserved. They represented a very important element of our railway heritage, the small Victorian six-coupled goods engines which ran long distances with many of the most important goods trains of the period.

Of the other Midland Railway classes which I fired, we can perhaps dismiss all but one class quite quickly. The 0–6–0T class '1F' was confined to shed shunting duties and I have no clear recollection beyond the feeling that they were really underpowered for moving a rake of 13 ton loaded loco coal wagons. We didn't have any of the larger class '3F' 0–6–0Ts of Midland origin at Saltley, but I did have a few turns on the LMS Standard version during my very early days. I recall they were efficient, easy to fire and performed well, being in steam for the best part of 24 hours from leaving the depot until returning for coal and service. The fireman on the first and second shifts cleaned the fire while at Washwood Heath, with the third crew disposing the locomotive when they returned to Saltley, providing they had sufficient time and would not be on overtime before the job was completed.

Another class with members resident at Saltley was the class '2P' 4–4–0 which we have often referred to as the '483' class rebuilds. I had two or three days with a member of this class, almost certainly No. 40511. One job upon which it was employed, and for which it was totally unsuited, was a trip working which included running tender first from Washwood Heath to Lawley Street. As we slipped our way across the main line I could not help wondering why a more suitable locomotive was not employed upon this working. The other job was West Pilot at New Street. This was a fairly 'cushy' job, you were there to bank any overloaded westbound passenger train up through the tunnels to Five Ways or, if the worst came to the worst, be coupled to the front of the train engine and assist it to Gloucester – not a prospect I relished. However, this was not to be and we spent most of our time standing with nothing to do. We moved parcels vans around and shunted the fish sidings and my memory of the '483' class was the distinctive sound they made when running, a kind of clanging which came from the side rods.

Of course, I never knew them in their prime and would have enjoyed the experience of working on them when they were on main line express trains.

I did, however, fire some members of the Midland's premier passenger class, or to be correct, the LMS version of it, and I have chosen one night's work with two of these locomotives to record my memories of the class and to conclude this brief survey.

It began one October evening in 1947 when I booked on and was told by the foreman's assistant that I didn't have a driver. At that time I had been passed for firing for but a few weeks and had been 'past the shed signal' on only three occasions, a night on '28 trip' with No. 8010, a trip to Water Orton with a class '4F' 0–6–0 No. 4525, and then later that night with a class '3F' light engine from Washwood Heath to the shed, and a day's work shunting at Washwood Heath with a class '3F' 0–6–0T. The remainder of my time had been spent preparing or disposing locomotives on shed. However, this was the first time I had booked on and didn't have a driver.

The foreman's assistant told me to go round to the cabin and wait for further instructions. The cabin was a very large room with a high ceiling. At one side there was an open fire which never went out. It fuelled an enormous kettle whose purpose in life was to provide boiling water for the engine crew's tea. In addition, there were numerous tables and benches at which enginemen could be seen eating their 'snap' (food), reading newspapers, or playing cards or dominoes. Walking in and sitting down unnoticed or unrecognised, I wondered what would happen next. After perhaps thirty minutes or so the foreman's assistant came into the cabin and said, 'You've got a job, you're on the Leicester parcels with Gilbert Church. Your engine is 928, it's prepared and in the yard.' With that he walked away, leaving me utterly speechless. No. 928 was a 'Compound', Leicester was miles away, and the 'parcels' was a main line train. I was, in modern parlance, on cloud nine!

Out into the yard I went and there was No. 928 standing on 'Woody's Siding', a short siding off the departure road. Climbing aboard, I stowed away my haversack and looked at the water, the boiler was full, and at the fire – it looked a big firebox! I really didn't know what to do next but had the bright idea that I should check the tools. It is doubtful if ever again I came onto a prepared engine and found anything missing but this time I couldn't find a $7/8''$ spanner. Now apart from being used to tighten up the smokebox door nuts I didn't know what else it might be required for, but felt that we ought to have one, and so I set off to find a $7/8''$ spanner as quickly as possible.

My search did not take long, two solid weeks of preparing engines had made one an expert and, quickly returning to the locomotive, I found driver Church on the footplate. He eyed me up and down and asked where I had been and I proudly displayed the spanner. His next question brought me to earth. 'How many times have you been past the shed signal?' I told him. All he said was that he would be gone for a few minutes, but while he was away I was to 'put some fire on'.

The coal comprised large slabs which responded to treatment with the coal pick. I found that if I used the point to split it and then hit it hard with the hammer end, it would break up, and so I started to break up the coal and to pile it into the firebox. After a short while I realised that this was hard work and had just paused for a short breather when Gilbert Church returned. He looked at me, then the fire, and said, 'Don't bother to break it up, if it goes through the firebox door it's small enough', and promptly picked up a big slab of coal and thrust it into the firehole with his foot. 'Keep putting it in', he said, 'You'll find it is much easier when standing still.' Never was a truer word spoken to me during my entire footplate career.

And so, redoubling my efforts, I began to build up a decent fire in the rear of the box, and then Gilbert said, 'Stop'. We were off. We set back under the water column and 'topped up' the tank. Then ringing off the shed we were off for Lawley Street where we backed onto the train. Confirming that I could couple up, watched carefully by the driver, I attached the van to the tender and screwed up the coupling and then connected 'the pipes' by first hooking them together and then 'clicking' them together, finally securing them with the pin. Next I set the locomotive head-lamps and returned to the footplate.

By now Gilbert was quite friendly. I presume his first trip from the engine had been to see if he could get a replacement, but with one not available had decided to take this 'green' fireman with him.

My instructions were very brief. 'When I tell you to put coal on, do so until I tell you to stop. When I tell you to put the injector on, do so until I tell you otherwise.' Thus armed and advised, we waited for the signal and then there was the green light held steady, the shout 'right away' and we were off, 'main line to Leicester'.

Quickly getting into her stride, No. 928 was soon at Saltley station and past Washwood Heath, Castle Bromwich fell behind and then the junction at Water Orton came into view with the signals showing the 'the road' was clear towards Coleshill and Whitacre Junction, where we turned onto the Leicester line.

Meanwhile the system worked. I put coal on when told and stopped when Gilbert tapped me on the shoulder, I worked the injector and, thank goodness, it was an exhaust injector which gave no trouble.

I hacked and smashed at the coal and tried to shovel it through the firedoors. To this day I'm sure that No. 928 had at least one square wheel, the footplate was all over the place. More than one shovelful of coal failed to find its mark and the contents of the shovel were strewn across the footplate — more work for my brush and slaking pipe. It was hard work but it was exciting — probably more exciting than any trip I ever made.

Taking the curve at Whitacre, we began to climb up towards Arley and ahead of us lay the tunnel. As we approached Gilbert told me to close the firedoors and the dampers as we rushed through.

On we went, the names of the stations meant nothing to me, and then Gilbert told me to stop putting coal on, to fill the bucket with hot water because we would soon be there.

Coming to a halt at Leicester, I was uncoupled by the shunter and while this was being done I adjusted the lamp code and we ran light engine into Leicester shed. Here, in the time honoured way, my mate and I washed up in the

bucket and, leaving our locomotive on the yard at Leicester, went to the mess room for our supper.

After a while we walked across to Leicester station to relieve the crew of another 'Compound', No. 1054, which had recently arrived, and we were shunted onto the carriage sidings where I coupled the train of non-corridor coaches to the tender. In addition, I connected the carriage warming pipe and, under Gilbert's instruction, turned on the heating.

We ensured that No. 1054 would 'stand' by tending to the fire and boiler and then returned to the leading compart-ment of the coach. Enginemen will never sit on their locomotive if they can find somewhere which is more comfortable -- we were no exception.

In due course, around 6.0 a.m., we went back onto No. 1054 to ensure she was ready to depart with her train, the 6.30 a.m. to Birmingham. We would work it as far as Saltley station where we would be relieved.

While Gilbert went round with his oilcan, I built up a good fire in the back of the box, broke up the coal and ensured that it was well forward. I don't recall filling the tank, but it must have been done sometime and then we pulled forward and stood at our departure platform.

It was a wonderful trip back. On receiving the 'right away', I stood and watched the train leave the platform, just in case a late arriving passenger tried to jump aboard. I presume that if he missed his step and fell between the coach and platform, my duty was to draw this to my driver's attention!

As we left the station, I shut off the injectors and put a quick eight around the box: two in the back corners, one under the door, two down each side and one towards the front. It seemed to work well and steam pressure remained just on or just below the red line.

All too soon we were back at Saltley and were relieved. As we walked back to the shed I felt that at last I had arrived as a fireman. As yet I had a long way to go and I was a long way off mastering the class '4s', but I had the confidence. After all, I had worked two main line trains.

Only once more did I work a 'Compound', on a passenger to Gloucester. To my intense regret I never fired one on an express. My impression of them was that they were big, but on the local jobs that I have described they were total masters of the job.

Gilbert and I were to work together again, this time some three years later, when I worked my first express train with a 'Crab', but that is really another story.

M.R. LOCOMOTIVE RENUMBERING OF 1907

It is often difficult to identify Midland Railway Locomotives from their pre-1907 numbers. This appendix is therefore an attempt to relate the old numbers carried in 1907 to the new numbers allocated in the renumbering scheme, which took place that year. However, it should be born in mind that prior to 1907, much renumbering of individual engines had taken place within the 'old' number series (see page ix). When studying old photographs, this fact should be born in mind. The list below gives the 'old' number carried *immediately* prior to the systematic 1907 reorganisation.

Readers interested in greater detail should refer to:- *British Locomotive Catalogue Volume 3A* by David Baxter, published by Moorland Publishing Co., Ashbourne, Derbyshire, which is the only published guide to early Midland Railway locomotive numbers known to the authors.

Old No.	New No.	Old No.	New No.	Old No.	New No.
145	633	206	499	267	3797
146	156	207	500	268	3798
147	1235	208	501	269	3799
148	91	209	502	270	3800
149	650	210	1720	271	3801
150	493	211	1721	272	3802
151	536	212	1722	273	3803
152	537	213	1762	274	3804
153	494	214	1763	275	3805
154	495	215	1723	276	3806
155	496	216	1724	277	3807
156	423	217	1764	278	3808
157	424	218	1725	279	3809
158	425	219	1726	280	3810
159	426	220	1690	281	3811
160	427	221	1691	282	3812
161	459	222	1765	283	3813
162	460	223	2704	284	3814
163	461	224	2693	285	2696
164	462	225	2794	286	2302
165	538	226	2684	287	2830
166	539	227	2679	288	2310
167	540	228	2687	289	2831
168	541	229	2793	290	2459
169	542	230	463	291	2832
170	651	231	464	292	2580
171	652	232	465	293	2685
172	653	233	466	294	2686
173	654	234	467	295	2697
174	655	235	468	296	2677
175	656	236	469	297	2678
176	657	237	470	298	2675
177	658	238	471	299	2680
178	659	239	472	300	2349
179	660	240	3770	301	2581
180	661	241	3771	302	2353
181	662	242	3772	303	2688
182	663	243	3773	304	2582
183	664	244	3774	305	Sold
184	443	245	3775	306	Sold
185	444	246	3776	307	2465
186	445	247	3777	308	2705
187	446	248	3778	309	2828
188	447	249	3779	310	2714
189	448	250	3780	311	2710
190	449	251	3781	312	2359
191	450	252	3782	313	Sold
192	451	253	3783	314	2829
193	452	254	3784	315	2394
194	453	255	3785	316	2476
195	454	256	3786	317	2354
196	455	257	3787	318	2350
197	456	258	3788	319	2351
198	457	259	3789	320	2797
199	458	260	3790	321	2352
200	1760	261	3791	322	2406
201	1761	262	3792	323	2827
202	1346	263	3793	324	2361
203	1780	264	3794	325	2391
204	497	265	3795	326	2392
205	498	266	3796	327	2362

Old No.	New No.	Old No.	New No.	Old No.	New No.
1	147	49	103	97	644
2	88	50	187	98	645
3		51	188	99	646
4	640	52	189	100	647
5	94	53	190	101	197
6	1226	54	191	102	198
7	113	55	192	103	199
8	630	56	193	104	200
9	148	57	194	105	201
10	149	58	195	106	202
11	401	59	196	107	203
12	95	60	523	108	204
13	150	61	524	109	205
14	402	62	525	110	206
15	1227	63	526	111	217
16	641	64	527	112	218
17	642	65	528	113	219
18	1228	66	529	114	220
19	690	67	533	115	670
20	691	68	534	116	671
21	692	69	535	117	672
22	693	70	151	118	673
23	694	71	152	119	674
24	634	72	114	120	675
25	600	73	153	121	676
26	601	74	154	122	631
27	602	75	665	123	677
28	603	76	666	124	678
29	604	77	667	125	679
30	605	78	115	126	680
31	606	79	668	127	681
32	607	80	393	128	682
33	635	81	394	129	648
34	609	82	395	130	683
35	636	83	396	131	684
36	637	84	397	132	632
37	614	85	398	133	649
38	638	86	399	134	
39	639	87	400	135	125
40	99	88	669	136	126
41	100	89	221	137	1229
42	116	90	90	138	531
43	101	91	104	139	532
44	118	92	92	140	1230
45	117	93	530	141	1231
46	102	94	643	142	1232
47	112	95	89	143	1233
48	119	96	155	144	1234

Old No.	New No.	Old No.	New No.	Old No.	New No.	Old No.	New No.	Old No.	New No.	Old No.	New No.
328	2826	392	2324	456	2712	520	2436	584	2491	648	2566
329	Sold	393	2835	457	2370	521	2437	585	2492	649	2567
330	2395	394	2325	458	2371	522	2438	586	2493	650	2583
331	2715	395	2326	459	2372	523	2439	587	2494	651	2584
332	2825	396	2327	460	2698	524	2440	588	2495	652	2585
333	Sold	397	2328	461	2373	525	2441	589	2496	653	2586
334	2702	398	Sold	462	Sold	526	2442	590	2508	654	2587
335	2387	399	2711	463	2374	527	2443	591	2509	655	2588
336	2701	400	2925	464	2375	528	2444	592	2510	656	2317
337	2343	401	2926	465	2376	529	2445	593	2511	657	2589
338	2469	402	2927	466	2377	530	2461	594	2512	658	2590
339	2824	403	2928	467	Sold	531	2482	595	2513	659	2591
340	2823	404	2929	468	2378	532	2471	596	2514	660	2791
341	2822	405	2401	469	2379	533	2396	597	2515	661	2526
342	2479	406	2334	470	2380	534	2477	598	2516	662	2527
343	2466	407	2474	471	2817	535	2467	599	2517	663	Sold
344	2398	408	2314	472	2798	536	2478	600	2518	664	2528
345	2301	409	2335	473	2381	537	2490	601	2720	665	Sold
346	2497	410	2813	474	2382	538	2483	602	2519	666	2529
347	2709	411	2336	475	2383	539	2694	603	2520	667	2699
348	2821	412	2303	476	2384	540	2446	604	2521	668	2530
349	Sold	413	2337	477	2820	541	2447	605	2522	669	2531
350	2799	414	2338	478	2385	542	2448	606	2523	670	2304
351	2800	415	2470	479	2386	543	2449	607	2524	671	2568
352	2795	416	Sold	480	2305	544	2718	608	2819	672	2569
353	2801	417	2339	481	2331	545	2450	609	2525	673	2570
354	2796	418	2814	482	2332	546	Sold	610	2532	674	2571
355	2802	419	2340	483	2703	547	2451	611	2533	675	2572
356	2473	420	2319	484	2707	548	2452	612	2534	676	2573
357	2803	421	2320	485	2333	549	2453	613	2535	677	2574
358	2804	422	2307	486	Sold	550	2454	614	2536	678	2575
359	2315	423	2321	487	2342	551	2455	615	2537	679	2576
360	2402	424	2346	488	2790	552	2456	616	2538	680	2577
361	3460	425	2347	489	2407	553	2457	617	2539	681	2578
362	3461	426	2322	490	2313	554	2458	618	2540	682	Sold
363	3462	427	2815	491	2408	555	Sold	619	2541	683	2579
364	3463	428	2341	492	2409	556	2309	620	2721	684	2672
365	3464	429	2312	493	2410	557	2348	621	2542	685	2673
366	3465	430	2462	494	2411	558	2498	622	2543	686	2674
367	3466	431	2355	495	2412	559	2499	623	2544	687	2792
368	3467	432	2816	496	2676	560	2682	624	2545	688	2681
369	3468	433	2356	497	2413	561	2500	625	2546	689	2683
370	3469	434	2357	498	2414	562	2501	626	2722	690	1401
371	2403	435	2358	499	2415	563	2502	627	2547	691	1402
372	2399	436	2708	500	2416	564	2503	628	2548	692	1403
373	2318	437	2360	501	2417	565	2504	629	2549	693	1404
374	2404	438	2716	502	2418	566	2505	630	2464	694	1405
375	2344	439	2363	503	2419	567	2506	631	2550	695	1406
376	2300.	440	2308	504	2420	568	2695	632	2551	696	2689
377	2400	441	2364	505	2421	569	2507	633	2552	697	2690
378	2833	442	2316	506	2422	570	2475	634	2553	698	2691
379	2405	443	2323	507	2423	571	2397	635	2554	699	2692
380	2472	444	2365	508	2424	572	2393	636	2555	700	2592
381	2920	445	2388	509	2425	573	2468	637	Sold	701	2593
382	2921	446	2706	510	2426	574	2484	638	2556	702	2594
383	2922	447	2717	511	2427	575	2390	639	2557	703	2595
384	2923	448	2463	512	2428	576	2700	640	2558	704	2596
385	2924	449	2389	513	2429	577	2486	641	2559	705	2597
386	2306	450	2366	514	2430	578	2818	642	2560	706	2598
387	2713	451	2367	515	2431	579	2481	643	2561	707	2599
388	2329	452	2460	516	2432	580	2485	644	2562	708	2600
389	2330	453	2368	517	2433	581	2487	645	2563	709	2601
390	2345	454	2369	518	2434	582	2488	646	2564	710	2602
391	2834	455	Sold	519	2435	583	2489	647	2565	711	2603

APPENDICES

Old No.	New No.	Old No.	New No.	Old No.	New No.	Old No.	New No.	Old No.	New No.	Old No.	New No.
712	2604	776	2628	840	750	904	82	968	Sold	1031	2480
713	2605	777	2629	841	751	905	83	969	2756	1032	2837
714	2606	778	2630	842	752	906	84	970	2757	1033	2838
715	2607	779	2631	843	753	907	85	971	Sold	1034	2839
716	2608	780	1407	844	754	908	86	972	Sold	1035	2840
717	2609	781	1408	845	755	909	87	973	Sold	1036	2841
718	2610	782	1409	846	756	910	2770	974	2758	1037	2842
719	2611	783	1410	847	757	911	2771	975	2759	1038	2843
720	2632	784	1210	848	758	912	2772	976	2760	1039	Sold
721	2633	785	1211	849	759	913	2773	977	Sold	1040	Sold
722	2634	786	1212	840	760	914	2774	978	Sold	1041	Sold
723	2635	787	1213	851	761	915	2775	979	2761	1042	2844
724	2636	788	1214	852	762	916	2776	980	2762	1043	2845
725	2637	789	1215	853	763	917	2777	981	Sold	1044	2846
726	2638	790	1216	854	764	918	2778	982	2763	1045	2847
727	2639	791	1217	855	765	919	2779	983	2764	1046	2848
728	2640	792	1218	856	766	920	2780	984	2765	1047	2849
729	2641	793	1219	857	767	921	2781	985	2766	1048	2850
730	2642	794	1220	858	768	922	2782	986	Sold	1049	2851
731	2643	795	1221	859	769	923	2783	987	2767	1050	2852
732	2644	796	1222	860	770	924	2784	988	2768	1051	2853
733	2645	797	1223	861	771	925	2785	989	2769	1052	2311
734	2646	798	1224	862	772	926	2786	990	2805	1053	2719
735	2647	799	1225	863	773	927	2787	991	Sold	1054	2854
736	2648	800	705	864	774	928	2788	992	2806	1055	2855
737	2649	801	706	865	775	929	2789	993	2807	1056	2856
738	2650	802	707	866	776	930	2730	994	Sold	1057	2857
739	2651	803	708	867	777	931	Sold	995	2808	1058	2858
740	2652	804	709	868	778	932	2731	996	2809	1059	2859
741	2653	805	543	869	779	933	Sold	997	2810	1060	2860
742	2654	806	544	870	Sold	934	2732	998	2811	1061	2861
743	2655	807	545	871	2723	935	Sold	999	999	1062	2862
744	2656	808	546	872	2724	936	2733			1063	2863
745	2657	809	547	873	2725	937	2734	1000	1005	1064	2864
746	2658	810	720	874	2726	938	2735	1001	1006	1065	2865
747	2659	811	721	875	2727	939	2736	1002	1007	1066	Sold
748	2660	812	722	876	Sold	940	2737	1003	1008	1067	2866
749	2661	813	723	877	2728	941	2738	1004	1009	1068	Sold
750	2662	814	724	878	2729	942	2739	1005	1010	1069	2867
751	2663	815	725	879	Sold	943	2740	1006	1011	1070	127
752	2664	816	726	880	1795	944	2741	1007	1012	1071	128
753	2665	817	727	881	1796	945	2742	1008	1013	1072	129
754	2666	818	728	882	1797	946	Sold	1009	1014	1073	130
755	2667	819	729	883	1798	947	Sold	1010	1015	1074	131
756	2668	820	730	884	1799	948	Sold	1011	1016	1075	132
757	2669	821	731	885	1800	949	2743	1012	1017	1076	133
758	2670	822	732	886	1801	950	2744	1013	1018	1077	134
759	2671	823	733	887	1802	951	Sold	1014	1019	1078	135
760	2612	824	734	888	1803	952	2745	1015	1020	1079	136
761	2613	825	735	889	1804	953	Sold	1016	1021	1080	137
762	2614	826	736	890	68	954	2746	1017	1022	1081	138
763	2615	827	737	891	69	955	Sold	1018	1023	1082	139
764	2616	828	738	892	70	956	2747	1019	1024	1083	140
765	2617	829	739	893	71	957	2748	1020	1025	1084	141
766	2618	830	740	894	72	958	Sold	1021	1026	1085	142
767	2619	831	741	895	73	959	2749	1022	1027	1086	143
768	2620	832	742	896	74	960	2750	1023	1028	1087	144
769	2621	833	743	897	75	961	2751	1024	1029	1088	145
770	2622	834	744	898	76	962	2752	1025	1030	1089	146
771	2623	835	745	899	77	963	Sold	1026	1031	1090	1740
772	2624	836	746	900	78	964	2753	1027	1032	1091	1741
773	2625	837	747	901	79	965	2754	1028	1033	1092	1742
774	2626	838	748	902	80	966	Sold	1029	1034	1093	1767
775	2627	839	749	903	81	967	2755	1030	2836	1094	1743

MIDLAND LOCOMOTIVES

Old No.	New No.	Old No.	New No.	Old No.	New No.	Old No.	New No.	Old No.	New No.	Old No.	New No.
1095	1744	1159	2917	1223	2991	1287	162	1351	1684	1415	1705
1096	1755	1160	2918	1224	2992	1288	163	1352	1685	1416	1706
1097	1756	1161	2919	1225	2993	1289	164	1353	1686	1417	1707
1098	1757	1162	2930	1226	2994	1290	165	1354	1687	1418	1708
1099	1758	1163	2931	1227	2995	1291	166	1355	1688	1419	1709
1100	1759	1164	2932	1228	2996	1292	167	1356	1689	1420	1692
1101	1768	1165	2933	1229	2997	1293	168	1357	3020	1421	1693
1102	1775	1166	2934	1230	2998	1294	169	1358	3021	1422	1694
1103	1776	1167	2935	1231	2999	1295	170	1359	3022	1423	1695
1104	1777	1168	2936	1232	3000	1296	171	1360	3023	1424	1696
1105	1778	1169	2937	1233	3001	1297	172	1361	3024	1425	1697
1106	1779	1170	2938	1234	3002	1298	173	1362	3025	1426	1698
1107	1816	1171	2939	1235	3003	1299	174	1363	3026	1427	1699
1108	1817	1172	2940	1236	3004	1300	175	1364	3027	1428	1347
1109	1818	1173	2941	1237	3005	1301	176	1365	3028	1429	1348
1110	1819	1174	2942	1238	3006	1302	177	1366	3029	1430	1349
1111	1820	1175	2943	1239	3007	1303	178	1367	3030	1431	1769
1112	1821	1176	2944	1240	3008	1304	179	1368	3031	1432	3050
1113	1822	1177	2945	1241	3009	1305	180	1369	3032	1433	3051
1114	1823	1178	2946	1242	3010	1306	181	1370	3033	1434	3052
1115	1824	1179	2947	1243	3011	1307	182	1371	3034	1435	3053
1116	1634	1180	2948	1244	3012	1308	183	1372	3035	1436	3054
1117	1635	1181	2949	1245	3013	1309	184	1373	3036	1437	3055
1118	1636	1182	2950	1246	3014	1310	185	1374	3037	1438	3056
1119	1637	1183	2951	1247	3015	1311	186	1375	3038	1439	3057
1120	1638	1184	2952	1248	3016	1312	300	1376	3039	1440	3058
1121	1845	1185	2953	1249	3017	1313	301	1377	1660	1441	3059
1122	1846	1186	2954	1250	3018	1314	302	1378	1661	1442	3060
1123	1847	1187	2955	1251	3019	1315	303	1379	1662	1443	3061
1124	1848	1188	2956	1252	1256	1316	304	1380	1663	1444	3062
1125	1849	1189	2957	1253	1257	1317	305	1381	1664	1445	3063
1126	1850	1190	2958	1254	1258	1318	306	1382	1665	1446	3064
1127	1851	1191	2959	1255	1259	1319	307	1383	1666	1447	3065
1128	1852	1192	2960	1256	1260	1320	308	1384	1667	1448	3066
1129	1853	1193	2961	1257	1261	1321	309	1385	1668	1449	3067
1130	1854	1194	2962	1258	1262	1322	1341	1386	1669	1450	3068
1131	1649	1195	2963	1259	1263	1323	1342	1387	1670	1451	3069
1132	1650	1196	2964	1260	1264	1324	1343	1388	1671	1452	3040
1133	1651	1197	2965	1261	1265	1325	1344	1389	1672	1453	3041
1134	1652	1198	2966	1262	1236	1326	1345	1390	1673	1454	3042
1135	1653	1199	2967	1263	1237	1327	310	1391	1674	1455	3043
1136	1654	1200	2968	1264	1238	1328	311	1392	1675	1456	3044
1137	1655	1201	2969	1265	1239	1329	312	1393	1676	1457	3045
1138	1656	1202	2970	1266	1240	1330	313	1394	1677	1458	3046
1139	1657	1203	2971	1267	1241	1331	314	1395	1678	1459	3047
1140	1658	1204	2972	1268	1242	1332		1396	1679	1460	3048
1141	1659	1205	2973	1269	1243	1333	315	1397	1727	1461	3049
1142	2900	1206	2974	1270	1244	1334	316	1398	1728	1462	3070
1143	2901	1207	2975	1271	1245	1335	317	1399	1729	1463	3071
1144	2902	1208	2976	1272	1246	1336	318	1400	207	1464	3072
1145	2903	1209	2977	1273	1247	1337	319	1401	208	1465	3073
1146	2904	1210	2978	1274	1248	1338	320	1402	209	1466	3074
1147	2905	1211	2979	1275	1249	1339	321	1403	210	1467	3075
1148	2906	1212	2980	1276	1250	1340	322	1404	211	1468	3076
1149	2907	1213	2981	1277	1251	1341	323	1405	212	1469	3077
1150	2908	1214	2982	1278	1252	1342	324	1406	213	1470	3078
1151	2909	1215	2983	1279	1253	1343	325	1407	214	1471	3079
1152	2910	1216	2984	1280	1254	1344	326	1408	215	1472	222
1153	2911	1217	2985	1281	1255	1345	327	1409	216	1473	223
1154	2912	1218	2986	1282	157	1346	1766	1410	1700	1474	224
1155	2913	1219	2987	1283	158	1347	1680	1411	1701	1475	225
1156	2914	1220	2988	1284	159	1348	1681	1412	1702	1476	226
1157	2915	1221	2989	1285	160	1349	1682	1413	1703	1477	227
1158	2916	1222	2990	1286	161	1350	1683	1414	1704	1478	228

Old No.	New No.	Old No.	New No.	Old No.	New No.	Old No.	New No.	Old No.	New No.	Old No.	New No.
1479	229	1543	1277	1607	3105	1671	487	1735	1328	1799	3191
1480	230	1544	1278	1608	3106	1672	488	1736	1329	1800	3192
1481	231	1545	1279	1609	3107	1673	489	1737	1330	1801	3193
1482	232	1546	1280	1610	3108	1674	490	1738	358	1802	3194
1483	233	1547	1281	1611	3109	1675	491	1739	359	1803	3195
1484	234	1548	1282	1612	3110	1676	492	1740	360	1804	3196
1485	235	1549	1283	1613	3111	1677	1730	1741	361	1805	3197
1486	236	1550	1284	1614	3112	1678	1731	1742	362	1806	3198
1487	237	1551	1285	1615	3113	1679	1732	1743	363	1807	3199
1488	238	1552	1710	1616	3114	1680	1733	1744	364	1808	378
1489	239	1553	1711	1617	3115	1681	1734	1745	365	1809	379
1490	240	1554	1712	1618	3116	1682	1735	1746	366	1810	380
1491	241	1555	1713	1619	3117	1683	1736	1747	367	1811	381
1492	272	1556	1714	1620	3118	1684	1737	1748	368	1812	382
1493	273	1557	1715	1621	3119	1685	1738	1749	369	1813	383
1494	274	1558	1716	1622	3120	1686	1739	1750	370	1814	384
1495	275	1559	1717	1623	3121	1687	1745	1751	371	1815	385
1496	276	1560	1718	1624	3122	1688	1746	1752	372	1816	386
1497	277	1561	1719	1625	3123	1689	1747	1753	373	1817	387
1498	278	1562	328	1626	3124	1690	1748	1754	374	1818	388
1499	279	1563	329	1627	3125	1691	1749	1755	375	1819	389
1500	280	1564	330	1628	3126	1692	1750	1756	376	1820	390
1501	281	1565	331	1629	3127	1693	1751	1757	377	1821	391
1502	242	1566	332	1630	3128	1694	1752	1758	3150	1822	392
1503	243	1567	333	1631	3129	1695	1753	1759	3151	1823	1331
1504	244	1568	334	1632	1286	1696	1754	1760	3152	1824	1332
1505	245	1569	335	1633	1287	1697	1350	1761	3153	1825	1333
1506	246	1570	336	1634	1288	1698	3130	1762	3154	1826	1334
1507	247	1571	337	1635	1289	1699	3131	1763	3155	1827	1335
1508	248	1572	338	1636	1290	1700	3132	1764	3156	1828	1336
1509	249	1573	339	1637	1291	1701	3133	1765	3157	1829	1337
1510	250	1574	340	1638	1292	1702	3134	1766	3158	1830	1338
1511	251	1575	341	1639	1293	1703	3135	1767	3159	1831	1339
1512	252	1576	342	1640	1294	1704	3136	1768	3160	1832	1340
1513	253	1577	343	1641	1295	1705	3137	1769	3161	1833	1351
1514	254	1578	344	1642	1296	1706	3138	1770	3162	1834	1352
1515	255	1579	345	1643	1297	1707	3139	1771	3163	1835	1353
1516	256	1580	346	1644	1298	1708	3140	1772	3164	1836	1354
1517	257	1581	347	1645	1299	1709	3141	1773	3165	1837	1355
1518	258	1582	3080	1646	1300	1710	3142	1774	3166	1838	1356
1519	259	1583	3081	1647	1301	1711	3143	1775	3167	1839	1357
1520	260	1584	3082	1648	1302	1712	3144	1776	3168	1840	1358
1521	261	1585	3083	1649	1303	1713	3145	1777	3169	1841	1359
1522	262	1586	3084	1650	1304	1714	3146	1778	3170	1842	1360
1523	263	1587	3085	1651	1305	1715	3147	1779	3171	1843	1770
1524	264	1588	3086	1652	1306	1716	3148	1780	3172	1844	1771
1525	265	1589	3087	1653	1307	1717	3149	1781	3173	1845	1772
1526	266	1590	3088	1654	1308	1718	1311	1782	3174	1846	1773
1527	267	1591	3089	1655	1309	1719	1312	1783	3175	1847	1774
1528	268	1592	3090	1656	1310	1720	1313	1784	3176	1848	1781
1529	269	1593	3091	1657	348	1721	1314	1785	3177	1849	1782
1530	270	1594	3092	1658	349	1722	1315	1786	3178	1850	1783
1531	271	1595	3093	1659	350	1723	1316	1787	3179	1851	1784
1532	1266	1596	3094	1660	351	1724	1317	1788	3180	1852	1785
1533	1267	1597	3095	1661	352	1725	1318	1789	3181	1853	608
1534	1268	1598	3096	1662	353	1726	1319	1790	3182	1854	610
1535	1269	1599	3097	1663	354	1727	1320	1791	3183	1855	611
1536	1270	1600	3098	1664	355	1728	1321	1792	3184	1856	612
1537	1271	1601	3099	1665	356	1729	1322	1793	3185	1857	613
1538	1272	1602	3100	1666	357	1730	1323	1794	3186	1858	615
1539	1273	1603	3101	1667	483	1731	1324	1795	3187	1859	616
1540	1274	1604	3102	1668	484	1732	1325	1796	3188	1860	617
1541	1275	1605	3103	1669	485	1733	1326	1797	3189	1861	618
1542	1276	1606	3104	1670	486	1734	1327	1798	3190	1862	619

MIDLAND LOCOMOTIVES

Old No.	New No.	Old No.	New No.	Old No.	New No.	Old No.	New No.	Old No.	New No.	Old No.	New No.
1863	620	1927	3254	1991	1814	2055	3332	2119	3396	2183	403
1864	621	1928	3255	1992	1815	2056	3333	2120	3397	2184	404
1865	622	1929	3256	1993	1825	2057	3334	2121	3398	2185	405
1866	623	1930	3257	1994	1826	2058	3335	2122	3399	2186	406
1867	624	1931	3258	1995	1827	2059	3336	2123	3400	2187	407
1868	625	1932	3259	1996	1828	2060	3337	2124	3401	2188	408
1869	626	1933	3260	1997	1829	2061	3338	2125	3402	2189	409
1870	627	1934	3261	1998	1830	2062	3339	2126	3403	2190	410
1871	628	1935	3262	1999	1831	2063	3340	2127	3404	2191	411
1872	629	1936	3263	2000	1832	2064	3341	2128	3405	2192	412
1873	3200	1937	3264	2001	1833	2065	3342	2129	3406	2193	413
1874	3201	1938	3265	2002	1834	2066	3343	2130	3407	2194	414
1875	3202	1939	3266	2003	1835	2067	3344	2131	3408	2195	415
1876	3203	1940	3267	2004	1836	2068	3345	2132	3409	2196	416
1877	3204	1941	3268	2005	1837	2069	3346	2133	3410	2197	417
1878	3205	1942	3269	2006	1838	2070	3347	2134	3411	2198	418
1879	3206	1943	3270	2007	1839	2071	3348	2135	3412	2199	419
1880	3207	1944	3271	2008	1840	2072	3349	2136	3413	2200	420
1881	3208	1945	3272	2009	1841	2073	3350	2137	3414	2201	421
1882	3209	1946	3273	2010	1842	2074	3351	2138	3415	2202	422
1883	3210	1947	3274	2011	1843	2075	3352	2139	3416	2203	428
1884	3211	1948	3275	2012	1844	2076	3353	2140	3417	2204	429
1885	3212	1949	3276	2013	1361	2077	3354	2141	3418	2205	430
1886	3213	1950	3277	2014	1362	2078	3355	2142	3419	2206	431
1887	3214	1951	3278	2015	1363	2079	3356	2143	3420	2207	432
1888	3215	1952	3279	2016	1364	2080	3357	2144	3421	2208	433
1889	3216	1953	3280	2017	1365	2081	3358	2145	3422	2209	434
1890	3217	1954	3281	2018	1366	2082	3359	2146	3423	2210	435
1891	3218	1955	3282	2019	1367	2083	3360	2147	3424	2211	436
1892	3219	1956	3283	2020	1368	2084	3361	2148	3425	2212	437
1893	3220	1957	3284	2021	1369	2085	3362	2149	3426	2213	438
1894	3221	1958	3285	2022	1370	2086	3363	2150	3427	2214	439
1895	3222	1959	3286	2023	3300	2087	3364	2151	3428	2215	440
1896	3223	1960	3287	2024	3301	2088	3365	2152	3429	2216	441
1897	3224	1961	3288	2025	3302	2089	3366	2153	3430	2217	442
1898	3225	1962	3289	2026	3303	2090	3367	2154	3431	2218	1371
1899	3226	1963	3290	2027	3304	2091	3368	2155	3432	2219	1372
1900	3227	1964	3291	2028	3305	2092	3369	2156	3433	2220	1373
1901	3228	1965	3292	2029	3306	2093	3370	2157	3434	2221	1374
1902	3229	1966	3293	2030	3307	2094	3371	2158	3435	2222	1375
1903	3230	1967	3294	2031	3308	2095	3372	2159	3436	2223	1376
1904	3231	1968	3295	2032	3309	2096	3373	2160	3437	2224	1377
1905	3232	1969	3296	2033	3310	2097	3374	2161	3438	2225	1378
1906	3233	1970	3297	2034	3311	2098	3375	2162	3439	2226	1379
1907	3234	1971	3298	2035	3312	2099	3376	2163	3440	2227	1380
1908	3235	1972	3299	2036	3313	2100	3377	2164	3441	2228	1381
1909	3236	1973	1786	2037	3314	2101	3378	2165	3442	2229	1382
1910	3237	1974	1787	2038	3315	2102	3379	2166	3443	2230	1383
1911	3238	1975	1788	2039	3316	2103	3380	2167	3444	2231	1384
1912	3239	1976	1789	2040	3317	2104	3381	2168	3445	2232	1385
1913	3240	1977	1790	2041	3318	2105	3382	2169	3446	2233	1386
1914	3241	1978	1791	2042	3319	2106	3383	2170	3447	2234	1387
1915	3242	1979	1792	2043	3320	2107	3384	2171	3448	2235	1388
1916	3243	1980	1793	2044	3321	2108	3385	2172	3449	2236	1389
1917	3244	1981	1794	2045	3322	2109	3386	2173	3450	2237	1390
1918	3245	1982	1805	2046	3323	2110	3387	2174	3451	2238	1391
1919	3246	1983	1806	2047	3324	2111	3388	2175	3452	2239	1392
1920	3247	1984	1807	2048	3325	2112	3389	2176	3453	2240	1393
1921	3248	1985	1808	2049	3326	2113	3390	2177	3454	2241	1394
1922	3249	1986	1809	2050	3327	2114	3391	2178	3455	2242	1395
1923	3250	1987	1810	2051	3328	2115	3392	2179	3456	2243	1396
1924	3251	1988	1811	2052	3329	2116	3393	2180	3457	2244	1397
1925	3252	1989	1812	2053	3330	2117	3394	2181	3458	2245	1398
1926	3253	1990	1813	2054	3331	2118	3395	2182	3459	2246	1399

APPENDICES

Old No.	New No.	Old No.	New No.	Old No.	New No.	Old No.	New No.	Old No.	New No.	Old No.	New No.
2247	1400	2311	3497	2375	1874	2439	521	2503	2202	2567	3646
2248	1855	2312	3498	2376	1875	2440	522	2504	2203	2568	3647
2249	1856	2313	3499	2377	1876	2441	1900	2505	2204	2569	3648
2250	1857	2314	3500	2378	1877	2442	1901	2506	2205	2570	3649
2251	1858	2315	3501	2379	1878	2443	1902	2507	2206	2571	1890
2252	1859	2316	3502	2380	1879	2444	1903	2508	2207	2572	1891
2253	1639	2317	3503	2381	1880	2445	1904	2509	2208	2573	1892
2254	1640	2318	3504	2382	1881	2446	1905	2510	2209	2574	1893
2255	1641	2319	3505	2383	1882	2447	1906	2511	2230	2575	1894
2256	1642	2320	3506	2384	1883	2448	1907	2512	2231	2576	1895
2257	1643	2321	3507	2385	1884	2449	1908	2513	2232	2577	1896
2258	1644	2322	3508	2386	1885	2450	1909	2514	2233	2578	1897
2259	3545	2323	3509	2387	1886	2451	1910	2515	2234	2579	1898
2260	3546	2324	3510	2388	1887	2452	1911	2516	2235	2580	1899
2261	3547	2325	3511	2389	1888	2453	1912	2517	2236	2581	473
2262	3548	2326	3512	2390	1889	2454	1913	2518	2237	2582	474
2263	3549	2327	3513	2391	3570	2455	1914	2519	2238	2583	475
2264	3550	2328	3514	2392	3571	2456	1915	2520	2239	2584	476
2265	3551	2329	3515	2393	3572	2457	1916	2521	2210	2585	477
2266	3552	2330	3516	2394	3573	2458	1917	2522	2211	2586	478
2267	3553	2331	3517	2395	3574	2459	1918	2523	2212	2587	479
2268	3554	2332	3518	2396	3575	2460	1919	2524	2213	2588	480
2269	3555	2333	3519	2397	3576	2461	3600	2525	2214	2589	481
2270	3556	2334	3520	2398	3577	2462	3601	2526	2215	2590	482
2271	3557	2335	3521	2399	3578	2463	3602	2527	2216	2591	553
2272	3558	2336	3522	2400	3579	2464	3603	2528	2217	2592	554
2273	3559	2337	3523	2401	3580	2465	3604	2529	2218	2593	555
2274	3560	2338	3524	2402	3581	2466	3605	2530	2219	2594	556
2275	3561	2339	3525	2403	3582	2467	3606	2531	2220	2595	557
2276	3562	2340	3526	2404	3583	2468	3607	2532	2221	2596	558
2277	3563	2341	3527	2405	3584	2469	3608	2533	2222	2597	559
2278	3564	2342	3528	2406	3585	2470	3609	2534	2223	2598	560
2279	3565	2343	3529	2407	3586	2471	3610	2535	2224	2599	561
2280	3566	2344	3530	2408	3587	2472	3611	2536	2225	2600	562
2281	3567	2345	3531	2409	3588	2473	3612	2537	2226	2601	685
2282	3568	2346	3532	2410	3589	2474	3613	2538	2227	2602	686
2283	3569	2347	3533	2411	3590	2475	3614	2539	2228	2603	687
2284	3470	2348	3534	2412	3591	2476	3615	2540	2229	2604	688
2285	3471	2349	3535	2413	3592	2477	3616	2541	3660	2605	689
2286	3472	2350	3536	2414	3593	2478	3617	2542	3661	2606	700
2287	3473	2351	3537	2415	3594	2479	3618	2543	3662	2607	701
2288	3474	2352	3538	2416	3595	2480	3619	2544	3663	2608	702
2289	3475	2353	3539	2417	3596	2481	3620	2545	3664	2609	703
2290	3476	2354	3540	2418	3597	2482	3621	2546	3665	2610	704
2291	3477	2355	3541	2419	3598	2483	3622	2547	3666	2611	1411
2292	3478	2356	3542	2420	3599	2484	3623	2548	3667	2612	1412
2293	3479	2357	3543	2421	503	2485	3624	2549	3668	2613	1413
2294	3480	2358	3544	2422	504	2486	3625	2550	3669	2614	1414
2295	3481	2359	1513	2423	505	2487	3626	2551	3630	2615	1415
2296	3482	2360	1514	2424	506	2488	3627	2552	3631	2616	1416
2297	3483	2361	1860	2425	507	2489	3628	2553	3632	2617	1417
2298	3484	2362	1861	2426	508	2490	3629	2554	3633	2618	1418
2299	3485	2363	1862	2427	509	2491	3650	2555	3634	2619	1419
2300	3486	2364	1863	2428	510	2492	3651	2556	3635	2620	1420
2301	3487	2365	1864	2429	511	2493	3652	2557	3636	2621	1421
2302	3488	2366	1865	2430	512	2494	3653	2558	3637	2622	1422
2303	3489	2367	1866	2431	513	2495	3654	2559	3638	2623	1423
2304	3490	2368	1867	2432	514	2496	3655	2560	3639	2624	1424
2305	3491	2369	1868	2433	515	2497	3656	2561	3640	2625	1425
2306	3492	2370	1869	2434	516	2498	3657	2562	3641	2626	1426
2307	3493	2371	1870	2435	517	2499	3658	2563	3642	2627	1427
2308	3494	2372	1871	2436	518	2500	3659	2564	3643	2628	1428
2309	3495	2373	1872	2437	519	2501	2200	2565	3644	2629	1429
2310	3496	2374	1873	2438	520	2502	2201	2566	3645	2630	1430

MIDLAND LOCOMOTIVES

Old No.	New No.	Old No.	New No.	Old No.	New No.	Old No.	New No.	Old No.	New No.	Old No.	New No.
2631	1000	2695	3724	2759	1938	2767	1946	2775	1954	2783	712
2632	1001	2696	3725	2760	1939	2768	1947	2776	1955	2784	713
2633	1002	2697	3726	2761	1940	2769	1948	2777	1956	2785	714
2634	1003	2698	3727	2762	1941	2770	1949	2778	1957	2786	715
2635	1004	2699	3728	2763	1942	2771	1950	2779	1958	2787	716
2636	548	2700	3729	2764	1943	2772	1951	2780	1959	2788	717
2637	549	2701	3730	2765	1944	2773	1952	2781	710	2789	718
2638	550	2702	3731	2766	1945	2774	1953	2782	711	2790	719
2639	551	2703	3732								
2640	552	2704	3733								
2641	3670	2705	3734								
2642	3671	2706	3735								
2643	3672	2707	3736								
2644	3673	2708	3737								
2645	3674	2709	3738								
2646	3675	2710	3739								
2647	3676	2711	3740								
2648	3677	2712	3741								
2649	3678	2713	3742								
2650	3679	2714	3743								
2651	3680	2715	3744								
2652	3681	2716	3745								
2653	3682	2717	3746								
2654	3683	2718	3747								
2655	3684	2719	3748								
2656	3685	2720	3749								
2657	3686	2721	3750								
2658	3687	2722	3751								
2659	3688	2723	3752								
2660	3689	2724	3753								
2661	3690	2725	3754								
2662	3691	2726	3755								
2663	3692	2727	3756								
2664	3693	2728	3757								
2665	3694	2729	3758								
2666	3695	2730	3759								
2667	3696	2731	3760								
2668	3697	2732	3761								
2669	3698	2733	3762								
2670	3699	2734	3763								
2671	3700	2735	3764								
2672	3701	2736	3765								
2673	3702	2737	3766								
2674	3703	2738	3767								
2675	3704	2739	3768								
2676	3705	2740	3769								
2677	3706	2741	1920								
2678	3707	2742	1921								
2679	3708	2743	1922								
2680	3709	2744	1923								
2681	3710	2745	1924								
2682	3711	2746	1925								
2683	3712	2747	1926								
2684	3713	2748	1927								
2685	3714	2749	1928								
2686	3715	2750	1929								
2687	3716	2751	1930								
2688	3717	2752	1931								
2689	3718	2753	1932								
2690	3719	2754	1933								
2691	3720	2755	1934								
2692	3721	2756	1935								
2693	3722	2757	1936								
2694	3723	2758	1937								

DUPLICATE ENGINE NUMBERS

Old No.	New No.	Old No.	New No.	Old No.	New No.	Old No.	New No.
19A	98	151A	110	810A	43	1119A	1511
		152A	111	811A	44	1120A	1512
22A	66	153A	20	812A	45		
23A	67	154A	21	813A	46	1122A	1605
		155A	22	814A	47		
60A	28	156A	1	815A	48	1124A	1606
61A	29	157A	12	816A	49	1125A	1607
62A	30	158A	2	817A	50	1126A	1608
63A	31	159A	3	818A	51	1127A	1645
64A	32	160A	16	819A	52	1128A	1646
65A	33	161A	17	820A	53	1129A	1647
66A	34			821A	54	1130A	1648
67A	105	163A	18	822A	55	1131A	1515
		164A	19	823A	56	1132A	1516
69A	107	165A	23	824A	57	1133A	1517
		166A	24	825A	58	1134A	1518
76A	10	167A	25	826A	59	1135A	1519
77A	11	168A	26	827A	60	1136A	1520
		169A	27	828A	61	1137A	1521
79A	14			829A	62	1138A	1522
		201A	1601			1139A	1523
89A	4			880A	1610	1140A	1524
		203A	1600	881A	1611	1141A	1525
93A	65	204A	1198	882A	1612	1142A	1526
		205A	1199	883A	1613	1143A	1527
104A	6			884A	1614		
105A	7	222A	1602	885A	1615	1322A	1500
106A	8	223A	1604	886A	1616	1323A	1501
107A	9			887A	1617	1324A	1502
		690A	1200	888A	1618	1325A	1503
116A	15	691A	1201	889A	1619	1326A	1504
		692A	1202				
118A	5	693A	1203	1095A	1603	1428A	1505
119A	13	694A	1204				
120A	124	695A	1205	1102A	1620	1430A	1506
121A	106			1103A	1621		
		780A	1206	1104A	1622	1697A	1507
123A	96	781A	1207	1105A	1623		
124A	120	782A	1208	1106A	1624		
125A	93	783A	1209	1107A	1625		
126A	121			1108A	1626		
127A	97	800A	35	1109A	1627		
128A	122	802A	36	1110A	1628		
		803A	37	1111A	1629		
130A	123	804A	38	1112A	1630		
131A	108	805A	39	1113A	1631		
132A	109	806A	40	1114A	1632		
				1115A	1633		
138A	63	808A	41	1116A	1508		
139A	64	809A	42	1117A	1509		
				1118A	1510		

APPENDIX 2

OVERSEAS SERVICE

**Kirtley 0–6–0 Locomotives
sold to the Rete Mediterraneo Railway
August 1906**

281	455	870	953	978
284	462	876	955	981
305	467	879	958	986
306	486	931	963	991
313	546	933	966	994
329	555	935	968	1039
333	637	946	971	1040
349	663	947	972	1041
398	665	948	973	1066
416	682	951	977	1068

TOTAL = 50 locomotives
Allocated Italian Numbers 3801-50

Plates 270 & 271. A number of locomotives were 'called up' during the First World War and these pictures illustrate Kirtley goods engines in this guise. The first view illustrates No. 2717 with an enlarged cab. This locomotive was captured by the Germans at Cambrai in November 1917 and recaptured twelve months later. It was returned to Midland Railway service and was withdrawn at the end of 1932. The second picture shows No. 2742 at an unknown location. *Collection Ken Nunn*

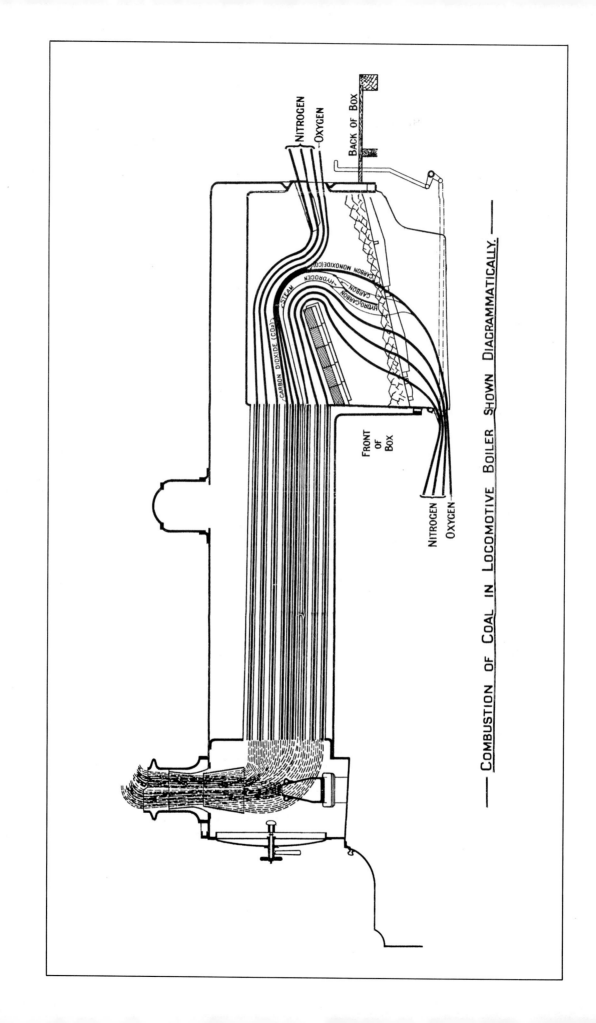

COMBUSTION OF COAL IN LOCOMOTIVE BOILER SHOWN DIAGRAMMATICALLY.

M.R. FIRING INSTRUCTIONS

*NOTE: Figure numbers in this Appendix are those used in the original
MR book and do not relate to the rest of this volume.*

This copy of the 1904 Midland Railway Locomotive Firing Instructions is a copy of a book issued to the company's footplate staff in that year.

'Instructions to firemen' in written form were not uncommon in the steam era but this is the oldest example of a Midland Railway edition which has come to the attention of the authors and we are indebted to Peter Truman who obtained this copy for use in this volume.

INTRODUCTION

THE success with which a driver is able to work his engine, as regards the punctuality of running and the loads hauled, depends largely upon the fire being managed in an economical manner, and the utmost heating value of the fuel being thereby obtained. Although long experience in the practical use of the shovel, fire-door, and damper, generally teaches firemen to act in a very skilful manner, it is certain that an intelligent knowledge of the changes which occur in the processes of combustion would enable them to secure better results. Every driver and fireman should, therefore, pay great attention to the study of combustion, and should satisfy their superiors that they have an intelligent knowledge of what is taking place in the fire-box, tubes, and smoke-box. Every fireman is aware that the passage of air through the damper and fire-bars causes rapid combustion of the heated fuel, that gases are given off which have to be burned by air entering through the fire-hole door, and that the resulting highly heated gases in their passage through the tubes give up a large portion of their heat to the water surrounding them. It is not, however, sufficient to know merely this; the following description of what goes on in the fire-box during the combustion of the fuel, and the methods to be adopted in the management of the fire, must be carefully studied, so as to enable the men concerned to take advantage of this knowledge, and to be able to give intelligent answers to the questions on pages 24 to 35. [201-203]

COAL AND ITS COMBUSTION

1. Coal is of vegetable origin, but owing to the changes which have taken place during its formation, it does not resemble anything which grows at present. If, however, a piece of wood is charred, partially burnt, or heated in a retort, it is converted into charcoal, which consists almost wholly of carbon – a dense form of which is the chief constituent of coal.

A body is said to burn when it unites with oxygen, giving out heat, and this is what the carbon in coal does when burnt in a fire. The oxygen is supplied by the air, which is a mixture of about 23 parts of oxygen and 77 parts of nitrogen in every 100 parts by weight (see Fig. 1). The nitrogen takes no part in the combustion.

2. When carbon burns, the combustion may take place in two ways. In a plentiful supply of air, 12 parts by weight of carbon unite with 32 parts by weight of oxygen, and a non-inflammable gas called carbon dioxide (carbonic acid gas) is formed. If the supply of air be limited, however, only half this amount of oxygen may be taken up, and a gas called carbon monoxide may be formed, which is inflammable and capable of uniting with more oxygen to form carbon dioxide.*

*To explain more fully how it is that carbon can burn in two ways, it must be remembered that combustion takes place by the uniting together of the smallest particles of substances, or 'atoms' as they are called. These minute particles have different weights; thus, each atom of carbon weighs 12 and each atom of oxygen 16, as compared with the atom of the lightest known substance, hydrogen, which weighs 1. In the incomplete combustion of carbon, each atom unites with one atom of oxygen, and the product is called carbon monoxide. In the complete combustion, two atoms of oxygen combine with one atom of carbon, and the product is called carbon dioxide.

Incomplete Combustion

Carbon	=	12 parts by weight
unites with Oxygen	=	16 " " "
forming Carbon Monoxide	=	28 parts by weight

giving off only $^3/_{10}$ ths of the heat of the fuel.

Also

Carbon Monoxide	=	28 parts by weight
unites with Oxygen	=	16 " " "
forming Carbon Dioxide	=	44 parts by weight

giving off the remaining $^7/_{10}$ths of the heat of the fuel.

Complete Combustion

Carbon	=	12 parts by weight
unites with two atoms of Oxygen	= (2 x 16) = 32	" " "
forming Carbon Dioxide	=	44 parts by weight

liberating the whole of the heat in the fuel.

In burning to carbon monoxide, carbon gives out only about three-tenths as much heat as it does in completely burning to carbon dioxide, and, therefore, if, through not admitting enough air through the fire-hole door, carbon monoxide only is formed, about seven-tenths of the heat is lost, or *about 7 out of every 10 lbs. of coal consumed in this way are wasted.* Heat may also be wasted by admitting too much air; but the reason of this will be explained further on. To completely burn 1 lb. of carbon, the 2 $^2/_3$ lbs. of oxygen contained in 12 lbs. of air are required, and this air, at the ordinary temperature, would measure about 156 cubic feet.

3. Coal does not consist wholly of carbon, not more than about 70 to 90 per cent of steam coal being composed of this substance. The remainder consists of hydrogen, oxygen, nitrogen, sulphur, ash, and water. (See Fig. 2.)

The hydrogen in coal is partly united to the oxygen, and these together are given off as water-vapour or steam, when the coal is burnt. Another portion of the hydrogen, when the coal is heated or distilled, is given off in combination with some of the carbon in the form of hydrocarbon vapours, and it is the burning of these vapours that causes the luminous flames. Coal, such as anthracite, which contains very little hydrogen, does not burn with a flame, and is useless for steam-raising in an ordinary boiler grate.

When a locomotive has been fired whilst standing without the jet* on, the hydrocarbon vapours can be seen issuing from the chimney as a yellowish smoke. At the high temperature of the fire-box,

*alternative name is 'blower'.

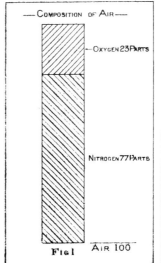

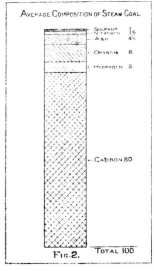

when running, these hydrocarbons tend to split up into carbon and hydrogen, and if sufficient oxygen is not present to completely burn the carbon, some of it escapes unburnt, causing a black smoke. If properly burnt, both the carbon and the hydrogen unite with the oxygen of the air, the former in the manner described above, and the latter forming water which passes off in the form of steam. (See Fig. 3.)

The heat given off by hydrogen in burning is much greater than that given off by an equal weight of carbon; but the amount of hydrogen in steam coal is comparatively small, whilst of this amount, some (often the greater proportion) is virtually already united with the oxygen in the coal, and therefore gives out little or no heat when the coal is consumed.

DIAGRAM SHOWING HOW HYDROCARBONS BURN

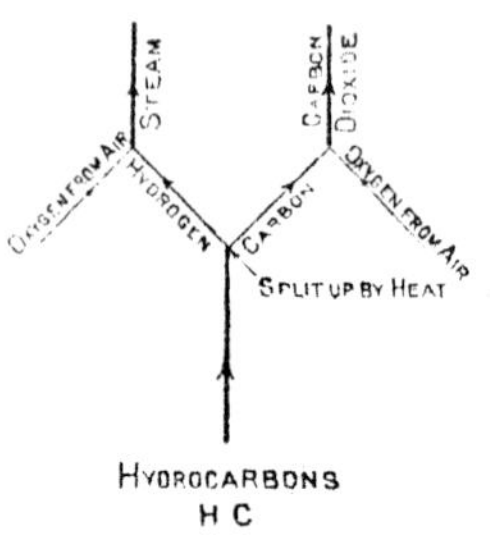

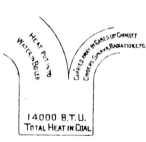

HYDROCARBONS
H C
FIG. 3.

4. The sulphur in coal is chiefly found united with iron in the 'Coal Brasses' or 'Iron Pyrites'. The sulphur itself burns out of the 'brasses', but the iron is left behind, and, in burning, tends to cause the ashes to run together and form clinker, thus preventing the air from getting through the fire-bars. This hinders, or checks, the supply of oxygen necessary for the combustion of the fuel, and, consequently, steam is not raised so readily as it might be. Some of the substances found in coal ashes do not clinker, but fall into the ash-pan in a powdery state.

5. The nitrogen in coal is small in amount and takes no part in the combustion; it simply passes up the chimney when the coal is burnt, carrying away some heat.

Of much greater importance is the enormous volume of nitrogen which has to pass through the fire-box in the air required to burn the coal. This will be readily understood when it is remembered that to burn 1 lb. of coal requires about 12 lbs. of air, of which over 9

WHERE THE HEAT IN COAL GOES TO.

14,000 B.T.U.
TOTAL HEAT IN COAL

FIG. 4.

NOTE

B.T.U. MEANS BRITISH THERMAL UNIT. THIS IS THE AMOUNT OF HEAT REQUIRED TO RAISE 1 LB OF WATER 1 DEGREE FAHRENHEIT. IT MUST BE CLEARLY UNDERSTOOD THAT THIS DIAGRAM SHOWS THE DISPOSITION OF THE HEAT WHEN THE COAL IS BURNT ECONOMICALLY; IF UNNECESSARY AIR IS ADMITTED THE AMOUNT CARRIED OFF UP CHIMNEY IS GREATLY INCREASED.

lbs. are nitrogen. This nitrogen does not itself burn, but it reduces the rate of combustion, and having to be heated up with the other gases in the fire-box, it causes a great deal of heat to be wasted. The temperature at which the gases leave the chimney is often over 800° Fahrenheit, and to heat 9 lbs. of nitrogen up to this temperature takes about one-ninth of the lb. of coal.

From this it will be readily seen that it is absolutely necessary, if economy is to be exercised, that only the amount of air requisite for burning the fuel is allowed to pass through the fire-hole and damper doors, owing to the loss arising from the heat carried away by any superfluous air which may be drawn in.

6. All coals contain more or less water, which in the fire-box has to be evaporated and converted into steam. This carries away useful heat. It can be shown that as much as $1/25$ part of the total heat given out by the coal in burning may be carried away in the steam formed by the evaporation of the water contained in the coal, and that formed by the combustion of the hydrogen.

7. In a locomotive fire-box the chemical reactions already explained are taking place continuously; the coal thrown in provides the carbon, hydrogen, etc., whilst the air supplies the oxygen necessary. This air, of course, enters through the damper and fire-hole door, being drawn in, when the engine is running, by the action of the blast.

HYDROCARBONS BURNING IN AN ORDINARY GAS FLAME

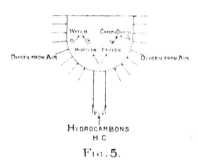

HYDROCARBONS
H C
FIG. 5.

Assuming that coal has just been put on a fire which was previously clear, what occurs is, approximately, as follows:— the hydrocarbons which are given off on heating the coal are distilled or driven off in the form of a crude coal-gas; they mingle with the air drawn up through the fire and that taken in through the fire-hole door, and burn. How they burn in an ordinary coal gas flame is shown in Fig. 5. The same action is shewn diagrammatically in Fig. 3.

If, however, the air supplied is not sufficient, the hydrocarbons either pass off as a yellow smoke, or, if the fire-box, etc., be hot enough, they are partially split up, and some of the carbon passes off as black smoke without being burnt, whilst the hydrogen is not completely consumed. These gases are not formed all at once, but naturally, the outside of the lump of coal is distilled first, the action going on gradually until the whole of the piece is incandescent or red through. The lumps of coal are, however, somewhat broken up by this time, and the oxygen in the air drawn through the bars, now unites with the carbon of the red hot fuel.

If sufficient air be present, the carbon will be completely burnt to carbon dioxide gas at the bottom of the box, but if not, it will only be immediately burnt to carbon monoxide gas, and the complete combustion can only take place above the fire (see frontispiece). Here the gases are thrown together by the brick arch and the fire-hole door deflector, and if too much oxygen has been drawn in at one part of the fire and too little at another, the gases have a chance of meeting and burning. In most cases, however, the air necessary for the proper burning of the coal cannot be drawn in through the fire itself, and an additional amount has to be taken through the fire-hole door.

COMPLETE COMBUSTION

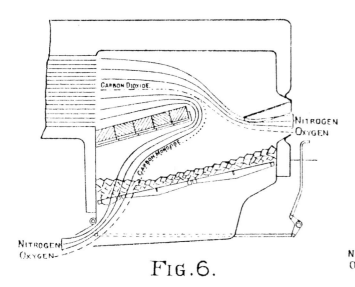

FIG.6.

INCOMPLETE COMBUSTION

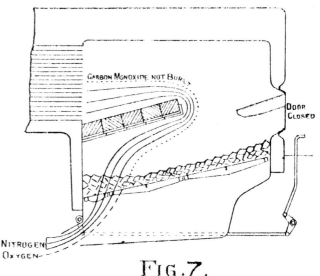

FIG.7.

8. The reason why some air must be admitted through the fire-hole door is, that when the carbon dioxide, formed by the complete combustion of the coal at the bottom of the fire, is drawn up into the fire-box through the mass of red hot fuel, it combines with more carbon and becomes converted into carbon monoxide. This carbon monoxide requires oxygen to burn it, which is supplied by the air entering through the fire-hole door.*

If air were not admitted through the fire-hole door, the carbon monoxide would escape unburnt up the chimney, and valuable heat would be lost as explained in paragraph 2. On the other hand, if too much air be admitted, a very considerable waste of heat naturally occurs, as will be readily understood from the amount of coal shown in paragraph 5 to be necessary to heat up the nitrogen in the air actually required.

Under some conditions, if the door be opened unnecessarily, the amount of coal required for heating the air drawn in is about 80 lbs. per minute. This seems a large amount, but it must be borne in mind that air is drawn in at the fire-hole door at a very high speed indeed, and under such wasteful conditions steam could not be maintained.

This waste is not the only one, for supposing the opening of the fire-hole door be too great, the extra air drawn in not only requires heating up, but lowers the temperature of the gases passing through the tubes. The water in the boiler is, of course, heated by the hot gases, and the heat given out to it depends largely on these gases being much hotter than the water, as, if they are nearly of the same temperature, the heat is transferred only slowly, especially as the passage of the gases through the tubes is rapid.

It would, perhaps, at first seem difficult to judge of the amount of air which should be supplied in this manner, but it is found that of the substances which burn, the last to be completely consumed is the smoke, or carbon in small particles. This being so, **sufficient air should be admitted through the fire-hole door to allow of the smoke being completely, or almost completely, consumed, and no more.**

With some coals which are almost smokeless, and in all cases where the fire is thoroughly incandescent, it is difficult to say when the right quantity of air is being introduced through the fire-hole door; in cases such as these the fire itself should be carefully watched.

*The same changes can be seen taking place in an ordinary house grate on a frosty night; when the fire is clear, a pale blue flame may often be seen, caused by the carbon monoxide, formed as described above, burning where it meets with the air at the top of the fire.

9. If it be found, whilst standing at stations, signals, etc., that steam is being made too rapidly, **the opening of the fire-hole door to cool the boiler is a very bad practice**; not only is heat wasted, but the tube plate may be cooled down so much that the tubes will start leaking. Now it will be readily understood from what has already been stated, that, as oxygen is necessary for the combustion of the fuel, if the supply be wholly stopped, the coal can no longer burn. It follows, therefore, that to prevent further steam being generated, all that is required is that both the damper should be closed and the fire-hole door be shut.

If, however, the supply of air were in this manner to be completely cut off, the fire would gradually go out, owing to no oxygen being supplied; the damper must, therefore, in practice, be left

EXCESS OF AIR

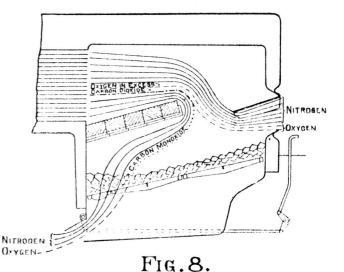

FIG.8.

sufficiently open to allow of the fire being kept in a satisfactory state.

10. Several points must be considered when deciding on the method of firing to be adopted in any particular case, the chief of these being the class of coal used, the strength of the blast, and the size and form of the grate.

In all cases, however, it should be borne in mind that the fire should be as thin as possible, without ever being allowed to burn into holes, whilst it should be somewhat thicker at the sides than in the middle. This allows of free access of air to all parts, whilst the slight thickening at the sides prevents any tendency of the gases to creep up the plates and pass away through the tubes without being properly consumed. A glowing centre also helps to burn any smoke formed.

The behaviour of coals when heated varies considerably, even when they are, approximately, of the same composition. As a rule, however, when they contain a considerable proportion of hydro-carbons they tend to soften before burning, and to run together or cake. When this is at all the case, it is necessary to have a very thin fire, or the blast will in no case be strong enough to draw the neces-sary air through the coal. If, on the other hand, a hard coal or a Welsh coal is being used, which does not soften at all, the fire may be somewhat thicker; but care must be taken to see that the fire is made and retained thoroughly incandescent, expecially with Welsh coal, otherwise it will not burn freely, as these coals are poor in hydrocarbons, and so do not tend to break up or become porous as softer coals do.

If a coal is dirty, and contains impurities which are liable to form into clinker, care must be taken to break the clinker up and remove it, or it will prevent the air passing up through the fuel, with the result that the coal cannot be burnt or steam raised as rapidly as it should be. See Fig. 9.

DECREASED GRATE AREA DUE TO CLINKER ON BARS

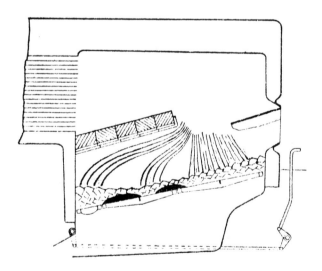

FIG. 9.

11. The blast has a very great effect on the character of the fire, as upon it depends the amount of air which is drawn up through the bars and in at the fire-hole door.

Where a boiler has a small grate, it will usually be found that the blast is keen. This will necessitate a somewhat thicker fire being used than would otherwise be the case, as the stronger blast will draw the requisite air through a greater depth of fire, and, as a result. more coal can be burnt on the same area of grate. There will be, however, a greater tendency to make the fire burn more quickly at particular points, owing to the air going the easiest and shortest way and burning the coal more quickly at this point. This, of course, may lead to the fire burning in holes, which not only will allow an excess of air to be drawn in, but also will cause the rush of air to carry some particles of glowing coal with it through the tubes and out of the chimney as sparks. If the blast is keen, even more care must be exercised with regard to the fire-hole door, as, if left open longer than is necessary, more air will be drawn in than would be the case with a gentle blast.

If the grate be large and the blast gentle, the fire must be kept as thin as possible, for if allowed to get at all thick, the blast will not be able to draw through it the air necessary for the combustion of the coal, and the boiler will not steam well.

12. The influence of the size of the grate has already been men-tioned. With a long narrow box, care must be taken to see that the front end is not neglected. With flat bars, it is, of course, easy to keep an even fire; but there is a tendency to overlook the back corners of the box, as they are deep down and somewhat out of sight.

With a box which slopes towards the front, the back of the box is, of course, the portion into which most of the coal is fed, as, in running, the fuel tends to run down towards the front end under the brick arch. Care must be taken, however, to see that the fire is not too heavy under the door, or smoke may be formed by the uncon-sumed gases passing round the deflector plate and away through the tubes. The fire must not be made so thick here that the front of the box cannot be readily watched, and, if necessary, any holes which form at this point must be filled up.

13. Before firing up, the actual state of the fire, both front and back, should be ascertained. This can often be readily determined by inserting the fire shovel through the fire-hole door, and by deflecting the entering air downwards, allowing the fire itself to be seen. After this has been done, the first care should be to fill the holes in the fire with coal, first at the front and then at the back, and then firing should proceed in the manner best suited to the box and coal.

It should be borne in mind that a little coal, frequently fed on, is far more conducive to economy than heavy firing, as it allows of the coal being consumed more completely and satisfactorily.

14. When approaching a station at which a stop is to be made, considerable economy can be effected by paying proper attention to the fire, so as to render it unnecessary to reduce the boiler pressure by passing cold air through the tubes, and yet prevent the boiler from blowing off whilst standing. It should be arranged that the coal is almost wholly incandescent some little time before steam has to be shut off. The damper and fire-hole door should then be more or less closed, by which means the generation of steam will be reduced, and, as steam continues to be used, the boiler pressure will fall before the station is reached.

The glowing mass of coal, whilst standing, will radiate, or give out, some of its heat to the water, but, as the pressure of steam has been reduced, there will be room for this in the boiler itself. The pressure will again rise, and, by careful manipulation, will be at full pressure when steam is again required.

If this course be adopted, there will be no necessity to open the fire-hole door in order to reduce the pressure by cooling the boiler, which has already been shown to be very wasteful and injurious.

At the end of a trip, every care should be taken to see that the fire is as low as possible, bearing in mind the necessity of returning to the shed.

APPENDICES

CATECHISM FOR ENGINE FIREMEN, &c.

1. *Q. Of what does the combustible matter in coal consist?*

   A. Chiefly of carbon, but also of hydrocarbons and a small amount of sulphur.

2. *Q. What do you understand by hydrocarbons?*

   A. Carbon and hydrogen in chemical combination. In gas coals these are the chief light-giving portions.

3. *Q. When coal burns, what really happens?*

   A. The carbon and other combustible ingredients unite with oxygen of the air and are said to 'burn'.

4. *Q. From whence is the oxygen derived in a locomotive firebox?*

   A. From the air drawn in through the damper and fire-hole door by the action of the blast.

5. *Q. What is formed when carbon burns?*

   A. If the combustion is complete, a gas called carbon dioxide (or carbonic acid gas), consisting of 32 parts, by weight, of oxygen, and 12 parts, by weight, of carbon.

6. *Q. You say, 'If the combustion is complete'. What happens if it is not complete?*

   A. The carbon is not completely consumed, and a gas called carbon monoxide is formed, which consists of 12 parts, by weight, of oxygen. If a further supply of oxygen is available, the carbon monoxide will burn with a blue flame forming carbon dioxide, but if not, it will escape unburnt through the tubes and up the chimney, and a large proportion of the heat will thus be lost, and more coal will be required to produce the same amount of steam.

7. *Q. How do the hydrocarbons in the coal burn?*

   A. In a similar manner to the carbon, but, in addition to the carbon uniting with oxygen, 2 parts of hydrogen unite with 16 of oxygen and burn, forming water which escapes as steam. These portions of the coal do not provide a great proportion of the heat, but the carbon in them is often responsible for smoke.

8. *Q. What amount of air is necessary for the complete combustion of one pound of coal?*

   A. If the coal is assumed to be pure carbon, about 12 lbs of air, by weight, is required. This air at ordinary temperature, has a volume of 156 cubic feet, but as it leaves the fire-box at a fairly high temperature, its volume then is much greater, and is about 500 cubic feet.

9. *Q. Is it correct to take coal as wholly combustible matter?*

   A. Not entirely. All coals contain, beside combustible matter, some incombustible substances, which either fall into the ash-pan as ashes (not cinders), are carried as dust into the smoke-box or up the chimney, or remain in the fire-box and form clinker, their final destination depending upon the class of coal which is being burnt.

10. *Q. The amount of air you mentioned as necessary for the combustion of one pound of coal seems large when the coal burnt per mile is considered. Where is it obtained from?*

    A. It is, as previously stated, drawn in by the blast, and comes past the damper through the fire, and also through the fire-hole door.

11. *Q. Is it necessary for it to come in by both these ways?*

    A. Yes, in nearly all cases; because the air drawn through the fire is necessary to keep it alight and alive, whilst the fire-hole door admits the air necessary to complete the combustion, to burn the carbon monoxide to carbon dioxide, and to help to consume any smoke and hydrocarbon vapours that may have been formed.

12. *Q. Is one to understand from this that so long as there is plenty of air admitted through the damper and fire hole door everything is satisfactory?*

    A. By no means. Every cubic foot of air admitted into the fire-box above the quantity absolutely necessary for the complete combustion of the coal, is heated up before it escapes from the chimney, and so carries heat away with it which should have been used to make steam.

13. *Q. What do you mean by this?*

    A. A certain amount of heat is given out by every pound of coal, and if part of this is used for warming up a quantity of air, which passes away hot, this portion must be entirely lost. In addition, this needless air, increasing as it does the quantity of gases which are heated up, causes the temperature of the flame to be lower than it would otherwise be; this also means loss of heat, and therefore of coal, because the hotter the gases, the more readily they part with some of their heat to the water, providing, of course, they are not allowed to escape into the atmosphere at too high a temperature.

14. *Q. If, then, this is the result of too much air, how does an insufficient supply of air affect the working of a locomotive boiler?*

    A. In the first place, if sufficient air is not present, there is a tendency for the fire to smoke, owing to the particles of carbon not coming into contact, especially when hot, with the oxygen necessary for their combustion; then there is a great danger of the carbon being burnt only to carbon monoxide and being allowed to escape in that state up the chimney, whilst some of the hydrocarbons may also pass up the chimney in an unburnt state.

15. *Q. Is there any means of telling when just the requisite amount of air is being admitted?*

    A. It would appear that if carbon monoxide, hydrocarbons, and smoke are escaping up the chimney, and an additional supply of air is introduced, the last of these to be consumed is the smoke, and, therefore, when the last traces of this have disappeared, it may be concluded that the combustion is as complete as possible.

16. *Q. What, then, is the ideal state of a fire?*

    A. One in which no smoke is given off, but if the air supply were ever so slightly reduced, smoke would appear.

17. *Q. Is there, then, no waste whatever, except the heat carried away by the consumed gases?*

    A. By no means. The nitrogen which is mixed with the oxygen in the air carries away much heat, without fulfilling any useful purpose; but this is unavoidable.

18. *Q. What is the purpose of the damper?*

    A. To supply air under the fire which is necessary to cause it to burn and to keep it incandescent.

19. *Q. Why is it not possible to supply the whole of the air in this way?*

A. Because in any case the continual opening of the fire-hole door to put in fuel allows air to be drawn in. It is also impossible, owing to the large amount of fuel which has to be burnt per square foot of grate with a locomotive, to have a sufficiently thin fire to allow of the whole of the necessary air being drawn through it.

20. *Q. Of what use, then, is the damper?*

A. Of the greatest use in regulating the fire itself. If the damper were kept absolutely closed, and no air were allowed to pass through it, the fire would only burn very imperfectly, and from the top; if, on the other hand, no damper were provided, the amount of air admitted would often be too great, with the result that steam would be made when not required, and heat would be wasted by being carried away by hot gases.

21. *Q. When would this latter be likely to occur?*

A. In many cases, such as when running down banks, standing at stations and signals, and in fact, in all instances where steam is not being used as rapidly as produced. In these cases the damper should be nearly closed, so as to admit only sufficient air under the grate to just keep the fire in a satisfactory state, the fire-hole also being closed, if this can be done without smoke being given off.

22. *Q. Should the damper, then, be the sole means of regulating the amount of steam produced?*

A. By no means. It should always be used in conjunction with the fire-hole door, which, as previously stated, supplies the air necessary for the complete combustion of the gases given off by the coal.

23. *Q. What, then, should be the position of the fire-hole door when not open for firing?*

A. This depends entirely upon the state of the fire and the work the engine is doing. The position to be aimed at is one in which if the door be slightly further closed, smoke will be given off, as it may then be assumed that the fuel is being used economically.

24. *Q. What should be the position of the fire-hole door when little steam is required?*

A. Like the damper, nearly or wholly closed, only sufficient air being admitted to allow of the gases given off by the fire being consumed.

25. *Q. Is it possible for gases to pass off without being properly burnt, and yet no smoke be visible from the chimney?*

A. Yes, if smokeless coal is being used, or if the fire is wholly incandescent or clear. It is, however, difficult to judge when this is taking place, owing to the gases being colourless, and in these cases the fire itself should be carefully watched.

26. *Q. Should the fire-hole door ever be opened to check the generation of steam?*

A. No! In fact the practice of opening the fire-hole door to cool down the boiler is not only unnecessary, as has been shown, but one of the worst practices which can be indulged in.

27. *Q. Why is this?*

A. Because, in the first place, it leads to waste by causing a large quantity of unnecessary air admitted through it to be heated up and carried away without serving any useful purpose; and secondly, by cooling down the back tube plate, it may start the tubes leaking, owing to the strains thus set up.

28. *Q. Are there any other aids to the proper combustion of the coal?*

A. Yes. The brick arch and the deflector, which tend to throw together and mix the gases given off by the coal and the air admitted through the fire-hole door.

29. *Q. Can you give any definite rules for firing the boiler?*

A. No. It must depend on several points which may vary with different locomotives.

30. *Q. Are there any general points which should be aimed at?*

A. Yes: regularity of firing, and keeping the fire as thin as possible, bearing all the conditions in mind.

31. *Q. Under what circumstances, then, should a fire not be as thin as is possible for it to burn?*

A. When the grate, for some reason, is small, when it will be found that the blast is somewhat keen.

32. *Q. What would happen if a very thin fire were kept under these conditions?*

A. The keenness of the blast would tend to draw in through the fire-bars and fire-hole door more air than was absolutely necessary for the combustion of the fuel. The result of this would be that the extra air or gases would have to be heated up, and they would carry heat away up the chimney, causing waste. The fire would also tend to burn through in holes, however carefully watched, and an excess of air would be drawn in through these holes. This is one of the causes of sparks being thrown from the chimney.

33. *Q. What, then, is required in this case?*

A. The fire should be thickened somewhat, so as to prevent unnecessary air being drawn in in this way. Great care must also be taken to see that too much air is not drawn in through the firehole door, and yet that sufficient is allowed to enter to prevent smoke.

34. *Q. What other conditions are likely to be met with?*

A. A gentle blast with a large grate, when the fire should be kept as thin as possible, without allowing it to burn through in holes. This gives all the fuel a chance of getting direct the air and oxygen necessary for its complete combustion, and thus reduces the chance of smoke and prevents waste of heat.

35. *Q. Is there any other point to be considered?*

A. Yes, the kind of coal being used. If this has any tendency to settle closely or cake together, it will prevent the air passing readily through it, and, therefore, the fire must be thinner than would be the case if the coal burnt more openly.

36. *Q. What is the effect of clinker?*

A. If this forms on the bars, the space through which air can pass is reduced, and if not removed, the amount of fuel which can be burnt becomes less, and the boiler consequently steams badly.

37. *Q. How should the coal be put on during firing?*

A. This also varies with different grates, depending on the inclination of the latter, etc. In all cases the person firing should have in view the prevention of holes in the fire; as a rule, too, the corners and sides should be kept higher than the centre of the fire as this helps to burn the smoke by leaving a glowing mass in the centre. The thickened sides of the fire prevent gases creeping up the plates and passing away unconsumed. When firing is started, first the holes at the front and then those at the back should be filled up, and then the firing generally attended to. **It is far better to fire a few shovelfuls often than to put in a heavy charge every now and then.**

38. *Q. Is there any other evil caused by the fire being allowed to burn through in holes, besides the waste caused by more air than necessary being drawn in?*

A. Yes; if there is a hole in the fire the air naturally tends to pass in at this spot, as it is the easiest path for it. This results in a rush of air, which carries small particles of glowing cinders with it, which causes sparks to be thrown from the chimney.

Fig. 22. Finally, we have used this diagram from the LMS version of 'Instructions for Firemen' to illustrate some of the points described in Chapter 7 and Appendix 3.

SECTIONAL VIEW OF BOILER

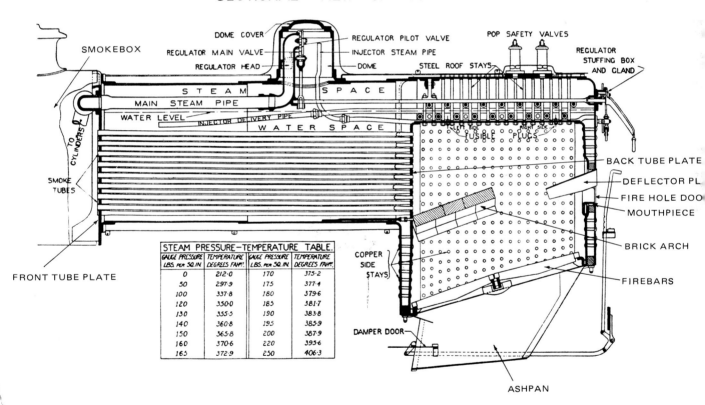

STEAM PRESSURE—TEMPERATURE TABLE.			
GAUGE PRESSURE LBS. per SQ.IN.	TEMPERATURE DEGREES FAH⁹!	GAUGE PRESSURE LBS. per SQ.IN.	TEMPERATURE DEGREES FAH⁹!
0	212·0	170	375·2
50	297·9	175	377·4
100	337·8	180	379·6
120	350·0	185	381·7
130	355·5	190	383·8
140	360·8	195	385·9
150	365·8	200	387·9
160	370·6	220	395·6
165	372·9	250	406·3

CONTENTS OF VOLUMES 2 and 3

The second and third volumes of *Midland Locomotives* summarize the history of each type and analyse the design variations within each class. Liveries are also discussed and the official diagrams and scale drawings are accompanied by a wide ranging collection of photographs.

VOLUME 2

PASSENGER TENDER LOCOMOTIVES

Power class 1	1-281, 300-327, 600-684	2—4—0, 4—4—0, 4—2—2
Power class 2	328-562, 695-694	4—4—0, 4—2—2
Power class 3	700-779	4—4—0
Power class 4	990-1044	4—4—0

PASSENGER TANK LOCOMOTIVES

Not classified	1198-1199	4—4—0T
Power class 1	1200-1430	0—4—4T
Power class 3	2000-2039	0—6—4T

ABSORBED LONDON TILBURY & SOUTHEND RAILWAY LOCOMOTIVES

VOLUME 3

GOODS TANK LOCOMOTIVES

Power class 0	1500-1537	0—4—0T
Power class 1	1600-1899	0—6—0T
Power class 3	1900-1959	0—6—0T

GOODS TENDER LOCOMOTIVES
(all 0—6—0 except where stated)

Power class 2	2200-2239 (American 'Mogul', all 2—6—0, extinct by 1915)
Power class 1	2300-2867 (Some class 2 within this series)
Power class 2	2900-3764 (Three locomotives were class 1 and many were class 3 within this series)
Power class 3	3137-3764 (Many were class 2 within this series)
Power class 3	3765-3834
Power class 4	3835-4026
Not classified	2290 (0—10—0 banking engine)

SOMERSET & DORSET JOINT RAILWAY LOCOMOTIVES
BUILT TO MIDLAND DESIGN